Oboe Art and Method

Oboe Art and Method

Martin Schuring

OXFORD
UNIVERSITY PRESS
2009

OXFORD
UNIVERSITY PRESS

Oxford University Press, Inc., publishes works that further
Oxford University's objective of excellence
in research, scholarship, and education.

Oxford   New York
Auckland   Cape Town   Dar es Salaam   Hong Kong   Karachi
Kuala Lumpur   Madrid   Melbourne   Mexico City   Nairobi
New Delhi   Shanghai   Taipei   Toronto

With offices in
Argentina   Austria   Brazil   Chile   Czech Republic   France   Greece
Guatemala   Hungary   Italy   Japan   Poland   Portugal   Singapore
South Korea   Switzerland   Thailand   Turkey   Ukraine   Vietnam

Copyright © 2009 by Oxford University Press, Inc.

Published by Oxford University Press, Inc.
198 Madison Avenue, New York, New York 10016

www.oup.com

Oxford is a registered trademark of Oxford University Press

Library of Congress Cataloging-in-Publication Data
Schuring, Martin.
Oboe art and method / Martin Schuring.
    p.   cm.
Includes bibliographical references and index.
ISBN 978-0-19-537458-2; 978-0-19-537457-5 (pbk.)
Oboe—Instruction and study. I. Title.
MT360.S38 2009
788.5'2193—dc22   2008045311

9 8 7 6 5 4 3 2 1

Printed in the United States of America

Dedicated to the memory of my father
Dieterich J. Schuring
and
the memory of my teacher
John de Lancie

Preface

It has been nearly fifty years since the appearance of the last comprehensive oboe technique book from a major publisher written by a
North American author. The world at large, the world of music, and the
much smaller world of oboe playing have all changed in significant ways
since then. Today, almost every university of any size and ambition has
a music school, with many of those institutions offering degrees special-
izing in oboe. School music programs, though suffering from inadequate resources in many places, are nonetheless ubiquitous. There are
many more oboe teachers, oboe players, and oboe students than ever
before. Still, the oboe is not nearly as popular as the flute or the piano,
never mind the guitar or the drums, so expert instructors are sometimes
difficult to find outside of urban areas. Although a book can never take
the place of private lessons from a specialist, it can help to guide students toward organizing their thinking and to enable them to ask intelligent questions once they find a good teacher.

While much of music making and oboe playing is rooted in a tradition at least a century old, today's demand for the most recent information makes a new text desirable. The alphabet remains the same, but
the vocabulary has increased, and some of the usage and spelling has
changed.

This book is not an attempt to be a comprehensive resource on the
entire world of oboe. Others have written eloquently and comprehen-
sively on the history of the oboe, so I refer to it only as it applies to a
specific musical or technical issue. Repertoire lists are obsolete as soon

as they are printed and can never be complete in any case, so I have not included one. Interested readers can find very thorough resources on extended techniques; these are addressed, but in a general rather than an exhaustively specific way (the bibliography has suggestions for further reading on all of these topics). Others are much more expert than I on improvisation and on popular, commercial, jazz, and world music, so these issues are covered only to the extent that they relate to music making on the oboe.

The information in this book is all practical. All of it can be applied by any student of the oboe (of whatever age and experience) to the craft and the art of making music on the oboe. Much of it can be transferred to performers on any instrument—practicing and phrasing are universal and will not change much whether one is playing the oboe or the euphonium. The text is liberally supplied with exercises and illustrations to make sure that the information can be readily absorbed and, if necessary, practiced in an organized way.

Much of the book is written in the first and second person. Sometimes this makes me sound like a drill sergeant rattling off instructions: "do this, don't do that." That isn't my intention; the intent is to be economical. Saying, "Put your feet flat on the floor" seems better to me than, "The student should make sure that his or her feet are placed flat on the floor." So, as you read, remember that all of the instructions are spoken in a kindly tone.

If there is one central concept to all of my thinking about making music on the oboe, it is that of efficiency. The oboe, while not an easy instrument, can nonetheless be made to sound easy. It can sing and speak effortlessly. The vexing difficulties of reed making and practicing can be streamlined to eliminate error and to provide maximum benefit to the player. Some of the journeys are necessarily quite laborious, but they should never be tortuous or confused. The most important premise in this book is that successful oboe playing depends on doing the very basic, simple (not easy!) things well. Every suggestion in the book, even the most time consuming, is in fact the short cut to success. Learn it right the first time, and then you can move on to learning the next thing.

While the text is all my own, much of the material is, of course, not my invention. Everything musical (and some nonmusical things) I have ever heard or seen or learned is in some way contained in this book. If what you read merely confirms what you already know, good. If you teach the same thing yourself, better still. But if you read something you have never thought of before, or even something you disagree with, give it a try. It has been tested in a harsh laboratory—up there on the stage in front of lots of audience members. It all works.

Acknowledgments

I am grateful to my oboe students at Arizona State University who read the entire manuscript and gave very helpful feedback: Carly Aylworth, Katie Mordarski (who also assisted very capably with the photographs), Dane Philipsen, Mary Simon, and Ashley Steves. My wife, Gail Schuring, in addition to taking care of me and making it possible for me to complete this project, also read the manuscript and made many important observations. I owe special thanks to Elizabeth Buck, whose careful and detailed reading of the manuscript changed the book very much for the better.

Contents

I

FUNDAMENTALS

1

Posture, Breathing,
and Support

Much of this information will seem obvious (and probably should seem obvious to anyone who has studied the oboe for some time)—"Oh, I knew that. . . ." But when oboe playing sounds bad or feels bad, the remedy is rarely found in the examination of detail or in the acquisition of tricks. Instead, some basic fundamental technique of playing either is defective or has been forgotten. There are no tricks. My teacher, John de Lancie, used to say, "You really don't need to know very many things to play the oboe." (Left unsaid was just how long and difficult the road to this little bit of knowledge would be.) Improvement on the oboe depends on a thorough and constant effort to master the very basics of playing the instrument—the "simple" things you were meant to learn from your first teacher in your first few lessons. Over time, oboe playing can become so automatic, so habitual, that a periodic self-examination is worthwhile. Often you aren't doing what you think you are.

In a moment of frustration, after trying for weeks to improve the matter, I once asked a very tense and contorted student, "Doesn't that feel awful?" "No," came the reply. "It feels like playing the oboe." So do look at yourself and your students and make sure that what seems normal and familiar is also efficient.

Efficiency and ease are the key words in this discussion. But they do not mean that oboe playing should be lazy. Playing the oboe can actually be quite strenuous, and oboe players should work hard, but every morsel of energy expended should be audible in the musical result.

Relaxation and efficiency are the result of using the right muscles to do the work so that the wrong muscles don't have to.

Oboists often jump to conclusions. A passage sounds bad, and blame is quickly assigned to the most popular scapegoat: the reed. It may or may not be the reed, but before concluding anything, read the following, and make sure that all of the basics are working correctly. Only then should the process of diagnosis proceed further.

Goals

Air is the foundation of everything we do on the oboe. Without proper, relaxed tone production, every aspect of playing the instrument suffers. Issues of inappropriate tension, unusual reedmaking styles, even awkward technical facility and articulation can usually be traced to inadequate or unhealthy air supply to the instrument. If the right muscles are not doing their work, the wrong muscles will have to step in and try.

It is possible to play the oboe without discomfort. Indeed, it's possible to sing through the oboe with complete ease and freedom while still meeting all the technical and dynamic demands of the music. Breathing and supporting that breath are the foundations. Our goals are:

- To maintain an erect, stable, posture.
- To inhale air to all portions of the lungs.
- To support the air firmly with an energy that matches the requirements of the reed (assuming the reed has been adjusted to match the requirements of the player).

Posture

Without excellent posture, the air has no space to occupy, and the muscles are unable to perform their proper tasks. Effective posture arranges the body in a straight line from the hips all the way to the head, as though it is suspended by a hook from above. Hold yourself with a straight back, with the shoulders above the hips and the head above the shoulders. Don't bring your head forward: bring the oboe to you, don't go to the oboe. If this posture is difficult to visualize, back up against a wall and try to touch the wall at every point between your hips and your head. It won't be possible to do it completely, but try to grow as tall as you can. The correct posture can be maintained either standing or sitting, although standing is preferable for now—sitting compresses the abdominal region slightly and makes it easier to cheat the breathing and support. If you stand, place your feet about as far apart as your shoulders, with one foot slightly in front of the other for stability and balance. Don't lock your knees or hold any tension in your legs. Imagine that your center of gravity is low—in your thighs—and that your feet are firmly rooted in the ground. Don't lean forward on your toes or back on your heels. Shifting weight slightly from side to side is a good idea to help keep your legs relaxed. Stand proudly; don't collapse your upper chest. You need a posture that is erect, relaxed, and stable. If you sit, keep your upper body in the same arrangement—a straight line from the hips to the head—and try to keep the angle of the fold at the hips to a minimum. Put your feet flat on the floor. Don't cross your legs; don't even cross your feet.

Once seated or standing comfortably (and straight), introduce the oboe. Hold it at about a 45 degree angle to your body (more about this later), with your shoulders relaxed (not bunched up around your neck) and your elbows comfortably away from your sides—say, three to six inches. Don't clench the elbows tightly to your sides, but don't let them fly away like bird wings either. Keep your head upright above your back without leaning forward to reach the oboe; bring the oboe to you.

Breathing

Now that you're upright, you can take a breath. The goal is to occupy all parts of the lungs with air. The breathing and support mechanism needs to work like a toothpaste tube—when you squeeze from the bottom, toothpaste should come out the top—so that pressure from the abdomen (this is called "supporting"—more about this in a few paragraphs) will result in air pressure at the reed. There must be air everywhere between the abdomen and the reed; it is impossible to support the air column otherwise.

Every student has heard, "Breathe from the diaphragm!" without really knowing what that means. Where is the diaphragm? What does it do? Why is it important to wind playing? The diaphragm is "the partition of muscles and tendons between the chest cavity and the abdominal cavity."[1] Its muscular action pulls downward when we inhale and relaxes as we exhale. The diaphragm cannot assist in forcefully expelling air; it merely relaxes during the exhale portion of the cycle. Indeed, all muscles work in one direction only; when required, they have opposing muscles to accomplish the reverse (for example, the body has both a biceps muscle to lift the arm and a triceps muscle opposite to extend it again).

During quiet breathing, the diaphragm moves only an inch or so; during more demanding applications, it can move up to four inches. During quiet exhalation, the diaphragm's relaxation is sufficient to expel the air; for more athletic situations (playing the oboe is certainly athletic in this regard), the motion of the diaphragm must be assisted by the abdominal muscles (supported). So the inhalation of air is the whole extent of the diaphragm's contribution to oboe playing. You cannot support from the diaphragm; you cannot vibrate from the diaphragm.

1. Neufeld, *Webster's New World Dictionary of American English*, p. 380.

I would honestly prefer to leave the diaphragm out of the breathing discussion altogether—nobody can really visualize or feel their diaphragm,
and it wouldn't help if you could—but the use of the term is so well established that this much discussion, at least, is unavoidable.

Instead of dwelling on the diaphragm, it is important to begin by
breathing as deeply as possible—all the way to the bottom of the lungs—
and to imagine filling to the top from there. Most students are adept
enough at taking a shallow breath, so the first goal is to bring air all the
way to the bottom of the lungs. Everyone frequently does this naturally
when sleeping, laughing, coughing, or gasping—in fact, when doing just
about anything besides playing the oboe. It's worth trying a few of these
natural things to observe how they feel. Yawn—a really deep, satisfying
yawn. Feel how the air goes all the way down. Do you feel how your
stomach goes out? Laugh. Feel how your stomach moves? Cough. Feel
the same thing. Gasp as if you're suddenly scared to death. Pant like a
dog. All should give the same basic sensation. Not surprisingly, many
students would rather not gasp and pant in front of their teacher, so we
will use the following exercise, which works flawlessly. I have never had
it fail to bring air to the bottom of the lungs immediately and correctly.

Exercise

To Promote Proper Deep Breathing

> Sit on the edge of a chair and fall forward until your hands
> touch the floor. Relax and inhale. Make sure that the posture
> is really relaxed and that your body is just hanging forward.
> Breathe. An observer should see your lower back expand;
> you should feel your belly expand against your legs. Repeat
> the breath a few times, especially if it is a new sensation. Sit
> upright again at intervals—you don't want to get dizzy. Now
> try it again a few more times. Then, while gradually moving
> to an upright sitting position, continue to take slow deep
> breaths while maintaining the same feeling. Remember to
> take deep, full breaths. It should be possible to maintain the
> proper sensation in any posture. If the feeling of breathing
> deeply is unfamiliar, you will need to repeat this exercise
> frequently to remind yourself of the proper technique.

Your abdomen should expand first, then your chest. The rib cage also
has muscles that can assist in expanding the lungs, and these should be
used second, not first. But they must be used. Many students, under the
impression that they must "breathe from the diaphragm," never fill up
the chest at all. Remember the toothpaste tube—not filling the chest is
as useless as filling only the chest; we must inhale air to all parts of the

lungs. A helper or a teacher should verify this by putting his or her hands on either side of your back just below the armpits. After the abdomen expands, the upper back should expand also, forcing the observer's hands apart. The idea is to expand the torso—to make it wider, not taller. If breathing makes you taller, reexamine your posture; it is likely too slumped over. Evelyn Rothwell, in her excellent book *Oboe Technique*,[2] describes the correct three-stage breath. First the belly expands; then the chest expands (shown by the upper back expanding also); and finally the upper chest just below the neck rises. At that point the stomach will probably come back in slightly, which is normal and correct.

This is a very large breath—unnecessary and rather uncomfortable for the oboe. The purpose of taking the large breath is to create expansion in the entire upper body, thereby teaching you the proper sensation so you can later take a partial breath with the same correct technique. So, before beginning to play, release a portion of the large breath. Not too much—just enough that you feel natural rather than inflated. It is not important to take a very large breath every time, but it is essential to take a breath that includes all parts of the lungs, or the support cannot work properly. Eventually, taking a correct partial breath will be easy. The large breath is just for practice. Remember, as with anything that requires practice, if you take a breath and it doesn't feel right, don't play. Exhale and try again. A new, correct habit can be developed very quickly if you never do it wrong.

Blowing (Support)

"Support," along with "diaphragm," is another word every student knows, usually without being able to describe it convincingly. Support is nothing more than firmly pushing inward and slightly upward with the abdominal muscles. Aim at an imaginary spot about halfway up your spine. This pushing displaces the internal organs, which in turn displace the diaphragm upward; the diaphragm pushes against the bottom of the lungs, placing their contents under pressure, and this in turn creates air pressure at the reed. You can see from this description how essential it is to have air filling all parts of the lungs.

When the abdominal muscles are tensed, the entire region of muscle will feel activated and tight. But it is possible to identify one particular place where the main focus of the tension is felt: around the belt buckle, or a few inches below the navel. Pushing from too high creates a lot of tension, but no actual support. Some students have discovered that the diaphragm is somewhere around the bottom of the rib cage; armed with this piece of irrelevant information, they try to support from there with weak results. Feel the focus of the tension around the belt buckle or a bit below. Examine your technique very carefully where

2. Rothwell, *Oboe Technique*, pp. 5–6.

these matters of support placement and direction are concerned—many students push in the wrong direction and/or feel the focus of the tension much too high. Push inward and upward while feeling the focus of that tension a few inches below the navel.

Take a moment and read the previous paragraph again. Make sure that when you play, you are tensing the abdominal muscles around the belt buckle and pushing inward and upward. Any deviation from this technique means that the right muscles are prevented from doing their work, which forces the wrong muscles to step in and help. I have worked with very advanced players who were not doing this correctly and suffered from mysterious subtle problems they could not diagnose. The oboe is played with the whole body and can become a very complex puzzle if this basic technique is not properly learned. So, before proceeding, ask a few questions:

· Is your posture erect, yet relaxed?
· Are you breathing in a way that supplies air to every part of the lungs?
· Is your support focused in a spot roughly near your belt buckle?
· Are you supporting by tightening the abdominal muscles in an inward and slightly upward direction?

The tension should be firm, yet elastic—not rigid. The tension will vary to suit the dynamic and phrasing demands of the music. More sound requires more air; less sound requires less air, in the same way that speaking softly needs little energy and shouting needs a lot.

It is vital that every sound you make be supported. With a good ear and enough experience, it is possible to make an acceptable sound with little or no support—the beginning of a slippery slope that ends in uncomfortable playing without life or projection. Think of support like the engine in your car: sometimes it runs under heavy acceleration, sometimes it idles, sometimes it cruises on the freeway, but it is always running. Without the engine, the rest of the car is useless, no matter how luxurious the accessories. So tense your abdominal muscles, push inward and slightly upward, and make sure that this tension is felt around the belt buckle or slightly below.

Reeds and Resistance

The reed is an essential link in the sound-production chain. If the reed is uncomfortable or reluctant, no effort to produce a free singing tone can succeed. Our relaxed, ideal way of playing demands a good reed that vibrates freely and supports the pitch firmly.

The resistance of the reed must be suited to the player's capacity, allowing the player to play comfortably and naturally. You must be able to play against the resistance of the reed, not more and not less. If the reed needs, say, five pounds of air pressure to vibrate well, you should push with five pounds of pressure from the abdomen and allow that energy to transfer, unrestricted, into five pounds of pressure at the reed. ("Five pounds" is an arbitrarily chosen number.) Instead, many players are much less efficient than this: they push with ten or fifteen pounds (not real numbers, remember, just examples) and then find all sorts of ways to restrict the excess flow—with tension at the embouchure, in the throat, and in the upper chest—thereby artificially increasing the resistance of the reed. We all know players who work very hard to make very little sound by trying to regulate a hopeless system of opposing tensions. This has its origin in a very good intention: if X amount of air is good (like two aspirin), then surely 5X amount of air must be better (like ten aspirin?). Overblowing is just as dangerous as underblowing.

Exercise

To Find the Appropriate Amount of Air Pressure

Here's a simple exercise to find the correct effort: make a very slow breath attack—don't start the note with the tongue, just with the air—on an easy note (the orchestra tuning A is a good choice). Set the embouchure neutrally, making no effort to control either the dynamic or the tone color. Start by blowing very gently—the only sound will be air passing through the reed—and gradually increase the air until the reed speaks, which should occur at around mezzo piano. Adjust your reed until it speaks naturally at mezzo piano. If it speaks at a softer dynamic, the reed will feel limited; louder, and the reed will be too hard.

With the reed now properly adjusted, try the exercise again, and after the reed speaks, continue to increase the air until the tone firms up to a solid, resonant mezzo forte. You are now playing against the resistance of the reed. In other words, your production of air and the reed's consumption of air are correctly matched. With too little air, the sound will be lifeless and flat, and you'll be tempted to artificially support the tone with throat and embouchure tension. So, up to a point, more air is good. But with too much air, the tone will be coarse and spread, and you'll be tempted to restrain it with throat and embouchure tension. Play against the resistance of the reed. Blow very hard only to get more intensity, not as a matter of routine. Giving a consistent 150 percent effort is every bit as dangerous as giving only 50 percent.

The reliability of this exercise depends on a reed that resists your efforts in a way that is natural and comfortable for you. Hence the importance of adjusting the reed until it speaks at mezzo piano for you, not for anyone else. If mezzo piano seems a bit soft, remember that you will always have to work hard to play loud; if you also have to work hard to play soft, your dynamic range will tend to stay in the middle. So adjust reeds to speak naturally at mezzo piano. We will discuss this idea more thoroughly when talking about tone concept.

Breathing while Playing

Now that you know how to take a good breath, make sure to do it much more often than you need to. Breathing is not merely a chance for air; it provides relaxation. Breathe often. Breathing lets blood back into your embouchure and relaxes the muscles, provides fresh oxygen and relaxes you, and allows for improved endurance and tone. On the oboe, you will never use all the air you inhale with a normal breath; you will always need to exhale to remove the excess air that is sitting in your lungs losing oxygen and making you feel suffocated. Don't wait until you need a breath to take one. If there is time, disengage the reed from the lower lip completely; this will allow blood back into this vital contact patch.

Plan your breathing. The most common reason for player exhaustion is a failure to plan breathing. Once the plan is settled, mark all of it in the music and follow it consistently. You cannot produce a consistent performance with inconsistent breathing. When planning, consider these things:

1. *Where to breathe*. Often, the places are indicated by rests and are completely obvious. When they are not, plan the breathing places to cause minimum disruption to the phrasing. Many times the breaths can be planned to actually enhance the phrasing. Listen to any good singer and notice how often he or she breathes and how little the breathing disturbs the music. If the phrasing is not immediately apparent to you, the "Expression" chapter later in this book should be helpful.
2. *What to do when you breathe*. On the oboe, you must always exhale first and then inhale. If there is time, complete the full breath cycle of exhale/inhale. But there is often not enough time. If that is the case, consider what to do—exhale or inhale? If there are two small breathing places relatively close together, you can exhale at one place, play a little longer, and inhale at the second. If you are uncomfortable arriving at a breathing place and exhaling, practice this until it is completely natural. Being able to exhale only and continue playing is an essential

Example 1.1   Exercise to practice alternation of exhales and inhales.

technique vital to good playing. Practice the simple exercise shown in example 1.1 until you are able to do this with complete comfort.

If you are undecided about whether to inhale or exhale—exhale; your body will remind you to inhale soon enough. Avoid the tendency, exacerbated by hasty breathing, to exhale a small amount of air and inhale a large amount of air. If you do this repeatedly, it will result in suffocation and exhaustion.

3. *Gauge your breath.* Remember that the breath you take now is to prepare you for the phrase to come; it is not to help you recover from the phrase just completed. This may seem obvious, but it is often overlooked. Many people play entire movements one breath behind, getting more and more tired as they go along. So gauge the size of your breath. If the next phrase is very long, take a full breath; if it is not, take a smaller breath. If you leave less excess to exhale, your breathing will be much more efficient.

4. *Prepare to breathe.* Breathing can be much better disguised and made much less obtrusive if it occurs with purpose and preparation. Carelessly gasping as quickly as possible is bad both musically and physically. The breath will be less obvious if it is given plenty of time, with a beautiful release preceding it and a smooth reentry following it. So, just as you would make certain physical preparations in advance of a subito piano or a large register shift, you can prepare to take a really excellent breath.

You will know that your breathing plan is successful if you feel refreshed every time you inhale. If you accumulate a large quantity of stale air, or if you arrive at the end of the piece just bursting to exhale, the breathing plan is not yet effective enough. Make some adjustments and try it again. When the plan seems reliable and consistent, mark it in the music. You will need to develop some system of shorthand to distinguish "in" breaths from "out" breaths and large breaths from partial breaths. Mark the plan in the music and then *follow the plan.* Too often players accidentally skip a breath, breathe in when they meant to breathe out, or make some other crucial error. Always be sure to do this; it can make the difference between completing the movement and not. When the consequences are that serious, it is not smart to trust to your memory.

With enough planning and careful execution, even very taxing pieces will become playable. For the few pieces that remain, you can always learn to circular breathe.

Circular Breathing for Oboe: A Step-by-Step Guide

Circular breathing is an essential part of oboe technique. Anyone who has learned to do it will never give it up. But it is not without controversy. Laypeople view it as some sort of magic trick—how can air go in and come out at the same time? Of course, glass blowers have been doing it for centuries, and it was almost surely used while playing some very ancient instruments. It is in no way a radical, avant-garde technique. Yet circular breathing is still regarded with suspicion by some who dismiss it as a virtuoso party trick that distorts the natural, human qualities of music. So it is important never to use it that way. Circular breathing is not really intended to increase the distance between breathing points, which should remain within the realm of comfort (yours and the listener's). Rather, it is a wonderful technique to enhance playing and increase comfort. Increased comfort gives increased endurance, more stability, better tone quality, and less tension. It allows players to reach the end of the concert with their power and control still intact. Everyone has sometimes wished for just a little more air (or a little less air) while playing a phrase. Circular breathing is the answer to these dilemmas; it can assure almost constant comfort.

Circular breathing can be abused and applied without sensitivity, just like any other technique: we have all heard insensitive tonguing, poor rhythmic discipline, bad intonation, uneven technique, and so on. In each case, it is not the technique that is at fault, but the mastery of the technique. An artistic player will play artistically in every case, and a dull one will not. Circular breathing has no effect on this result.

The description that follows is somewhat detailed. Actually, though, circular breathing is not very difficult, and some players are able to learn it very quickly with only a little guidance. So, if your result feels correct and the application of the technique seems effective, feel free to skip steps as you like.

There are two elements to the technique. You must be able to spit air through the reed instead of blowing. And you must be able to breathe in and out through your nose while spitting the air in your mouth. "Spitting" means using the cheek muscles and the tongue to force the air inside of your mouth through the reed.

First, we get comfortable spitting. . . .

Seal your lips and fill up your cheeks with air. Really puff them out. Then, using just the cheeks, force the air out of your mouth quickly and aggressively. Make a raspberry noise if you like, do it with enthusiasm, and repeat it until you are comfortable using just the cheeks to expel air through your lips. This is a primitive preliminary exercise to show that it is possible to expel air stored in the mouth without blowing any air stored in the lungs.

For a more refined exercise, take a mouthful of water and spit it into the sink through a coffee straw. A hollow coffee stirrer approximates the resistance of the oboe reed. Practice this until you can spit a continuous, energetic stream for two or three seconds.

Try the same thing with air. Take the coffee stirrer, submerge it in a glass of water, and see how long you can keep the air bubbles going. Don't blow air, spit it. You may have to puff your cheeks a fair amount. Observe that a forward movement of the tongue also propels the air. Since the oboe doesn't need a large quantity of air, that tongue motion will eventually be all that is needed to push enough air through the reed. The cheek puffing will not be necessary; it is merely a preparatory exercise to help you isolate the spitting from the blowing.

Initially, separating the spitting from the blowing will be the main difficulty. We are so used to blowing air and not spitting it that it is easy to revert to blowing without even being aware of it. So return to using water and the coffee stirrer as necessary. Continue to puff the cheeks to heighten the awareness that only what is in the mouth is being expelled.

Now try to spit air through a reed. Try to sustain a sound for two or three seconds. The sound needs to have good energy and intensity and to be around a C in pitch (two octaves above middle C on the piano). Remember to make sure you are spitting air and not blowing air. Practice the spitting until the sound has good duration and intensity. This may take a little time. Most initial attempts on the reed sound rather weak, but they quickly improve with regular practice.

Now try it with the oboe. Adding the oboe to the equation adds some resistance to the picture, but again, you should be able to sustain a sound for two or three seconds just spitting. Try to use mostly (or entirely) the tongue to push the air through the reed. For now, don't worry if the sound is unstable or distorted.

Once you're comfortable spitting, practice breathing in and out while doing it. You may want to return to practicing with the coffee stirrer if the oboe's resistance is too distracting. Then go back to the reed and eventually to the oboe. It is important to practice breathing while spitting until it works as one motion, not two.

Now comes the tricky part. You want to transition from blowing to spitting to blowing again. Take your time. Most beginners feel like they have to do this all in a big rush: do three things at once, and take the breath in a split second. You don't. If you can make a sound for two to three seconds while spitting, that gives you a lot of time to take your breath. Relax.

There will almost always be a small bump in the sound as you make the transitions. At first, there may be a large bump or even no sound at all. Relax, take your time, and do everything smoothly. It can take time (a year is not too long) before you are confident enough to use circular breathing in a recital situation. In the meanwhile, practice it during scales, during long tones, and during loud tutti passages in ensemble rehearsals (Don't ever waste time in ensembles. You can always do something productive to keep your mind occupied, even if nobody can hear a note you play. Think of it as free practice time.) Don't think of circular breathing as a special technique, nor as something particularly difficult. It is neither. And, as with anything that requires a complex synchronization of events, do not be troubled by unsuccessful attempts; rather, pay very close attention to the times the technique works beautifully, making sure to learn something each time you do it correctly. Think of it like learning to ride a bicycle—very awkward at first, hard to forget later.

Then, after you can do it, pick your spots carefully to keep the small bumps from being heard. Trills and fast scales are great places to circular breathe. Soft, long, low notes are bad. Some things are very difficult to do while circular breathing. Tonguing while circular breathing requires an adaptation of the technique—since the tongue is now busy articulating, the air has to be pushed through the instrument using the cheeks rather than the tongue. This technique can be learned, but it usually isn't too hard to find an alternate place to circular breathe.

I have never figured out how to create a vibrato while circular breathing, so expressive exposed passages are not good candidates unless you learn how to do this. But applied selectively and executed smoothly, circular breathing can be completely unobtrusive; even your neighbor onstage might be unaware that you are doing it.

Don't forget that you can exhale through your nose just as easily as you can inhale. Often using circular breathing to get rid of a little air is even more refreshing than inhaling.

Now you can enjoy your newfound freedom. For example, the first long statement of the Strauss Oboe Concerto has several easy and logical places to breathe. Use these to exhale only, and use circular breathing to inhale while playing the sixteenth notes. It makes the opening statement much easier from a physical perspective and leaves you enough energy to actually play fortissimo at the end.

Summary of Chapter 1

Think about breathing and blowing every time you play. Never do it wrong. Remember that if oboe playing sounds bad, it is seldom because of some detail. It is almost always because something fundamental was forgotten. If you don't sound good, before you embark on any process of correction (often jumping to conclusions), take a little inventory of the fundamentals:

- Use good posture.
- Take a proper three-stage breath.

- Exhale a portion before playing if the breath was very large (remember that the very large breath is not necessary once you consistently breathe in a way that brings air to all portions of the lungs equally).
- Support well: elastic, not hard. Feel the focus of the tension around the belt buckle, and push inward and upward from there.
- Make sure your reed resists your breath comfortably.
- Stay out of your own way. If the right muscles are doing their work, that should be easy.

If you take care of those few things and have an instrument and a reed that function well, you should sound good most of the time with little discomfort. Make sure to check yourself (and your students) on a regular basis; these good habits can fall by the wayside as the necessity for preparing this solo or that audition intrudes. Be vigilant. Until the technique of blowing through the instrument is stable, nothing else can be.

2

Embouchure and Other Matters of Tone Production

Three factors regulate the quality (dynamic, tone color, etc.) and/or the pitch of the tone: air, reed placement, and embouchure formation. The basic ground rules are: the air should be energetic; as little of the reed as is practical should be placed in the mouth; and the embouchure tension should be minimal. After reading the preceding chapter to make sure that the air production is healthy, adjusting the rest of the tone-production chain should be much more effective.

These three factors must work in balance; any deviation in one area will require compensation by the others. But each element has its primary, though not exclusive, area of responsibility. I assign these duties as follows:

- *The air is responsible for the dynamic.* Just as you exert more energy when shouting than when whispering, you blow more air for a louder sound and less air for a softer one. Refer to the breath attack exercise described in chapter 1 to make sure that the air energy is appropriate.
- *The embouchure is responsible for the tone color.* Of course, this is closely related to dynamics, since softer playing will want a duller tone color, while louder playing will require a more brilliant one. To find the basically correct embouchure tension, hold the reed (just the reed) in your mouth (no hands) while blowing firmly and tonguing hard. The reed should bounce only slightly from the tonguing, and the pitch of the sound should be C (two oc-

taves above middle C on the piano). If the reed bounces and the pitch is lower than C, firm the embouchure (possibly in conjunction with increasing the air) until everything is correct. If the pitch is too high and the reed won't move no matter how aggressively you tongue, the embouchure is too firm.

· *The reed placement is responsible for the pitch.* More reed in the mouth will produce a sharper pitch, while less reed will produce a flatter one. It is also necessary to gradually take more reed into the mouth for higher notes. To find the correct reed placement, start with what you know is too little reed—the sound will be flat and spread. Make sure the air production is healthy and the embouchure has been adjusted as described in the previous paragraph. Then gradually feed in slightly more reed until the sound just begins to firm up and resonate. In matters of reed placement, a millimeter is a large adjustment, so proceed with care. Stop and listen. If the pitch is still slightly low, try to blow the note into place. Now take in just a tiny bit more reed and notice how much more shallow the sound becomes. Avoid that placement; use the riskier one. In other words, the best place to play is with a reed placement that is just barely not flat.

Of course, these responsibilities inevitably overlap: the reed placement will alter the tone color, the embouchure formation will alter the pitch, and the air will alter almost everything. My goal in describing primary roles for each of these considerations is to encourage the player to regard air as the chief agent motivating the tone, with everything else arranged to support that role. In other words, the air is in charge, not the embouchure nor anything else.

Embouchure Formation

Embouchure formation is difficult to diagram or illustrate, since most of the action takes place out of view. Instead, I will discuss a few general concepts that will promote an efficient configuration.

The jaw should not be thrust forward. Keep it in a relaxed position, creating the largest possible space inside your mouth. Try this exercise: Place your hand, with the palm facing upward toward the ceiling, on your chest. Then, without looking down, blow on your hand. The resulting jaw position, though slightly exaggerated, is a good starting point for forming the embouchure.

The shape of the embouchure is round. Imagine a pucker shape, or a whistle shape turned inward. Imagine you are sucking a very thick milk shake through a straw, and turn that shape inward. Do not "smile."

To form the embouchure, place the tip of the reed near the pink line (the line where the lip meets the skin) on your lower lip. The reed tip should rest a millimeter or two into the red part of your lower lip.

Gently roll the lips over the teeth, taking the reed in with them, and close your mouth. The tip of the reed should extend just beyond the lower lip, allowing the tongue to find it rather easily. When the embouchure is formed, the pink line of the lower lip will be exactly even with the lower teeth. Players with very full lips may need to start by placing the reed a little further up on the lower lip—the goal is to have only a millimeter or two of reed tip exposed inside the mouth.

This formation will give the reed a fair amount of lip coverage, preventing the noisy tip vibrations from being heard too noticeably. The tip of the reed is the thinnest part, vibrating the most freely and also the most harshly. Some lip coverage of the tip is necessary to muffle and sweeten the sound. Forming the embouchure by placing the reed tip too far in will leave too much of the reed's tip free inside the mouth, giving a harsh sound.

All muscle tension is held at the corners of the mouth. Any tension in the middle of the mouth where the reed rests should be eliminated. Try saying "mmmmm," pressing the lips firmly together and creating muscle tension in the middle of the lips. If any of that same feeling is present while playing, get rid of it. Support the tone with firm corners, energetic air pressure, and proper reed placement—not with biting.

"Biting" is another word most young oboists know, primarily because so many of them are guilty of it. It does not have to mean that the jaw or the teeth are doing anything; it is enough if the middle of the embouchure is pinching, even slightly, from above and below the reed. All energy should come from the corners of the mouth, not from above and below the reed.

Most young players bite with the best of intentions. Usually their air production is too weak to support the tone by itself, making the biting almost essential to produce anything tolerable. So simply telling the student not to bite is useless: you have to combine that advice with really effective breathing lessons and active air support.

Forming the embouchure as just described should result in an embouchure that leaves none of the red part of the lips exposed. The lips themselves have little musculature; the muscles that work the embouchure surround the lips and are especially felt at the corners of the mouth, extending slightly into the cheeks. If there is too little of the lips inside the mouth, the muscles at the corners of the mouth have nothing to act upon, leaving the player little choice but to apply tension to the reed from above and below. The action of the embouchure should come from the corners of the mouth moving toward the reed. The more pronounced this action is, the more muffled the tone color will be.

It has never worked for me to hold the chin flat. The idea behind this concept is to free the reed of excess lip coverage, allowing it to vibrate more freely. For me, the result is that the sound is too shallow and harsh, and I don't have enough control over the tone color. Many good players swear by this setup, so if your teacher teaches it, go ahead and follow it. But, if it feels unnatural to you, you are not alone.

Manipulating Dynamics

Dynamics are regulated primarily with air, with the embouchure joining only when the softest sounds require additional support. As much as possible, control the dynamics with air. Try an experiment: Play a diminuendo using only air. Start mezzo forte and gradually diminish the air (not the support!) until the note quits, sags, or both. The end won't be pretty, but that isn't the point; this is an exercise to find the threshold of the reed's vibration. Try it a few times to get a good feel for the threshold and the warning signs of its arrival. Adjust your reed if necessary; the sound should fade to at least mezzo piano, even piano, before faltering. It is only at this threshold that the embouchure should intervene—not before.

Try the diminuendo again, and this time, just before the note begins to sag, gradually begin to muffle the sound slightly by bringing the corners of your mouth toward the reed. As the embouchure closes, the air will have to increase slightly to compensate for the artificially increased resistance of the reed. Continue to bring the embouchure in toward the reed and continue to blow, with very good attention to support and blowing through the oboe. Do not bite or apply any muscle tension with the middle of your mouth. (As you bring the corners of your mouth toward the middle, the pad in the center of your embouchure, where the reed rests, will become thicker and firmer. That is natural and correct and should not be confused with active muscle participation by the middle of the mouth. But you must avoid applying any additional muscle tension.) Keeping the air and the embouchure balanced should permit you to make a diminuendo to complete silence with little effort. Keep your attention on focusing the air forward and upward, rather than on closing the embouchure. Think of using the embouchure to muffle the tone color. If the note stops before you intended it to, pay even more attention to the air, since the only logical reason for the sound to stop is that there is not enough air. When you practice diminuendos in this way, you will have many failed attempts. Ignore them. Instead, learn from the times when the result is really beautiful and easy.

Reed Placement

It is important to play with as little reed in the mouth as possible. The advantages of playing on the tip of the reed are clear. The reed is thinner and more pliable there, and thus more easily manipulated with the embouchure. More important, placing too much of the tip of the reed inside the mouth emphasizes the short, brilliant tip vibrations too much.

A bit of tip muffling warms up the sound considerably. So play as close to the tip of the reed as you dare. Arrange your embouchure tension and reed placement so that if you were to accidentally miss the center of the note, you would miss flat.

Flat playing is the great fear of oboists. It sounds spread and wild and incompetent. If you play flat, everyone can hear it, and everyone knows that something is wrong. Many oboists protect against this embarrassment by playing just a little sharp all of the time. That doesn't sound as bad, but sharp playing is just as out of tune as flat playing is. And by playing sharp, oboists are depriving themselves of something very valuable: resonance. The greatest resonance of the oboe, and the finest control, lies in that placement of just-barely-not-flat.

The higher the note, the more reed you need in your mouth. As you take in more reed, roll the lips and the reed together. Then, when you return to a lower note, the reed can come out of the mouth without distorting the embouchure. This movement is controlled by the right thumb; the lips are passive and merely follow the reed.

Always play as near the tip as you can without the pitch sagging. Make sure the air is correct, or nothing can be evaluated with any accuracy. If the pitch is a bit low, especially in the upper register, try to blow the note up into place before adjusting anything else.

A Few More Important Things

Rather than worry about the thousands of places in your body that should be relaxed, be aware of the two places that require tension: the abdominal muscles around the belt and the facial muscles at the corners of the mouth. Relax everything else.

The interior vowel shape in the mouth should be "awh." "Oh" and "ah" also work, though not quite as well. Avoid tight sounds like "eh" and especially "ee." "Awh" works for the range of the oboe up to high E-flat (on the third ledger line above the treble staff). Higher than that and a tighter vowel shape is needed to voice the notes. Of course, a different vowel shape can be used anytime the tone color demands it; but the "awh" vowel shape is a basic position giving maximum resonance and fullness. Many players unconsciously close the vowel shape as they go higher; this can be helpful in keeping the notes focused but should not be done unconsciously. Maintaining an open "awh" vowel shape all the way to high D or E-flat places an unusual demand on the air supply, something that every player should be able to manage even if they do not use it all the time.

In the extreme high register (high E and above), all bets are off. To produce a firm, focused high F or G requires an embouchure firmly stretched over the teeth, lots of air pressure, lots of reed in the mouth, and a tight vowel shape—"ee" works quite well here.

Do not allow any air to puff into the cheeks, nor between the teeth and the lips. Even the smallest amount will force the embouchure to distort and weaken.

The tongue, even when not being used for articulation, should be drawn well back in the mouth. If you imagine your mouth cavity as a sphere, the tip of the tongue should be in the exact center of it. From there it will arch upward to nearly meet the roof of your mouth at the back. The tip of the tongue should need only a short motion directly forward to meet the tip of the reed for tonguing. If the tongue is held underneath the reed while playing, articulation will suffer, of course, but so will tone support and stability. If the tip of your tongue is anywhere near your lower teeth, draw it back.

Every player has an ideal angle at which he or she holds the oboe. Experiment with raising and lowering the instrument to find your best spot. The goal is to have the upper and lower lips meet their respective reed blades at the same spot. The three basic positions could be described as head up, oboe down; head down, oboe up; and in between. While sustaining a good warm forte tone, sweep the oboe up and down until you find the most resonant place.

Keep in mind that it is easily possible to overdo all of the recommended actions. It is possible to overblow, it is possible to play with too little reed in the mouth, and it is certainly possible to play with an embouchure that is relaxed to mush. An experienced teacher is essential for helping young players find the right balance and maintain steady progress toward a healthy tone production.

Tone Concept

The goal of the preceding ideas is to allow players to produce a free, singing tone that comes from the reed and the air doing most of the work. The embouchure should support the reed and support the tone, but it must not interfere with the vibrancy of the reed. It must allow a sound as rich in overtones as possible. It is an important characteristic of oboe tone that the overtones are relatively strong compared with the fundamental, which is what gives the oboe its distinctive sound quality. The flute, by comparison, has relatively weak overtones when compared with the fundamental, giving it a more pure sound. A brief digression will show how to use this information to good purpose.

One of the great difficulties of music making is finding a way to make subjective things (like tone quality) objective. How do we decide when a tone has quality? If we think about other things of great quality—say, poetry or wine—why are some better than others? Why is a poem by T. S. Eliot better than an advertising jingle? Why are some legendary vintages better than the everyday glass of wine? It has nothing to do with what we might like better at that moment—certainly we don't drink great wine every day, nor do we always read poetry—but there is an intrinsic quality to these things that is just better. What is it? The key ingredient, I think, is density—the poem conveys more information on more levels using fewer words, while the great wine has more flavors of greater intensity and longer duration.

Applying this to oboe tone, then, it stands to reason that the most beautiful sound on the oboe will be the one with the greatest complexity —in other words, with the greatest saturation of overtones present: "Any of the attendant higher tones heard with a fundamental tone produced by the vibration of a given string or column of air, having a frequency of vibration that is an exact multiple of the frequency of the fundamental."[1] Some of these overtones will be rather brilliant and sound harsh to your ear; do not reject these. Many players, in their effort to produce a dark sound, will produce a dull one instead. A beautiful sound is not necessarily dark or bright—rather, it is one that contains the most resonance and complexity without sacrificing control. A truly beautiful tone has the entire spectrum of color, ranging from a warm fuzziness at the bottom to a brilliant, piercing quality at the top. That brilliance or ringing in the tone is precisely the ingredient that needs to be encouraged. It is the most vulnerable part of the tone—any little deviation in reed placement or embouchure action will cause it to disappear. Its presence is your clue that everything is working properly—that you have struck the bull's-eye of the note. It can be very difficult to know how you really sound, since the sound in your ear is not the sound in the listener's ear. Being alert to the presence of this ringing quality can give you guidance about when your sound is working well and when it is not. It is much easier to hear this on some notes than others (upper G and F-sharp at the top of the staff are good places to start), and it is much easier to hear it when playing loud rather than soft. Eventually, though, the ringing sound becomes the vehicle that transports your tone and projects it to the listeners at any dynamic or in any register.

Listen to anyone whose sound you really admire, regardless of the instrument or voice. Listen as closely as possible, and you will find ingredients in that sound that on first impression are not noticed. These are what propel the sound into even large auditoriums. For a truly frightening experience, stand a foot or two away from a really great dramatic opera singer while he or she sings. The impression is deafening, but it isn't just loud—there is a brilliant quality to the sound that is almost painful at close distances. We should cultivate a similar projection in our tone.

While the previous two or three paragraphs may sound like I am encouraging loud playing, that is not at all my point. Resonance is not about power; it is about focus and placement. A big sound and a loud sound are not the same thing. On the contrary, a big sound results from the expansion of a pure compact sound, not from the compression of a

---

1. Neufeld, *Webster's New World Dictionary of American English*, p. 966.

raucous sound. Work to make the most beautiful piano sound possible with no effort. Insist that you and your reeds do this. Then, gradually allow that dolce sonority to grow and expand until your fullest sound still has that same sweet, focused quality. Until you can play piano with freedom, projection will be a spotty proposition. When you can play piano with freedom, you will notice that your sound contains a full spectrum of variety and color.

Of course, tone concept is formed not just by awareness of your own sound; it is also formed by awareness of every sound. Listening to players and singers of all kinds will help you develop a larger vocabulary of the tone elements you want to cultivate; it should also help you develop a sense of things you would prefer not to do. Gradually, by addition and subtraction, you will end up with the sound you want. It is really important not to limit your listening and awareness to oboe tone or to oboe players. Great singers and instrumentalists of all kinds will expose you to things you will wish you could do.

Every sound concept on the oboe is a balancing act between flexibility and agility on the one hand and, for lack of a better word, what we might call darkness on the other hand. Indeed, this compromise defines the central tension implicit in reed making: how do we balance the need for a reed that is vibrant with the need for stability? Again, careful listening and lots of practicing will help each individual find his or her place on this continuum. Every sound made by every successful player is an artistic choice; no one ever sets out to make a tone that spreads or distorts or that others regard as consistently ugly. Every player demands a sound that complements his or her artistic vision and, as such, deserves respect.

Pitch versus Resonance

On the oboe, pitch and resonance are almost the same thing. The resonance "bulls-eye" of a note will probably also be its pitch center. This helps players in two ways. If you aren't happy with the tone of a note, determine whether it is flat or sharp. Make the pitch correction, and the tone will probably improve also. Then, learn to improve your ear by becoming sensitive to the timbre deviations that accompany out of tune playing (thin or shallow for sharpness, weak and whiny for flatness). Most people react more quickly to timbre variations than to minute pitch deviations. All flat notes have a distinct tone quality in common, as do all sharp notes. Use your tuner to learn them, and look for the resonance center of every note. This topic is discussed further in chapter 6 on practicing.

Reeds Again

Without a good reed, none of these ideas will work. The reed needs to respond cleanly and readily at any dynamic; it should play in tune and hold its pitch at any dynamic, any level of air pressure, and any reasonable variation of embouchure tension or reed placement in the mouth. It needs to have a warm, resonant tone that will not flap or spread when pushed, nor die suddenly when diminished; and it needs to have an opening and a resistance that are comfortable. Failure in any of these areas will cause excess physical tension and result in fatigue and dull playing.

Vibrato

Perhaps vibrato is a subject more wisely left alone. The eminent French oboist and teacher Pierre Pierlot once said in an interview that he could say "nothing sensible about it"[2]—a sobering caution for someone about to say something about it.

Vibrato on the oboe is like a vocal vibrato: it is the natural result of a mature and efficient tone-production technique. Thus, although it is rare to find a twelve-year-old singer with a decent vibrato, it is just as rare to find a thirty-year-old singer without one. As technique and physique develop, so does vibrato. The placement of the vibrato—the long-standing rivalry between "throat" and "diaphragm" vibratos—is largely imaginary. The actual vibrato is created around the larynx, felt high in the chest. The player may perceive the origin differently, but that's where it ends up. Diaphragm vibrato does not exist.

I prefer to teach tone production and let the vibrato come naturally, which it usually does. For those occasions when it doesn't, a regimen of controlled abdominal thrusts usually gets it started. The following exercise is likely familiar to anyone who has ever studied the oboe—it is a gradual increase in the speed of abdominal bumps until they reach four or five per second. At that point, the pulsations will begin to be felt at the bottom of the neck. It is this sympathetic reaction to the abdominal thrusts that will become the vibrato we want. Once that is reliable, refinement can begin.

Exercise

To Develop a Natural, Singing Vibrato

> Use a metronome setting of 60 as your pulse. Begin by sustaining a tone (use an easy, free note in the middle of the staff) and "bumping" it very hard from the abdomen once each pulse. In other words, make a very fast crescendo and dimin-

2. "A Living Legend—Pierre Pierlot: An Interview," p. 84.

uendo once each second. It needs to be very quick and firm—
rather like driving over a speed bump too fast—not just a
swelling and a decrease. When the bump is consistent, increase the speed to twice per second, then three times, then
four, up to five. As the speed increases, the bumps will gradually become less violent.

At around four pulses per second, the sympathic vibrato
will begin to be felt around the larynx. The player will perceive it at the base of the neck, where it meets the chest. It is
this vibrato that we want to encourage. The whole point of
the abdominal pulsing exercise is to create this sympathetic
vibrato. Once it does occur, the abdominal pulses can cease
and the support held steady, while the vibrato takes place in
the upper chest. It will take the student some time to learn
to control and refine this, but he or she will eventually gain
a beautiful singing vibrato.

Some variation in placement is to be expected. If the result of the
preceding exercise is a pleasing vibrato that feels like it originates an
inch higher or lower, this is not important. Indeed, moving the vibrato
up or down and altering the perceived expansion of the throat are
useful ways of controlling the speed and the amplitude of the effect.
Moving it higher will speed up the vibrato, while a feeling of greater
expansion—I feel an almost bullfrog-like expansion near the bottom of
my neck—increases the amplitude.

Vibrato produced in this way is very natural, but rather dependent
on air speed: the more air intensity required to produce the tone, the
faster the vibrato tends to be. This helps us in many ways, since high
notes on the oboe sound better with faster vibrato than do low notes on
the English horn. If the air intensity drops too low (which it will when
you are playing very softly, for instance), the vibrato will cease to occur
by itself. However, after enough experience with producing it naturally,
the student will also learn to mimic the same mechanism to artificially
apply vibrato in any situation.

An important musical note on the use of vibrato: it is decoration. As
oboists, we are fortunate that there is no traditional expectation govern-
ing our use of vibrato. Flutists use it almost constantly; clarinetists rarely
do. For us, it is not an essential part of the sound, but an expressive device used to help explain the music. Be sure to use it with intelligence.
Vibrato used continuously is no more interesting than no vibrato at all.
Be sure to use it only after the basic tone and phrase are beautiful.
Think of it as painting a piece of furniture. If the piece is ugly or damaged, or even merely scratched, paint won't help it look better. Be very
attentive that you are not using vibrato to hide either an underlying
lack of integrity in your intonation or a lack of intensity in your tone
production.

Exercise

Very Difficult

> Play any slow Ferling etude with no vibrato at all. Make all
> of your dynamic and color changes; play all the nuances and
> inflections you want, but don't use any vibrato. Only after
> you can play in tune without vibrato, and play with true
> propulsion and intensity in your phrasing with no vibrato,
> should you allow it back in. Then it will fulfill its true purpose
> of making your playing more beautiful.

> This exercise may prove to be very difficult, and some students re-
> port that their support and blowing feel different when playing without
> vibrato, an indication that the vibrato is being applied to a sound with-
> out proper integrity and support.

Conclusion

The oboe is played with your whole body. You shape a note not just
with your mouth or your reed or your breath, but with your whole physical and mental attitude. The oboe is a treacherous instrument; it is entirely possible to do everything correctly and still get an unexpected
result. Do not let this make you cautious. Much unpleasant and tense
oboe playing is merely the result of fear, of an attitude that strives to
prevent bad things rather than to create good things. To play where the
real resonance and beauty of the oboe lie, you must take risks—you must
miss once in a while. If you never miss, you will never know where the
limits are, and you will never approach them. Your playing will feel safe
(a desirable goal) and sound dull (a very undesirable one). Work to
improve your ear, your reeds, your technique, and your imagination,
so that you become a successful risk taker, not a risk avoider.

3

Finger Facility

The preceding chapters describe a method of sound production that should result in a free and easy tone that functions well in all registers and at all dynamic levels. If those techniques are mastered, the only remaining aspects of basic playing technique are finger facility and articulation. Finger facility is discussed in this chapter, articulation in the next.

Technique is like money: it's hard to have too much of it. But the lack of technique (or money) is painful, even when the shortfall is only a few dollars a week. Applied correctly, technique becomes an artistic tool—you have so many more possibilities you can exploit and utilize. Moreover, technique is a measure of your devotion to your art and your craft. Technique takes work, and work takes persistence and time. There are many aspects of playing that improve at an irregular rate: tone quality, intonation, phrasing, reed making—the list goes on. But the more hours you spend on technique, the better it will become. A player with a consistently excellent technique is someone who will be in demand. Orchestral auditions reward those players who can make the right sound at the right time, and playing the right notes is an essential element of this competence.

Technique

First, begin by bringing the hands to the oboe in a comfortable, efficient position. To establish this, stand comfortably straight and let both hands hang easily to your sides. Observe the curvature of the fingers when the hands are hanging, relaxed. This same gentle curvature should be present when holding and playing the instrument. Set the thumb rest on the upper side of the right thumb (in other words, the thumbnail should face more toward your body than toward the ceiling) between the nail and the knuckle. If done correctly, the weight of the instrument will be supported by the limit of the thumb's range of motion and will not need the hand muscles to hold it up. Holding the instrument on the top of the thumb, with the nail facing the ceiling, requires too much muscular participation and can cause hand strain. Also, do not allow the thumb rest to stray too close to the end of your thumb (resting above the nail rather than between the nail and the knuckle), because that will amplify the weight of the instrument. See figure 3.1 for the correct hand position.

Notice that if the instrument is allowed to hang on the right thumb with no additional support, it will fall forward. Bring it back toward you with your left hand. The finger pressure created by this motion is all the pressure you should need to close the holes. Do not squeeze the oboe— if you can feel thumb pressure against the wood, you are squeezing. While not advisable, it should be possible to play with the left thumb completely off the wood. If more finger pressure is needed to make the oboe cover and play reliably, have it repaired. Technique will be severely compromised if the fingers are rigid and tense.

Cover the keys with the pads of your fingers. This is the same part of the finger that is often used to hold a pencil or grasp a fork—in other words, not the very tip, but rather the softer part just behind. Using the very tips of your fingers gives an exaggerated, spidery hand position and should be avoided. Neither should the fingers be completely flat, flailing at the oboe.

Observe your wrists. They should be nearly straight: the hand should be neither higher nor lower than the wrists. It may be necessary to rotate the hand slightly away from or toward the oboe, or you might have to turn the reed slightly to the right or the left to give the hands the proper approach to the oboe. Bent wrists often go hand in hand with incorrect finger orientation: if the player uses the tips of the fingers to cover the keys, the wrists are more likely to be wrong as well. And if the elbows are too far from the body, the wrists will again be forced into the bent position. The elbows should be no more than three or four inches away from the body.

The knuckles should be parallel to the instrument or slightly raised. The side octave key (on the left hand) and the alternate A-flat key (on the right hand) should each be felt lightly under the corresponding index finger. To get the correct position, place your right index finger on the F-sharp key, put your right little finger on the C-sharp key, and let the other fingers fall naturally into place. At this point you may notice that there is nothing especially "natural" about this—that the hand has to

Figure 3.1 Correct hand position.

stretch to reach the keys. The oboe has an unusually large finger span—larger than that on most wind instruments—and players with small hands can find it uncomfortable. Even players with fairly large hands sometimes feel discomfort if their approach to the instrument is tense or contorted.

Some players are "double jointed," meaning that their fingers collapse at the first knuckle, which distorts the required smooth curvature. This really has nothing to do with the joints; rather, it means that ligaments which should restrict the range of motion are too weak, allowing fingers to move in opposing directions. This limitation can be overcome by building up muscle strength. A simple isometric exercise is usually enough to correct the flaw. Place the hand with the palm facing downward on a tabletop. Press the affected finger firmly against the table for a few seconds and release. Do not allow the joint to collapse—keep it curved. Repeat this exercise many times. It can be done almost anywhere at any time to build up the required strength. Of course, too much finger pressure on the keys, which should be corrected before taking any other measures, can easily cause breaks in the finger curvature.

Keep the fingers as close to the oboe as possible. This is feasible only if you use light pressure. If pressure is heavy, you will need to lift the fingers aggressively. Now they will likely be too far away from the instrument and will need to be re-placed aggressively to arrive on time for the next note. Tension is the enemy of technique.

Relaxation in technique flows from a relaxed and efficient tone production. If tension is required to make the sound, the tension will spread through the rest of the body. Habitual tension, combined with hours of repetitive activity, can eventually cause discomfort or even injury. The arms and shoulders are the most commonly afflicted, with the right arm affected more frequently than the left. I am not a medical expert, so I will not advise on specific maladies or remedies, but I will issue this practical caution: if you begin to feel pain, stop what you are doing. The maxim, "no pain, no gain" does not apply to playing a musical instrument. If the pain persists after you stop playing, seek advice from your teacher or a colleague about therapeutic options. Do not try to play through it; do not wait for it to get better. Seek help. Regrettably, overuse injury is common enough that finding recommendations for therapists or other medical professionals should not be too difficult.

Too many players wait until the symptoms of the injury are undeniable before trying to find a remedy. By that time, the injury might have been months in the making, which means that relief will be months away. Occasional temporary discomfort is normal when playing; pain that persists after the playing stops is not. Do not try to be a hero in this regard—if you think something is wrong, seek help immediately. It is not an admission of weakness to be very open and honest about this. Start by having a conversation with your teacher or a trusted colleague; you will not be the first player who has had a complaint. If playing hurts, that is an important clue telling you that something is not working efficiently and needs to be further examined.

Practice technique slowly. You need control and ease. Without control and ease, speed cannot be achieved. When you have practiced enough, fast will be exactly the same as slow, just faster. The fingers will stay close to the instrument and move with light motions. Ideally, it will feel as light and easy as drumming your fingers; an observer sitting more than a few feet away won't really be able to see your fingers move.

Example 3.1 Simple finger exercises to develop speed and fluidity.

In addition to practicing slowly, you also need to practice going fast. If you have never played extremely fast, no amount of slow practice will promote the right sensation of whizzing through scales and passagework. Begin with very simple five-note patterns as shown in example 3.1 and repeat them as quickly as you possibly can.

Notice that these are deliberately chosen so that only one finger moves at a time. Try to stay with those simple patterns until things get easier. Don't worry too much about accuracy or evenness—this exercise is to give you the experience of going fast. Stay completely relaxed and let the fingers run. As you gain proficiency, expand the exercises to longer scale passages encompassing an octave or two.

Alternate Fingerings

An essential part of technical development is learning to choose the most intelligent and practical fingering sequences. Alternate fingerings can make otherwise unplayable passages feasible. Their use, however, is a matter of some controversy—when do the inferior tone, response, and pitch of the alternate fingering overcome the benefit of cleaner execution? The forked F is a good example. Many players urge that the forked F never be used, regardless of the resulting difficulty. But in many instances the inferior quality of the forked F simply cannot be heard, while the technical complexity added by the left F is only too obvious.

Choosing fingerings carefully can make all the difference in the playability of a passage. Fingered as shown in example 3.2, this solo from Dvořák's Symphony no. 9 is perfectly easy. Fingered any other way, with lots of left F's, it becomes nearly unplayable. Note the use of the right F to start the solo off. This gives the listener the illusion that the rest of the F's (E-sharps, actually) sound equally clear. In order for this suggestion to work, your oboe needs to have a split-D mechanism in proper repair. If the ring is sticking at all, or if your oboe doesn't have this mechanism, these fingerings will not work. Also, the F-sharp to G-sharp trill must be adjusted correctly, as well as the D-flat to E-flat trill. Refer

Example 3.2 Dvořák, Symphony no. 9, "From the
New World," oboe solo from the second movement.
Press the A-flat and left E-flat keys together with the
left little finger after playing the first two notes.

to chapter 10 for the adjustment procedures. "R" refers to the right-hand
F key, and "F" refers to the forked F fingering.

In addition to considering the usefulness of alternate fingerings (including trill fingerings), constantly look out for opportunities to reduce
finger motions. Professional oboes have three articulated mechanisms
that allow fingers to remain down while playing other notes: the A-flat
key, which can remain pressed while playing any right-hand note; the
left E-flat key, which can remain pressed while playing C-sharp or low
C; and the C-sharp key, which can remain pressed while playing low B
or B-flat. Taking full advantage of these capabilities can significantly reduce the number of finger motions needed to play some passages. If the
instrument is poorly adjusted or damaged, be sure to get it repaired.
Again, refer to chapter 10 for adjustment instructions.

The Dvořák excerpt shown earlier is a good example of how to take
advantage of the oboe's mechanism. The scale study shown in example
3.3 gives another illustration. When lines appear underneath the music,
the A-flat key should remain depressed. By my count, that eliminates
sixteen finger motions in this line of music alone. Careful attention to
these opportunities will make many passages easier and cleaner. Note
the use of the many forked F's to make this passage more fluent. In my
judgment, using forked F's in a quick technical passage like this is not
only permissible but necessary.

Example 3.3 Leave the A-flat key pressed whenever a line appears
underneath the music.

Leaving down fingers or using alternate fingerings can alter the tone quality of some notes slightly, as can the use of trill fingerings. The million-dollar question is: where do we draw the line between technical convenience and tone quality? In some cases, use of the alternate fingering is almost unavoidable. In the Dvořák example discussed earlier, avoiding the forked F makes the passage almost unplayable, and certainly messier (try it, and try to find a sensible and playable alternative). But players must make diligent efforts to play every passage with the purest, most beautiful-sounding fingerings possible. Never use alternate or convenient fingerings to facilitate passages that really just need more practice.

Once fingerings are chosen intelligently, use them consistently from that point forward. The same pitch will come out whether you use the right F key or the left, but to the brain, it is like learning a different note. Mark fingerings in your music if your memory is unreliable. All players develop a shorthand to indicate alternate fingerings: "L" for left, "F" for forked (or a little drawing of a fork), and so on.

It is very useful to apply a system of "fingering hygiene." In other words, try to use the same fingerings in the same situations every time. Never use left E-flats or left F's unless they are necessary. Do not slide from one key to another if there is any way to avoid it. The only exception is the slur between E-flat and low B or B-flat (in which case you should slide with the right-hand little finger, not the left). Prioritize your fingering choices: if the right F works, use it; if it doesn't work, try to use the left F; if that is inaccessible or too clumsy, then use the forked F. Using the same fingerings in the same situations every time will help you develop to consistent habits and therefore save you a great deal of indecision, especially while sight-reading.

Many times the choice of fingering will be dictated by the tempo. For example, in a slow tempo, the correct choice would be the one shown in example 3.4.

When switching from one fingering to another—from the left F to the right F in example 3.4—do it quickly and at the beginning of the note, even if you have plenty of time. The more rapidly you can execute this technique, the more often you will be able to use it.

However, if the same music is fast, the preferred fingering will change to that shown in example 3.5.

Example 3.4
Recommended fingering choice in a slow tempo.

Example 3.5
Recommended fingering choice in a fast tempo.

Since many fast passages must initially be practiced slowly, remember to use the fast fingerings even when the music is being played slowly. Do not change your decisions halfway through the process; be consistent.

Bloops

Bloops, or extra notes that sound briefly between two intended notes, are regrettably common in oboe playing. Indeed, they can be so pervasive that they begin to sound normal, and the player stops noticing them. If you have any doubts about how clean a finger change is, compare it to something where only one finger moves: compare A to C with A to B, for example. With time and practice, the coordination improves and the bloops become inaudible, but a few will remain lifelong companions if committed and regular efforts are not made to exterminate them. A-flat to B-flat, A-sharp to B, and A to C are among the most persistent. The opposing motion—some keys going up while others go down—and the coordination between the two hands makes these fingering combinations particularly difficult. Practicing to eliminate the bloops must be slow, patient, and impeccable. Begin with example 3.6.

After that is really clean, try example 3.7.

And, finally, reverse it as shown in example 3.8.

Example 3.6   Practice this slowly until it is clean and even.

Example 3.7   Speed up the upper note to develop lightness and facility.

Example 3.8   Then speed up the lower note.

Example 3.9 Suggested fingerings for slow and fast execution of a high-note passage.

The finger motions must be as light and smooth as possible. At the first sign of strain or tension, return to the slow, even alternation. Eventually, and I mean eventually, the coordination will improve. Practicing to get rid of this sort of sloppiness can take a maddeningly long time. Don't give up; the only way it won't get better is if you don't practice it.

High Notes

Younger students often resist learning the correct "long" fingerings for notes in the third octave. With some experimentation, any of us could find five or six different fingerings that will produce something like a high E. But the long fingerings have achieved acceptance because of their superior intonation, response, and tone quality. They should be learned and applied as soon as the higher notes are included in the student's range. They are not actually that difficult, merely unfamiliar. The sooner standardization and consistency can be applied to this register, the sooner it will be stable.

The simpler alternate or trill fingerings, which employ fewer fingers, should be used only for passages that are otherwise unplayable. Consult the fingering chart in Appendix 2 for alternate fingerings, but remember not to use them unless they are absolutely necessary. They cannot really be tongued, and their intonation is unreliable, as is their tone focus, so reserve them for very quick technical passages where these defects can be hidden. Example 3.9 shows one possible application of the alternate fingerings and recommendations for fingering a slower version of the same thing. "Alt" is the abbreviation for "alternate."

Octave Keys

Most oboes are equipped with a semiautomatic octave key system. This means that pressing the second (side) octave key automatically closes the first (back) octave key.[1] Therefore, the back octave key may remain

---

1. Fully automatic octave key systems exist also. These have only one key—the back octave key—to operate the two vents, with a linkage that automatically opens the correct vent when the appropriate note is fingered. These mechanisms are rare in North America but are used elsewhere.

Example 3.10   Recommended use of octave keys in the second octave.

pressed whenever the side octave key is being used. With very rare exceptions, this is the technique that should be followed. Leave the back octave key pressed whenever using the side octave key. To those who are already applying this technique correctly, the preceding paragraph will seem unnecessary. Those doing it incorrectly (roughly half of you, in my experience) can look forward to a difficult transition period followed by much-improved technique. By making this one correction, many dozens of finger movements can be eliminated and technical capacity increased significantly. Example 3.10 shows what I mean.

Many newer oboes also have a third octave key, which assists with the response of notes in the third octave—high E and above. Be sure it is adjusted properly; it should just barely open when pressed. When using it, make sure to touch only the third octave key, not the back octave and the third octave together. Then experiment with it; it will often improve high notes, especially at soft dynamic levels. Often closing the half hole while opening the third octave key will improve the quality of the note even further.

Half Hole

The half hole may be opened by either sliding the left index finger or rolling it. I prefer rolling the finger because it requires less motion. Do not lift the finger and replace it, but keep it in contact with the key. Move the finger as little as possible; do not be misled by the fairly large plate available for use (especially on English horn). To find the right movement, play a low D and very gradually start to open the half hole. The low D will jump the octave after you have moved your index finger only slightly. That is all the motion that is required.

Fingering for Tone Color

Altered fingerings can also be used to adjust intonation and tone color. I generally take a dim view of this practice. To my ear, the altered note seldom sounds better, just different. Students should learn to play in tune with the standard fingerings. Tone-color alterations are better and more honestly achieved through embouchure and air manipulation than by adding fingers. Besides distracting from the pure sound of the oboe, adding fingers adds to the technical complexity of a passage and can easily result in indecision and confusion while one is sight-reading. Try to avoid this practice until you really have some unusual demand that cannot be met any other way.

English Horn

Hand position on the English horn should be the same as for oboe, but it is complicated by the fact that the instrument is longer, requiring both hands, especially the right, to be held lower. For players with shorter torsos, this can cause a very cramped position for a hand that has to support the instrument while still fingering notes. A neck strap is a good remedy—the ones with elastic cords do a fine job of supporting the instrument while still giving the player some freedom—but even with it, some people may find the English horn too difficult to manage. It is better not to force the issue of English horn playing if the player complains of tension or pain.

Some players routinely use different fingerings for some English horn notes to help with pitch stability or tone focus. Consult the fingering chart in Appendix 2 for the fingerings I find most useful.

Summary for Chapter 3

- Keep fingers relaxed and near the instrument.
- Choose fingerings carefully and apply them consistently.
- Utilize every opportunity to reduce finger motions.
- Learn and use alternate fingerings as appropriate.

4

Articulation

First, verify that the tongue is correctly positioned in the mouth while playing. Make your most beautiful sound on an easy note. If we imagine the mouth cavity as having a spherical shape, the tip of the tongue should be in the center of that sphere, gradually arching back toward the roof of your mouth. From this position, it's a simple motion forward to touch the reed. If the tongue does not feel like it is moving forward—directly forward—to strike the reed, it is in the wrong place and must be repositioned. Some players hold the tip of the tongue under the tip of the reed (some even place the tongue as far forward as the lower teeth), which is incorrect. The correct tongue placement is important for focusing the tone as well as for facility in articulation. It should remain in this position regardless of whether the music requires tonguing or not.

Once positioned correctly, the tip of the tongue should strike the tip of the reed. A slight bias toward the upper side of the tongue tip striking the lower blade of the reed is permissible. Take note of the word "slight"—imagine a couple of taste buds worth of bias, not any measurable distance.

Do not tongue hard. Touch the reed gently and quickly. Keep the tongue close to the reed and bounce it off the reed tip. The air makes the tone; the tongue prevents it. Tonguing is often thought of as touching the reed with the tongue, but the tone starts when the tongue is released from the reed.

According to my way of playing, it is a rule that the tongue should always start the note and never stop the note. Breath attacks (starting the note by gradually increasing airflow until the reed begins to vibrate) certainly sound gentle and ethereal, but the arrival of the sound can never be predicted with complete assurance. With practice, a more predictable and equally smooth result can be achieved with the tongue. Stopping the note with the tongue is certainly accurate, but it sounds too choppy and abrupt. Instead, stop the note by making a very rapid diminuendo, giving it a nice round end. There will be exceptions to this rule, but they should be confined to the realm of special effects.

Speed of Articulation

The tongue is a muscle. It can be trained. If you have any doubt of this, observe the complex and rapid actions of the tongue while speaking. The tongue can learn to do nearly anything at any speed. But, for articulation to be rapid and clear, regular practice is necessary. The exercise in example 4.1 will help to develop speed. It has two virtues that are important: the range is moderate, with only minor response difficulties, and there are not very many repetitions of each note. Do not tongue twenty or thirty notes in a row, the tongue will tire and become tense, making further practice unproductive. If this exercise is too tiring at higher speeds, begin by playing only five repetitions, instead of nine, on each scale degree. You can easily invent your own exercises.

Begin by practicing the exercise at a speed that you know you can perform comfortably. Increase the metronome clicks one notch at a time (not faster!) until you reach your maximum speed. If you reach a speed that you feel you cannot exceed, try anyway—sometimes it is just a temporary ceiling. After you are sure you cannot go any faster, play the exercise two or three more times, decreasing the speed one notch each time. This will assure that the tongue is not too tense at the completion of the exercise. After only a week or so of articulation practice, you will notice that your maximum speed has increased somewhat, and that your control of the intermediate speeds has improved greatly. Increasing your maximum articulation speed significantly can take a year or longer. After that, regular maintenance is required to keep it in shape.

Example 4.1 Exercise to develop single-tongue articulation speed.

In order to meet the demands of the repertoire, you must be able to play this exercise at a metronome speed of at least 132 to the quarter note (faster, if possible). A few players will never be able to achieve this speed, and they should investigate the multiple tonguing techniques described later. But practice the single-tonguing exercise diligently for at least several months before exploring other options. The tongue is a flexible muscle capable of a very high level of training.

Two factors (besides lack of practice) will limit tonguing speed: holding the tongue too far from the reed and/or touching the reed too firmly. In practice, these two are related—if the tongue touches the reed too firmly, it must be removed with greater effort, leaving it too far back in the mouth. Tongue gently, leaving the tongue as close to the reed as practical—not more than a distance of a few millimeters. Make sure your reed responds quickly and cleanly, or the best technique will still fail. Do not tongue hard: a "tah" stroke that sounds clean and definite at a slow speed will sound harsh and pecky when sped up. This hard stroke is the only one in many players' repertoire (see "Variety of Articulation"). The reason is simple: if you tongue firmly, you will never miss the reed. But for fast articulation to be facile and consistent, a much gentler stroke must be mastered first. So practice "duh, duh, duh, duh" at a speed slow enough to ensure perfect consistency. If you miss the reed now and then, it means that you are exploring the right sort of finesse. Gradually, as your control becomes more consistent, increase the speed. Finally, use that stroke for your fast articulation; it will give much more lightness and propulsion to your playing. To avoid tonguing harder as the speed goes faster, think of making the tongued notes longer as the speed increases. There is no need to play fast, tongued notes short. Their speed makes them short enough.

Variety of Articulation

Variety of articulation is as important as speed. In skillful combination with tone color, vibrato, rhythm, and other expressive equipment, articulation variety is an essential part of an oboist's expressive vocabulary.

From our first few lessons, we are taught that an articulation begins with T. Various syllables are given—tee, tah, tuh, and so on—but they all begin with the consonant T. As a basic articulation on the oboe, this is too explosive and unpleasantly harsh. If the composer's instruction is sforzando, forte, with a big accent, by all means use "tuh." But, as a basic stroke, "duh" is much more useful. For the softest articulations, something like the "th" in "then" is required.

The exercise shown in example 4.2 contains some commonly found articulations. You can easily invent your own variants. Practice scales and other patterns employing these and other articulations, working for complete consistency of stroke within each articulation, to develop a variety of articulation that ranges from the softest consonants to the most aggressive with complete control.

Example 4.2   Exercise to develop a wide variety of articulation strokes.

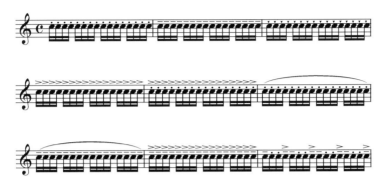

Example 4.3   Bach, Brandenburg Concerto no. 2, first movement.

Then apply your newfound variety of articulation to music. In example 4.3, for instance, three different strokes are employed: a short definite one (the first note, for example), a somewhat longer but still definite one (the second note), and lighter strokes the length of which is unimportant since they are quite fast (the sixteenth notes). My notation, like all notation, is imprecise, but it should give a clue to what I mean. Note that staccato does not always mean short—in many styles of music, it merely means light and separate, with no real implication of length. Often staccato refers more to lightness of attack than brevity of duration (Mozart wrote staccato whole notes and half notes—surely those aren't short). That is the staccato intended here on the sixteenth notes: light and brisk, but not short or pecky. The accents accompanying the tenuto lines are meant to be expressed with vibrato rather than impact.

Articulation and Music

Example 4.4 shows something that is rather difficult to perform: maintaining the direction of the music while also observing the silences of the rests.

Solutions to this problem are varied and represent one of the few significant disagreements among the world's oboists. Many players advocate stopping each note with the tongue, allowing the air pressure to continue behind the blockage, thereby continuing the musical line through the rests. Many American players regard this as unsatisfactory,

Example 4.4 Air must be kept
active during rests.

finding the note endings too abrupt. Another possibility is one pre-
sented by Robert Sprenkle in his book *The Art of Oboe Playing*.[1] Sprenkle
advocates turning the oboe slightly in the mouth so that the tongue
touches only the corner of the reed, allowing air to continue flowing
through the reed while the sound is stopped. For me, this is awkward,
difficult to execute, and tricky for the embouchure. My solution is based
on what John de Lancie once said in a lesson: "Blow hard enough to
start the note, but not hard enough to keep it going." In other words,
the air support still provides the shape of the phrase, and functions with
its usual energy. But the air speed is less—the reed won't vibrate until
the impact from the tongue sets it in motion.

You will notice that each of the approaches described earlier depends on a continuous line of air motivating the phrase; where they differ is in how to manage the silences. So whatever you do, do not "wind"
(rhymes with "pinned") the notes—do not give each note its own separate impulse of air. As you make your way through a phrase, you want
the tonguing to sound like you're flipping your finger through a stream
of water, not like you're turning the faucet on and off. If early attempts
to create continuity in tongued passages require you to play longer notes,
then by all means play longer notes. The direction of the phrase and the
flow of the air are more important than the element of staccato; your ear
will eventually demand a shorter note length, and your body will adjust to produce it. Remember, again, that staccato does not necessarily
mean really short, nor is there any standard directive about how much
it shortens the note (half the printed note value is a popular idea). Staccato merely means that the notes cannot be slurred together, and it
implies a bouncy lightness free of accent. If the passage sounds better
with the notes a bit longer, then play them a bit longer.

Multiple Tonguing

Multiple tonguing—double and triple tonguing—is a bit more difficult
on the oboe than on some other instruments (flute and brass, for example) where it is a standard technique, but this should not deter any-

---

1. Sprenkle and Ledet, *Art of Oboe Playing*, p. 14.

one from learning. The oboe reed has the highest resistance of any of the reed instruments, making it more difficult to cleanly interrupt the air with the rear stroke (the one that does not touch the reed). Moreover, our clarity of articulation depends on interrupting the vibration of the reed, not merely the passage of the air, so many oboists notice a distinct difference in response between the front and the back strokes. Diligent practice and free-blowing reeds can help to overcome these difficulties. Double tonguing is as liberating as circular breathing; it removes so many compromises caused by insufficient articulation speed that it is worth spending the time to gain facility with it.

In order to minimize the distance the tongue travels, employ very short and emphatic syllables, like the word "kitty" said backward: the syllables "tee" and "kee." In order to get the maximum clarity of articulation and to allow you to practice the technique slowly and gradually speed it up, make sure that the start of the next syllable ends the previous one, in other words: not exactly "tee" and "kee," but rather "tik" and "kit," with the syllables as short and definite as possible: "tik-kit-tik-kit-tik-kit," and so on. Keep the air pressure firmly engaged during the silences between the notes. The distance the tongue travels should be as small as possible. Following are some sample exercises, which you can easily supplement with your own. Practice these at various speeds, ranging from moderately slow to very fast, until they can be produced clearly. The exercises shown in example 4.5 can be practiced on the reed alone or the oboe, whichever seems more comfortable to you. When starting with the oboe, use easy notes with comfortable response and little resistance—the short notes in the middle of the staff, such as A, B, or C, would be a good place to start.

Example 4.5   Double- and triple-tonguing exercises.

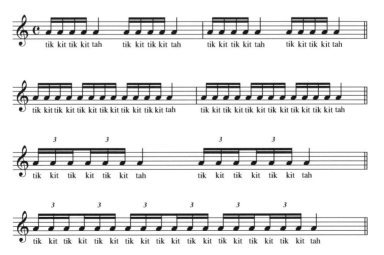

Example 4.6 Changing notes on the front stroke while double tonguing.

Example 4.7 Changing notes on the rear stroke while double tonguing.

Of course, you will never double tongue slowly, so the slow practice is only to help you get maximum clarity and definition from each stroke. Once that seems reasonably consistent, increase the speed.

At slower speeds, remember to distinctly stop each syllable with the start of the next one: "tik-kit." Be quite definite about this. At faster speeds, the distinction will blur: the result we are hoping for is a back stroke (the "kit") that sounds almost as distinct as the front one.

The next difficulty is changing notes while double tonguing. Changing on the front or "tik" stroke (example 4.6) is not so hard, since we have been doing that for many years.

Changing on the "kit" stroke, however, will require more practice (example 4.7).

Once these preparatory exercises can be performed with facility, it should be possible to introduce double tonguing into some carefully chosen real-world situations. At first, avoid extended tongued passages and places that require frequent pitch changes. Using it for a few notes at a time, mostly on the same pitch, will help build confidence. Brief fanfare flourishes are ideal: "tik-kit-tah."

Notice that triple tonguing isn't really "triple" at all—it is merely rearranged double tonguing: "TIK kit tik KIT tik kit." Occasionally, for clearer metric emphasis, it may be better to say "TIK kit tit TIK kit tit." For really complex, tongue-twisting patterns, it will prove very helpful to just practice speaking the patterns out loud a few times until they feel comfortable in the mouth.

With lots of practice and plenty of time, most players are able to develop a serviceable double tongue. Still, I have only rarely heard someone double-tonguing on the oboe without its being apparent. The uneven emphasis is usually there, more or less. So for most people, double tonguing will remain a tutti technique, not a solo technique. Still, it can be extremely helpful in keeping up with flute and bassoon colleagues in the orchestra, when the single tongue articulation is that little bit too labored.

5

Expression

Expression is not wholly the result of inspiration. It is also the result of study, practice, and the lifelong acquisition of taste. Many students are confused by what it means to play "musically." This chapter is intended to explain some basic concepts of intelligent musicianship and to provide tools that anyone can use to make his or her playing more expressive and convincing.

Begin by studying the music. I don't mean just play through it; I mean really look at it and figure out what you want to do. You should know the structure of every single phrase and have a plan for every note in every phrase. You also need a plan for the whole movement, the whole work, even the whole concert.

Let's say you're going on a trip: you get in the car, but you wouldn't start driving until you know where you are going and how you mean to get there. Careful drivers might also have a back-up plan in case the preferred route is blocked or congested. Then, if you want to stop at a scenic overlook, or make a detour through the park, or pick up your dry cleaning, it is still part of the big plan, and the trip will be successful. Your musical preparation must be every bit as careful, with about the same amount of room left for improvising. With practice, this planning becomes easier and easier until it becomes almost second nature. But do not start to play until you know what you want to do. You cannot get what you want until you know what you want.

Phrase Shape

Music must sing. Each phrase must have a beginning, a high point, and an end. Look at the phrase and decide how you want to shape it. Let's consider the first phrase from the Barret Melody no. 1 shown in example 5.1.

Playing or singing this a few times reveals that there are really two smaller phrases in these four measures. Before we decide how to shape the phrase, we should reduce it to its smallest unit. Example 5.2 shows the phrase with the intermediate punctuation point observed.

Now we have a phrase unit seven beats in length. Next, we must find the most important note of this phrase unit. (For now, we are going to ignore the printed diminuendo, which is explained later.) We are looking for the note that the preceding notes propel toward and that the following note(s) relax(es) away from. As shown in example 5.3, the C was chosen because of its placement on a strong beat and the underlying harmonic tension (all of the Barret studies are furnished with bass lines to make this sort of analysis easier. Example 5.3 shows this bass line.). Be careful to design the phrase shape according to these logical musical processes, and not for arbitrary reasons (giving higher notes preference, for example).

Example 5.1   Barret, *40 Progressive Melodies,* no. 1, first phrase.

Example 5.2   Phrase with the intermediate punctuation shown.

Example 5.3   Phrase with the high point indicated and bass line shown.

Example 5.4 Phrase shape
played on one note.

We will shape the phrase by making a crescendo toward the downbeat of the second measure, followed by a diminuendo to the end. To
practice this, play the phrase on one note to develop the right shape with
the air:

Repeat this, with excellent contrast between the loudest and softest dynamic, as often as necessary to get a really smooth result. Don't
be afraid to exaggerate the contrast. You should play a very beautiful
long tone with a slightly lopsided contour (that is, the climax is not exactly in the middle).

When the single tone sounds really beautiful, add Barret's notes to
the shape you have created with the air. Make the same shape with your
air and mold the phrase onto that shape. Finger the notes, play the slurs
as printed, but don't meddle with the shape of the air. Do it exactly as
you had it when it was just a single tone, except that now you will move
your fingers and your tongue. Try very hard to make it really pure: an
excellent long tone with notes on it. Often students will anticipate problems (the slow response of the downward slur to the A and the more
strident tone color of the C, for example) and unconsciously make corrections. Play the long tone with your air and place the notes on it. You
will probably find that you need to make no corrections at all; at most,
there will be one or two very small adjustments. Do not fix mistakes
before you've made them. Play the pure version first, then make any
minor adjustments necessary.

Many, many phrases work in just this way: as a long tone with notes
on it. The contour of the long tone will vary—sometimes the peak comes
near the beginning, sometimes near the middle, sometimes right at the
end. But the concept is the same every time: make the shape with your
air and place the notes on that shape.

A word about notation: do not be distracted by the diminuendo
printed in the first measure. Barret often treats diminuendos as brackets
to indicate note groupings. This diminuendo indicates that the G and
the following notes are upbeats to the C on the downbeat of the second
measure; in no way does it prevent a crescendo. Many pieces of music
present just this difficulty. Do composers mean what they have written,
or do they mean something else? In Barret's case, there are so many
diminuendos printed throughout the book with such frequency and
care for their placement that they have to mean something else—if the
diminuendos are observed as diminuendos, some passages cannot be

Example 5.5   Bach, Sonata in G Minor, BWV 1030b, second movement.

played. If they are seen as indicators of note groupings, then the marks make perfect sense. See the "Note Groupings" section in this chapter for a more complete discussion of this idea.

The concept of placing notes on the stream of air always applies, regardless of the speed of the notes or their difficulty. Whether you are playing one single note, a simple melody like the Barret, or an elaborate run, the sound and shape of the phrase should have the same simplicity and integrity each time. Do not allow energy, dynamics, or phrase shape to be influenced by whether the phrase is technically easy or difficult.

If the music is rather elaborate, simplifying the phrase—reducing it to a sort of skeleton, as shown in example 5.5—can be a useful first step to finding the correct shape.

Dynamic Control

Shaping phrases successfully, with a truly singing contour, depends on having an effective dynamic range to work with. Strive every day to develop more dynamic and color contrast in your sound. Try to play both a little softer and a little louder than you could the day before, always without compromising your beautiful sound. When searching for more dynamic range, look for it in the soft end of the range. There will always be a limit to how loudly you can play the oboe (there is certainly a limit to how loudly you *should* play the oboe); there is no limit to how softly you can play the oboe. This is true both theoretically and practically.

But even with diligent practice, we oboists have a disadvantage: almost every orchestral instrument (except for perhaps the bassoon) can play both louder *and* softer than the oboe. So, in addition to developing a large dynamic range, we must also develop an acute sense of dynamic control. Young players have basically two dynamics: not very loud, and not very soft. More advanced players improve this to three: the piano family, the mezzo family, and the forte family. These are not enough. Whatever your dynamic range is, it must have at least six or seven different levels within it that you can control precisely. Do not let piano and mezzo piano be the same thing. Play the dynamics indicated for the duration requested by the composer. Don't begin piano and then get lazy after a measure, letting the dynamic relax to mezzo something; you will have nowhere to go when the crescendo comes. When trying to create contrast, put the contrasting elements close together: play louder just before a subito piano, loudest at the start of a diminuendo, and softest just before a crescendo, for instance. Even very small differences in color are noticeable if they occur right next to each other. Effectiveness of dynamics is all about contrast. Loud and active playing is not interesting by itself until it is contrasted with soft and calm. Control your dynamics, and your playing will be much more exciting. Pay attention during large-ensemble rehearsals to how infrequently conductors request anything truly original or creative. Most of the time they ask only for what is already printed in the music, often reminding musicians of nothing more than how loud or soft they should be playing. This should be embarrassing for the players. Control your dynamic level with as much intensity as you can bring to it. You and your whole ensemble will sound better.

This idea will improve your playing immediately and significantly without requiring you to learn any new techniques, but only that you use what you already know. If you want to improve your control, however, example 5.6 is a very challenging exercise. Do it slowly and feel free to stop for breaths.

After deciding on phrase shape and making that shape with their air, players sometimes fail to verify that the result really matches their intention as vividly as they would like. Many times I have listened to a student performance in a lesson, made a few insightful comments about how the phrasing could be improved, and found that most of my suggestions were already marked in the student's music but had not been executed well enough to be heard. The problem is partly psychological: the player sees a crescendo and works to make a crescendo. From there it is simple to conclude that the crescendo must have been audible. The listener, unfortunately, did not hear it and cannot read your mind—the gestures must be very vividly drawn to get the desired reaction. John de Lancie frequently talked about the necessity for actors to wear stage makeup—from the theater, they look like normal people. From close up, however, the features are luridly exaggerated. They are not distorted, nor are the unimportant features highlighted, but the salient features are given special prominence, almost like the big ears or big noses in

Example 5.6 Exercise to develop dynamic control.

political cartoons. Our playing must be similarly expressive. Make your message overly clear. Do not worry about doing too much—how often have you left a performance feeling that it was too expressive or too powerful? Your playing is like a huge movie screen with an enormous sound system, not like a little tabletop television set.

Note Groupings

Music must sing. Play with the notes riding on the air, and your phrases will have more power and more integrity. But the idea of singing through phrases using the air is only the primary layer. Music must also speak. You must find punctuation marks within the phrases that give the music grammar and inflection. Speech, whether written or spoken, is full of punctuation and inflection. There are commas, full stops, colons, quotation marks, paragraphs, and other marks placed in the text to show the reader how it is meant to be spoken.

I saw John with Clara.
I saw "John" with Clara.
I saw John. With Clara.
I saw John. With *Clara?*
I *saw* John! With Clara!

Each one is spoken a little differently, and, more important, each one means something unique. Music has punctuation marks as well, but only rarely are they printed in the text. You must find them for yourself. Two important questions must be answered before the music can make sense: Which notes belong together? And what inflection (up or down) should they be given?

Notes are grouped into little "phraselets"—words and phrases that accumulate into sentences and paragraphs. These words and phrases rarely conform to the bar lines.

In examples 5.7 and 5.8 we see two ways of thinking about the same passage. The second, in example 5.8, is grammatically correct, while the first, in example 5.7, is very clumsy. Why is the second example right? The downbeat is always the most important beat of the measure and is always approached by a note (or several notes) before it. Downbeats have upbeats even when the music is continuous. The question is, how many upbeats should there be? In this case, punctuating after the first

Example 5.7 Punctuation placed without regard
for musical grammar.

Example 5.8 Punctuation placed to help express the phrasing.

note of each measure provides the most propulsion. We can have legitimate disagreement about the number of upbeats—this is very much a matter of judgment in many cases—but we cannot disagree that there must *be* upbeats. Breathing on the bar line puts the punctuation in the wrong place, resulting in an ungrammatical presentation.

Bar lines give very important metrical information, which we will explore later, but in terms of musical grammar, they are no more important than the end of a line of text in a book. You don't stop reading at the end of the line of text; you stop reading when you see a period or other punctuation mark. Likewise, you do not stop playing or phrasing when there is a bar line.

Beats and beam groupings are two other small containers for notes that have no bearing on the grammatical presentation of music. Music almost always moves *over* bar lines, *across* beats, and *across* beam groupings. Barret shows this very clearly in the twelve short articulation studies near the beginning of his *Oboe Method*. He uses diminuendos to indicate the beginning of a note grouping and carats to indicate each resolution (see example 5.9). The brackets are mine. I am convinced that Barret would have used brackets instead of the many diminuendos had the musical typography of his day been more flexible.

Example 5.10 shows an equally straightforward example from Etude no. 12 by Ferling, this time without such explicit guidance from the composer. Again, the brackets are mine.

Example 5.9 Barret, *12 Articulation Exercises*, no. 1.

Example 5.10 Ferling, *48 Famous Studies*, no. 12.

Example 5.11   Vivaldi, Sonata in C Minor, RV 53, second movement.

Example 5.11 shows the same idea applied to the second movement of the Vivaldi Sonata in C Minor, RV 53. It is possible to arrange the groupings a little differently than I have done, but the important thing is to have some arrangement clearly in your mind as you play. Note in all examples that every note group goes over a beat, over a beam grouping, or over a bar line.

Inflection

After you know which notes belong together, it becomes much easier to decide how to inflect them. Inflection on wind instruments is based upon the string technique of changing bow strokes. Simply put, the bow must travel either up or down. Observe a good string player and notice how bow direction changes inflection. Upbows are usually preparatory in nature, while downbows are more emphatic. Of course, many bowing choices are made for reasons of technical facility, but the musical sound of the result is always the paramount consideration. (We can also develop tone color from observing bow technique: bow pressure, bow speed, and the bow's proximity to the bridge all affect the quality of the sound). Take a look at the first two notes of each line in example 5.12 and see which seems the most natural and musical. In example 5.12, ⊓ means downbow and ∨ means upbow.

Clearly, the third example (up-down) is the only reasonable possibility. Everything else will sound and feel very awkward. Merely mimicking the wrong motions should be uncomfortable for anyone who has ever observed string players.

Not all examples will be as clear-cut as this one. Often the arrangement of up and down strokes can be complicated and open to debate. The important thing is to make an intelligent decision and present it convincingly. String players have a decided advantage in that their inflections are not only musical but also visual. Even if the musical effect is weak, it is at least partially bolstered by the visible motion of the arm. As wind players, we do not have this advantage, so our presentation of the musical gesture must be very clear and audible.

It should be clear from the preceding that the common habit of breathing on the bar line is almost always a mistake. Or, to put it more precisely, any time you breathe between an up impulse and a down impulse, it is wrong. Breaths must occur only where there are natural musical punctuations.

Example 5.12 Mozart, Oboe Quartet, K. 370, first movement.

Example 5.13 Barret, *16 Grand Studies,* no. 2.

   To confirm this practice of intelligent phrasing and punctuation, when beginning in the middle of a piece, it is a good idea to begin playing after the appropriate number of notes, not right on the bar line. Thus, if you were asked to play the passage shown in example 5.13, you should begin playing from the second note. The first note belongs to the previous phrase.

Elements of Music

Music is not just made of notes. It is made of four very important building blocks, or elements, which must be considered when developing an interpretation. Usually the interpretation comes much more easily when these considerations are taken into account. The four elements of music are, in order of importance:

   1. Meter
   2. Rhythm
   3. Melody
   4. Harmony

Example 5.14   Barret, *12 Articulation Exercises,* no. 10.

Example 5.15   The notes grouped to agree with the meter.

Example 5.16   The notes grouped incorrectly.

Meter is listed first because it is impossible to have music without it. Even musics that contain only rhythmic elements have meter (African drumming, for instance); without it, the music has no tension and no release. Meter is often the least carefully observed instruction printed in the music, but composers think very hard about the meter they assign to a composition. Meter assigns a hierarchy to the beats in the measure. If there are two pulses to the measure, the second is lighter than the first; if there are three, they are emphasized heavy medium light; if there are four, the emphasis should be heavy–light–medium–lightest. The very end of the measure often contains upbeats to the next measure, propelling toward the next downbeat emphasis and pushing the music forward.

Besides imposing a hierarchy of beats, the meter tells us how the notes must be organized. So the music in example 5.14 must be played as shown in example 5.15, and never as shown in example 5.16.

Quick quiz question: Example 5.16 would be right if the meter were different. What does the meter need to be to make example 5.16 correct? (See the note for the answer.)[1]

Composers sometimes use accents or other marks to indicate temporary shifts of metric emphasis. Because of the accents, it would be correct to play example 5.17 like example 5.18.

Hemiola is a subtler version of the same idea. Especially in baroque music, composers frequently intend a shift of metric emphasis but do

1. 18/16. Or, if we change the notation to include a lot of triplets, it could be 3/4. But if are only changing the meter, it must be 18/16.

Example 5.17 Barret, *12 Articulation Exercises,* no. 9.

Example 5.18 The notes grouped to observe both the accents and the meter.

not specifically indicate it in the score. It is most frequently found at cadences, such as in this example from the Alessandro Marcello Oboe Concerto. Example 5.19 shows what is printed. It should be played as shown in example 5.20.

Examples of hemiola can be found in almost any baroque piece, and in many classical and romantic works as well (Brahms was especially fond of playing with the meter in this way). Hemiolas are never indicated by the composer and must always be discovered by the performer.

Example 5.19 Alessandro Marcello, Oboe Concerto in D Minor, third movement.

Example 5.20 Alessandro Marcello, Oboe Concerto in D Minor, third movement, rewritten to observe the hemiola.

Example 5.21   Richard Strauss, *Till Eulenspiegel's Merry Pranks,* opening
horn solo.

Example 5.21, the opening horn solo from Richard Strauss's *Till Eulenspiegel's Merry Pranks,* illustrates all these considerations: the relation
of the notes to the beats, the inflections resulting from them, and the
temporary shift in meter in the fourth measure. If you have never seen
this music written down but are familiar with it from listening, the metric arrangement may surprise you. Rarely is it performed with the right
notes sounding as though they are on the beat.

Awareness of the meter should be combined with intelligent note
grouping and punctuation to make clear which notes are on which
beats. In music, communication depends on inflection and animation,
just as it does in speech. Do not mumble or speak in a monotone, and do
not speak with an impenetrable accent. Be very clear. The listener must
never be bored—or, worse, confused.

Reading Music

Music, as we have already seen, is a language. As such, it demands literacy. You must learn to read it and to give it life. You must develop a
large vocabulary of musical sounds motivated by informed reactions to
the marks on the paper.

When preparing a new piece of music, instead of first finding a recording or attending a performance, look at the music as if you are giving the world premiere. Even the most admirable recording or performance was prepared from a replica of the piece of paper on your music
stand (assuming you have a good edition—see my later discussion).
Later, after you have prepared the piece fairly well and feel like you
have a good grasp of it, listen to as many performances as you can find.
You should learn the tradition, and it can be helpful to hear how other
performers have solved problems. But if you begin with sound recordings, you may never develop any thoughts or ideas of your own.

Learn to see all of the marks on the paper and react to them automatically. Many young players apply a system of priority to what they
notice: first the notes, then the rhythms, then the slurs, then perhaps the
dynamics, finally the little subtle marks. Some marks are not observed
because they are simply overlooked. Learn to see all of the marks from

the very beginning. Do not learn one thing at a time (first the notes, then the rhythms . . .); instead, learn everything all together. This requires slow playing and fast thinking, but it will give you a result in which the performance instructions are embedded in your playing, as they should be.

Sometimes a mark is ignored because the student doesn't know what it means. Learn to read music. Know what all of the instructions mean, and have an idea of how they will influence the sound you make. This is especially important with instructions in foreign languages. Do not take these for granted or assume that you know approximately what they mean—many foreign words sound like familiar English words but mean something entirely different. For example, in the Barret *40 Progressive Melodies*, no. 23 is marked with a tempo of "Allegretto flebile." What does "flebile" mean? Some English words jump to mind immediately. Flexible? Feeble? The real meaning, which changes the interpretation of the piece completely, is "mournful." So if you are not absolutely sure—and I mean *absolutely* sure—look up the word. If your music dictionary doesn't contain the word, find a French, German, or Italian dictionary. If the French dictionary is no help or gives a confusing answer, find a French person. Do not continue preparing the music until you know exactly what the composer wrote. Usually an inexpensive pocket music dictionary (which you can carry with you everywhere —it's much more useful than half of the junk in your oboe bag) will solve the problem. After a few years of looking up every unfamiliar word, you will develop a good working vocabulary of Italian, French, and German that will cover almost every situation.

Look at every mark with care. Composers think long and hard about the instructions they give to performers. Imagine if you were to write a piece of music: you want it to sound a certain way, with a certain atmosphere and color and tempo. But you do not have the luxury of meeting with the performers and explaining everything to them. You have to communicate it all by writing on the page using signs. So the question of whether to write a dot or a dash, or a dot with a dash, for instance, is of paramount importance. If a passage is marked with dots in one place and repeated later with no dots, that discrepancy is worth noting. Should you play it differently the second time? It seems subtle, but it is a crucial clue toward performing what the composer intended.

You need to know the style of the music you are performing— figuratively speaking, what sort of costume should you wear? Early music (on oboe, mostly baroque music) requires the most creative approach: the notes on the page are only an approximate description of what the music is supposed to sound like. Many questions are left to the performer to determine—tempo, articulation, instrumentation (since "continuo" is an ensemble, not an instrument, it can be performed with various instrumentations), even the notes themselves (since ornaments are common). Music from 1850 onward, on the other hand, usually has careful and deliberate markings that should be observed exactly.

In another example, Mozart typically marks only two dynamics—piano and forte. Does this mean you should play only loud and soft with abrupt transitions between the two? Or does it mean something different? You need to learn the style—absorb the performance practice of the era—and decide for yourself.

As a musician, an interpreter of music, you have two responsibilities. You have to observe every mark on the page, and you have to make it sound good. It is possible to observe an accent, for instance, by making an explosive start to the note, making it sound quite harsh and unpleasant. Instead of beginning the note with a bang or just ignoring the accent, try to find a different way to emphasize the note. Perhaps the accent needs to start after the note has already sounded. Perhaps the accent can be accomplished with air or vibrato, and not with the tongue. Perhaps the accent means that another, normally stronger note should not receive an accent. Work hard to find a way to observe the composer's instructions that also sounds beautiful. Often, as we learned from Barret's use of diminuendos, we have to go even a step further and figure out what composers *mean*. Sometimes, literally observing what they've written doesn't work.

Marking Music

If the skill of reading music is properly developed, making pencil markings in the music should be largely unnecessary. If there is a dynamic printed in the music, circling it does not make it any more visible. Learn to see it. Nor should you write little lectures to yourself in the music. You won't have time to read them as you play. If you want to make notes (say, during a lesson or master class), make them on a separate sheet of paper or on the title page. Keep the actual music as clean as possible. The goal is that every mark on the page should change your sound. If you need to circle markings just to see them, then you don't read music well enough yet.

Obviously, some personal markings are necessary. Breath marks are essential. So are alternate fingerings, especially in some tricky technical passages. Often it is helpful to mark reminder accidentals in some very long measures. If a conductor asks for a change in dynamic or articulation, mark that in as well, sometimes with the conductor's initials alongside if the request is particularly unusual. But keep your markings to a minimum. A clean page is easier on both the eye and the brain. Once you've learned to read music properly, a clean page actually lets you think less, rather than more.

Editions

The more keenly you develop your musical literacy, the more you depend on the integrity of the material you read. Buy excellent editions.

As much as possible, you need to know what the composer actually wrote, not someone else's reading, however intelligent it might be. This is particularly important with baroque and classical music. This music certainly requires editing, because the conventions of musical notation have changed so much over the centuries—the material needs to be made to conform to modern practice. But you want to be sure that you are making the edition for yourself and not playing someone else's idea. Broadly speaking, there are three kinds of editions available: scholarly, *Urtext,* and performing.

Best are the scholarly editions. These are sometimes facsimiles of original manuscripts and sometimes large multivolume collections devoted to the works of one composer, region, or time period. They are essential references and are usually supplied with supplementary volumes containing exhaustive discussion of every editorial decision, no matter how seemingly insignificant. Frequently the editors work from several primary sources—the composer's manuscript, the first publication, the parts used at the first performance, and so on. There are often minor discrepancies between the sources and determining which should take priority is a tricky business, hence the detailed discussion. These editions are usually large and hardbound and are not supplied with individual parts, so using them for performance is impractical. And, since they are large and hardbound, they can be extravagantly expensive to own, so you may need access to a good university library if you want to refer to them. But if you have a question about a dynamic, an articulation, or a possible wrong note, referring to one of these will get you the closest answer you can find without access to the primary source material.

The *Urtext* editions are the ones recommended for performing use. These are frequently drawn from the scholarly editions and sometimes have minimal additional editing. If editorial marks are inserted, then some typographical system (dotted slurs, for example) is used to distinguish the composer's marks from the editor's. Buy these whenever possible. They are usually not much more expensive than the performing editions discussed in the next paragraph but have superior typography and legibility.

There are also many performing editions available. A performing edition is one editor's interpretation of how the piece should be played. Baroque music in particular is not usually supplied with dynamics and articulation marks by the composer, so the performing editions provide these instructions just like any more modern piece of music. Many of them are quite intelligently done by well-known musicians, while some are lamentably bad. I object to them, good or bad, because they give you insight into the mind more of the editor than the composer, and because they give you no way of knowing which marks are from the composer and which are from the editor. Get the clean edition and make your own decisions.

Style

Style, as actors say, is knowing what play you are in. You don't use a Brooklyn accent in Shakespeare; you don't wear Elizabethan ruffles in a prime-time television police show. Your knowledge of musical style must likewise be constantly refined and developed. A forte-piano in Mozart sounds different from the same marking in Beethoven or Schumann. In Mozart it could be quite light—a sizzling little accent at the beginning of the note, like flicking a drop of water onto a hot stove. In Beethoven the same marking will be heavier, still applied only to the beginning of the note but with more weight and duration than the Mozart. In Schumann the emphasis might shape the entire note, with the actual swell somewhere in the middle of the note's duration.

Likewise, a routine harmonic progression in one composition will be shocking and radical in another. For example, a fully diminished sonority is commonplace in Liszt's music, but in the baroque period it is an expression of great pain or drama. It is your task to know the difference. Developing your knowledge of history and style and applying it intelligently to your playing requires a lifetime of study, reading, and listening. Attend as many concerts as possible. Listen to recordings. Don't listen exclusively to oboe music, listen to everything: opera, chamber music, symphonies, violin concertos, song cycles, and so on. If you listen to jazz, pop, or other more commercial music, still listen with attention. When something sounds beautiful (or when it doesn't), try to determine what makes the sounds effective and communicative. Learn the repertoire for as many instruments and voices as possible. Nobody would dream of playing drums in a rock band without listening to rock and roll, but some classical musicians try to play in an orchestra without enough listening to music related to what they are playing. We have four centuries of music to play, not just fifty years of rock and roll.

At first, this effort at information gathering will feel quite unfocused. Since there is so much to learn, where do you begin? As a starting point, refer to David McGill's book, *Sound in Motion*, which contains a list of his favorite recordings with annotations describing what to listen for.[2] After digesting all of that, you will love some of the music, like some of it, and feel lukewarm about the rest. Follow the paths from there: if you love a particular performer, find more of his or her work. If you are inspired by hearing a Schubert symphony, find other repertoire by Schubert; he wrote hundreds of songs, for instance, and large quantities of chamber music. Gradually the path you're exploring will develop more and more branches as you discover new directions to investigate.

2. McGill, *Sound in Motion*, pp. 303–46. David McGill is principal bassoonist with the Chicago Symphony Orchestra.

Do not expect that your teachers will teach you everything you need to know. No curriculum, no matter how advanced or sophisticated, has enough time to cover all of the material necessary to develop a literate and informed musician. To become a good musician, it is not enough to be a good student, to "pass the class." You have to be at the head of the class, or better still, ahead of the class, to stand a decent chance at professional success. Listen and read constantly.

Musings on Expressive Markings and Music Notation, with Performance Examples

The history of music has seen a sort of continuum in which composers through the centuries gradually applied more and more expressive markings, leaving less and less of the decision making to the musician. To a large extent, the necessity for this grew out of obvious historical factors: for instance, as a performing musician in 1720, you were expected to play music from your region written during the past few years. That was all. You would have known all of the composers personally, been intimately acquainted with their style and their preferences, and known without being told how to translate the marks on the page into a pleasing performance. Composers then were like jazz composers of today: they provided a framework for what the piece should sound like, but the players felt free to improvise many elements, so individual performances had the potential to sound quite different from each other. As a composer in this circumstance, you would not feel compelled to give detailed instructions, and most composers did not.

Gradually, three things happened: composers and musicians traveled more, composers began to insist on greater fidelity to their notation, and music from earlier periods came to be played alongside modern works. (It is ironic to think, in this age where "new music" is almost a frightening word to audiences, that until the mid-nineteenth century, new music was the only music performed.) So it gradually became necessary for composers to include careful instructions in their music, since it was likely that sooner or later a performance would take place that they could not personally supervise. Today the inclusion of detailed performance instructions in the music is a given. Composers for the past hundred years have dotted every "i" and crossed every "t," leaving the performer very little room for improvisation.

The preceding is not meant as a philosophical or aesthetic dilemma, but rather as a problem for students, especially those with little knowledge of history and repertoire. One day the teacher is correcting the student for not following a subtle dynamic in a piece by Debussy or Stravinsky. In the next lesson the teacher is telling the student that he or she need not obey any of the instructions in a heavily edited copy of a Telemann work. And if the student has acquired a good edition of

Telemann, there will be no performance instructions at all, which could lead to a very dull reading of the piece. How can a student create a musical performance from just a bunch of notes without any additional help from the composer?

The thoughts expressed earlier in this chapter will help enormously: first make a phrase with shape, and group and inflect the notes to propel that shape. Notice the meter: if the meter is 6/8, play strong beat–weak beat; do not play a series of 3/8 measures.

Then reflect on the historical circumstance described earlier. I'm sure it has never occurred to any composer that he or she was providing insufficient information to the performers. Composers undoubtedly felt that they were giving all of the direction that experienced performers familiar with the style would require. A few simple rules will help us to create an interpretation of music not provided with performance instructions by the composer.

We begin our process by identifying repetitions of material. I don't mean large repetitions that help to delineate formal structures such as ABA form; rather, I mean short episodes a few notes or a few measures in length. Composers use some repetitive devices frequently, and recognizing these can help shape an interpretation a great deal. Music from the baroque and classical eras (precisely the music with the fewest expressive markings) is especially rich in these features.

The first repetitive device is an echo: the same material is repeated at the same pitch level—the notes are repeated exactly. This is composer shorthand for "play me differently." It is not necessary for the echo to be literally loud followed by soft. It could be soft followed by loud; it could even be sharply articulated followed by something gentler; it could be plain followed by an ornamented version. In any case, try not to play echoes the same.

The second repetitive device is a sequence: material is repeated at a different pitch level—the music has the same contour and the same types of intervals, but each repetition starts on a different note. When this happens, it almost always works to simply follow the direction of the sequence with your dynamics. If the sequence goes higher, play each repetition louder than the one before. If the sequence descends, play each one softer.

Then take note of the harmony. Dissonance is meant to create tension; consonance is meant to resolve it. Complete understanding of this concept takes time to learn, since a diminished chord would be a dissonance in Telemann and a commonplace sonority in Wagner; but in earlier music, dissonances usually are easily distinguished and should be given extra prominence.

In addition to having few notated dynamics, good editions of early music (for our purposes, "early music" is any music before ca. 1800) rarely provide specified articulations. That is not to say that the music

Example 5.22   Articulation patterns recommended for music from the baroque era.

Example 5.23   For baroque music, the articulation pattern of the second line is preferable to the first.

should not have articulations, but that they should be carefully added by the performer. Many performers on early instruments do indeed tongue a great many notes, but the baroque and classical oboes allow a fantastic variety of articulation that is better mimicked on the modern instrument by adding slurs.

But be discreet in performing the articulations. Articulation in baroque music is not a foreground feature of the music as it sometimes became later. If you play a short note long in Stravinsky, for example, you have made a bad mistake—Stravinsky's music depends on articulation for its distinctive character and sound. In baroque music, articulation is more a surface feature intended to enliven the texture of the sound.

Resist very strongly the temptation to use the ubiquitous two-notes-slurred, two-notes-tongued articulation pattern in baroque music. This is a common pattern in classical music but is never used in music from the baroque era. Everything else, shown in example 5.22, is permissible.

If you work creatively to design articulation patterns that follow the music, the two slurred–two tongued pattern will not be missed. Example 5.23 illustrates how easily an articulation can be designed that follows the contour of the music and actually delineates it more clearly. The second line shows the preferred articulation.

We are now ready to proceed to our specific examples. I have chosen a couple of movements from the standard oboe repertoire: the first movement of the Marcello Oboe Concerto, and the third movement of the Mozart Oboe Quartet. To follow my comments you will need a copy of the music furnished with measure numbers. There are good editions of the Mozart Quartet with only Mozart's markings; the Bärenreiter edition is easily found.[3] There is an edition of the Marcello Concerto in D Minor from Musica Rara that is free of dynamic indications and presents an unornamented version of the second movement.[4] The edition in C minor by Richard Lauschmann, originally published by Forberg and reprinted by International Music, Southern Music, and others, is heavily edited but has become ubiquitous.[5] If that is the copy you have, start with the assumption that none of the dynamic markings originated with the composer, and that you are therefore free to design your own dynamic plan.

I do not intend to present these thoughts as the last word on the subject; other interpretations are certainly possible. But I hope that by offering them, I can help students to see that they do not need a heavily edited score—all of the performance instructions are already contained in the music itself when we apply our knowledge of musical style, history, and theory. The repetitions in the Marcello are more obvious, so let's begin with that.

Alessandro Marcello: Concerto in D Minor, First Movement—Andante e spiccato

The first thing we need to decide is, should this piece be in C minor or D minor? Is one more correct than the other? The work was published by Roger in Amsterdam around 1716, with the composer named as Alessandro Marcello and in the key of D minor. Bach made a solo keyboard arrangement of it (BWV 974), also in the key of D minor.

In addition, there is a set of manuscript parts (in an anonymous hand) at the library in Schwerin, Germany. These parts name the composer as Benedetto Marcello and are in the key of C minor. It was this version that was published first, in Richard Lauschmann's edition, so it gained precedence. However, the D minor version has the weight of evidence on its side—a publication versus an anonymous manuscript—and should be given preference, no matter how well established the key of C minor is in the minds of oboists.[6]

I chose this movement because it is an easy illustration of how composers use sequence to build phrase shape. The sequences are plentiful and plain to see, linking together in a way that makes for a completely satisfying movement.

---

3. Mozart, *Quartet in F Major, KV 370 (368b)* (pl. no. BA4867).
4. A. Marcello, *Concerto in D Minor* (pl. no. MR 1891a).
5. B. Marcello, *Concerto in C Minor* (1923); *Concerto in C Minor*; and *Concerto in C Minor* (n. d.).
6. Stolper, "Robert Bloom Collection"; and Ruiz, e-mail to IDRS-L mailing list, April 20, 2001.

The opening statement in measure 4 is repeated in measure 7, suggesting that the echo idea could be applied. Since the second entrance has an extension, it makes sense to play it more strongly than the first, and perhaps with a little ornamentation. Any printed ornamentation in your music (grace notes, etc.) is editorial, so we can either delete those ornaments or elaborate them as desired.

The first sequence occurs in measure 14. The pattern is eight notes long and is repeated three times, for a total of four statements. The repetitions descend, suggesting that the dynamic should gradually get softer. So begin with a nice, warm, rich sound and play each half measure a little less loud, finishing softly. Now, notice what happens next. Another sequence begins immediately, but this one ascends, so begin it softly and gradually play louder. There are two repetitions (three statements altogether) with a cadence at the end. The next sequence begins with the upbeats to measure 26. This one goes higher with each repetition, so begin softly and crescendo until it climaxes halfway through measure 28. The end of this sequential pattern immediately elides into the next sequence, which descends by half measures to the downbeat of measure 30, where we will arrive rather softly to prepare for the crescendo to the cadence. The next oboe entrance is in measure 34, where the fifth sequence begins. Start with a full sound so the sequence and your dynamic can descend. The sequence ends on measure 40, where we find a harmonic elaboration of a descending circle of fifths for the next two measures. The harmonies gradually work their way further from the home key of D minor (or C minor), so a gradual intensification to emphasize the growing dissonance is appropriate. The next oboe entrance is the upbeat to measure 47; here the second measure looks at first like it will be an exact repetition of the first, but instead it continues more elaborately (both melodically and harmonically) until halfway through measure 49, after which we can begin to relax toward the cadence. The final phrase of the movement may be similarly shaped: first toward the downbeat of measure 56, then to the third beat of measure 57, then relaxing to the cadence.

So just by observing how the sequences are arranged and taking note of a few harmonic high points, we can arrive at a whole and completely satisfying interpretation without any editor to help us. The Mozart quartet movement is a little more complicated, but will respond to a very similar approach.

Mozart Quartet in F Major, K. 370,
Third Movement—Rondeau: Allegro

Throughout this movement, be aware that the meter is 6/8, and be sure to play the second beat a little weaker than the first and then propel toward the next downbeat. Too much emphasis on too many beats will deprive the movement of the necessary lightness and momentum.

There is no dynamic indicated at the beginning (indeed, in this movement Mozart wrote no dynamics in the oboe part at all), but the cheerful mood and brisk tempo suggest something with good energy and lively sonority—perhaps mezzo forte with good, crisp articulation to chase away the nocturnal mood left behind by the second movement. Measure 3 should be a little louder than either measure 2 or 4, following the higher contour of the shape.

Measures 5 and 6 are a sequence, so measure 6 should be louder than 5, with an arrival in measure 7, where the dissonance is found. Measure 8 is the resolution and so is a little softer. The idea of a cadence as the climactic moment of the entire phrase or movement is a highly romantic notion that has no place in earlier music. Here, the cadence is a place of repose, with all of the action taking place beforehand.

Note the absence of slurs in measure 8; this does not prevent you from adding some. I would suggest slurring the first two notes and tonguing the next four—a pattern that can be consistently applied throughout the movement to the many groups of six sixteenth notes.

Enter gently in measure 13; the oboe is not the melody yet. Make a crescendo toward the eighth notes—an idea supported by the rising sequence in the strings. There is a dissonance on the downbeat of measure 15, which is not entirely resolved until the middle of measure 18. The downbeat of that measure is an appoggiatura and so must be emphasized: that G-sharp should probably be the destination of the whole phrase.

The entrance in measure 23 can be explained with a short digression. Mozart was a very great composer who made a huge contribution to every genre of music. But he will be most remembered for his magnificent operas, an art form he completely transformed. All of his instrumental works can be better understood and performed if we also remember that they have a vocal and theatrical basis. The next oboe entrance, in measure 23, is made much more interesting if we give it a dramatic presentation. It is a series of short fragments—each is one to three measures long—that should be treated like a conversation in which each participant has a slightly different point of view. Give each little fragment a different character—you decide what they are—and make sure that they remain connected, like a conversation, not like a succession of brief monologues.

The music in measures 35–36 and 37–38 is exactly identical. Here is our first example of an echo. Should the first statement be louder or the second one? Mozart gives us the answer in measure 39, where a long sequence begins its descent. Since the sequence goes down, it should get softer. In order to get softer, measure 39 must start loud, which also means that measure 37 should be louder than measure 35 to prepare the forte in measure 39.

The sequence begun in measure 39 ends in measure 43. Make a little crescendo to the beautiful harmony in measure 44, saving room for a larger crescendo to the diminished (dissonant) harmony in measure 48. The trill in measure 50 should begin from the note above, as explained in the next paragraph.

It is worth including a small digression here on the subject of trills. The proverbial rule book says that trills in the baroque and classical eras should always start from the note above. First of all, be skeptical whenever someone says that music must be played only one way and cannot be played any other way, with no exceptions. Music is an art, and there is no bulletproof solution to every problem. Performance decisions should be based on informed, sensible observations of the musical surroundings. When looking at a trill, decide what its function is—does it provide activity or dissonance? Many trills only provide activity—a little sparkle added to a note—and do not alter the melodic or harmonic progression. Those trills can start from the main note. Most trills at cadences, however, are meant to add dissonance and increase the tension just before the relaxation of the cadence itself. This trill in measure 50 is a good example. The upper note of the trill, the E, is very much a dissonant note, creating a sonority of D, E, and F at the same time, and it is this clash that we want to emphasize. So place the E heavily on the downbeat, give it some duration—an eighth note or so—and then begin the trill itself. Don't rush the *Nachschlag* (a German word for the finish of a trill) at the end; although it is printed in small grace note–sized notes, it can be played as two sixteenth notes, allowing a soft landing on the next downbeat.

Measures 51½ through 55½ are exactly the same music as measures 55½ to 59. Mozart again answers the question of whether to play the first repetition louder or softer. An ascending sequence begins in measure 59. This must begin softly or the crescendo is not possible, so it makes more sense to play the echo loud–soft rather than the other way around. Also, the downbeat of measure 55 is a dotted quarter note, while the downbeat of measure 59 is only a quarter note, a circumstance that could argue for making the first repetition more intense than the second.

Build the sequence from measure 59 to the downbeat of measure 63, where it turns around and begins a descent, allowing a smooth and elegant return to the rondo theme in measure 65. Measures 63 and 64 are unaccompanied and should be played with a little bit of freedom. Whatever you choose to do, be sure that the last five eighth notes before measure 65 are back in tempo or you will confuse your ensemble, which has to enter together on the downbeat of measure 65.

The next rondo theme is not exactly the same as the others—measure 71 is a little different from measure 7. This is not a mistake. In Mozart's manuscript, the alteration is clearly visible. Indeed, the oboe part is the only part Mozart wrote out in this section. The string parts are left blank, with only the remark "same as the beginning."

The next new entrance is in measure 89. This introduces the most extraordinary passage in the piece: the oboe plays in 4/4 while the strings

Example 5.24   The turns in measure 98 organized rhythmically.

remain in 6/8. The music beginning in measure 89 is clearly an ascending sequence leading to a diminished harmony in measure 95, which
should be the peak of the phrase. From there we can gradually relax to
the resolution in measure 102.

In student performances the turns in measure 98 are frequently a
mess of disorganized tangles. But these turns are really a perfect illustration of how an ornament can be given an organized rhythm and then
practiced like any other technical problem.

We digressed earlier on the subject of trills; now we should discuss
turns and other ornaments. Many young students initially regard ornaments as optional (some teachers even teach them to omit the ornaments) and do not learn what the signs mean, nor what pitches to play,
nor what rhythm should be assigned to those pitches. Most ornaments
are no more difficult than the material that surrounds them and can
be learned easily by any student advanced enough to learn the piece he
or she is studying. The best way to start is to have firmly in mind an
organized picture of how the ornament should sound. Make sure to
identify exactly the pitches, and the order, and the rhythm. Write it out
if necessary, and then practice it.

So, in measure 98 (example 5.24), once the rhythm and the pitches
have been decided upon, the preparation of the passage is accomplished
easily. Practice it carefully and slowly until it becomes effortless. Do not
play something approximate.

The sixteenth-note passage that follows is quick but not too difficult.
The two places that require attention are where the motion changes
from stepwise to skipwise in measures 104 and 106. Take very good care
not to rush, and get used to counting in two rather than in four; coordination with the strings will be much easier if you are already well prepared in this way, since the cello is the only instrument you should be
listening to during this passage. Even though the passage is fast, the
overwhelming tendency is nonetheless to rush it. Be careful.

When the 6/8 meter resumes, the ascending sequence requires a
crescendo to the high D in measure 111, with a relaxation afterward to
the cadence. Measure 113 should again crescendo to the high C on the
downbeat of 114.

The next few measures require a bit of historical explanation. On
the classical oboe in the 1780s, high F (three ledger lines) was a really
high note. The oboe had only two keys, and neither of them was an
octave key. High notes were accomplished by overblowing lower notes,

which worked quite well up to high D—a note found routinely in all early oboe music. Notes higher than D were not unheard of before this piece, but they were certainly unusual (incidentally, the next piece from the standard repertoire by a major composer that includes a high F is Beethoven's only opera, *Fidelio*, written more than forty years later). The important thing for the modern performer to know is that the high F could only be produced strenuously, and quite likely loudly as well. That was the sound Mozart would have heard and the sound that he was writing. He was not writing the delicate little squeak that has become something of a modern performing tradition. So measures 117 and 118 must be loud. Measure 114 must be loud. In between, it is very effective to play the C-sharp and D rather softly and questioningly—an idea supported by the vague harmony—with the E and F providing an emphatic answer and launching another repeat of the rondo theme.

By now, my careful measure-by-measure descriptions of sequences, echoes, and harmonies should make it relatively easy to design a plan for the rest of the movement. I will conclude with just a few more observations. The passage from measures 152 to 155, with its many octave leaps, is rather tricky; it is also not the melody, which is found in the violin. Here is a relatively rare example of a place where the second octave key (the side octave) should be used by itself and not in combination with the back octave key. The third and fourth measures can be a little louder than the first two to support the rising sequence in the violin.

The ending of the piece is our last problem. Again, a modern performing tradition exists that plays the end very softly, letting the piece sort of evaporate. This is pretty, but it is not what Mozart would have expected. We should make a plan that allows the last two measures to be loud. So measure 172 should be quite soft, beginning in the strings. The strings should play louder in measure 174, and the oboe louder yet to the downbeat of 176. Notice that the downbeat of 176 is a quarter note, while the downbeat of 174 is an eighth note. Again, those details argue in favor of an intensification. From 176 to the end there should be an energetic crescendo in all instruments, allowing the piece to end with a brilliant flourish.

I hope that this little examination has shown that we really don't need an editor to decide how our music should sound. It's much more fun to make your own edition than to play someone else's. Mozart has already told us everything we need; we just need to look through a slightly different lens. All of the various performing editions marked up with dynamics and articulations and hints are not nearly as valuable as taking a careful look at the score and finding the clues that the composer has left there for us.

6

Practice

The most important thing to learn is how to practice. If you learn how to practice, you will certainly learn how to play. Many students (and professionals too, for that matter) don't like to practice, don't do it enough, and don't use their practice time productively. Many students don't even know what to do when they are supposed to be practicing. A lot of doodling and messing around masquerades as practicing. We all know players who assert that they practice three or four hours a day, and yet they are rarely prepared for lessons, much less concerts. This chapter is intended to help with these problems. While reading this, some may feel that the suggestions are excessively strict and that there must surely be some sort of a shortcut. On the contrary, these suggestions *are* the shortcut. Anything else will take longer and not work as well.

How to Practice

How you practice is the essential point of the entire subject. If you don't do it well, it doesn't matter how much you practice, what you practice, or how often you practice. Practicing is essential to progress, but done inefficiently, it can actually become a barrier to progress.

For many people, practicing is a process where they take something new, play it badly, and try to improve it through repetition. The reason they play it badly is simple: they can't play it yet. So they begin again, play it badly some more, maybe twenty times more, and quit for the day, having learned little except various ways of playing badly. There is no other process in life that people begin in this way. If I ask you to build a bookshelf, you wouldn't just collect a pile of scrap lumber, nail it together quickly, and then look at it—it's crooked, isn't it? Instead, you would likely make a drawing, decide dimensions, buy the correct amount of wood, measure and cut carefully, and so on. Done this way, the assembly of the bookshelf becomes the easiest part of the process, just as the performance should be the reward for careful preparation. Practicing needs to be a process of learning the music—both intellectually and physically—until success is assured.[1]

Accomplishing this goal is not as difficult as you might imagine. The key is four simple words: NEVER DO IT WRONG. Never do it wrong. Every time you play the oboe, do it right. Of course, you should use good posture and play with a healthy sound production on a comfortable reed. But you must also play the right notes in the right place with the correct fingerings. Every time. The secret lies in repetition—frequent, correct repetition. Both words are important—*frequent* and *correct.* Never do it wrong, and do it right many, many times. Whenever your brain detects any repetitive physical activity, it begins an acquisition mode: it starts to store the repetitions in anticipation of learning something. Feed it well.

If you play something ten times right and ten times wrong, even slightly wrong, you've just wasted the time it took to do it. Even worse, those ten wrong repetitions are stored in your brain for future retrieval —usually during the concert, when you might be a bit nervous and have less conscious control over the playing process. Ninety times right and ten times wrong is much better, but remember that those ten wrong ones are still in there lurking. Play it right every single time. You have only one chance to play it right in the performance. Knowing this, students sometimes settle for being able to play something once or twice— "I could play it at home." But playing it right once in the performance really means that you must be able to play it right every single time, no matter what. It means that whichever version of the passage is retrieved from the storage unit in your brain, it will still be correct. Never do it wrong.

Playing it right every time is not impossible. Usually, all you have to do is slow it down. Play at a speed at which your brain can operate faster than your body and fingers. Anytime you can no longer control everything coming out of the oboe, you will make mistakes. Use your metronome and slow down. Speed up only when you start to feel confident that nothing could cause you to make a mistake. Or, to express the concept more generally, find a way to reduce the demands on yourself.

1. Jack Nicklaus was asked once if he was nervous before putting on the last hole with the United States Open Golf Championship on the line. He said (this is a paraphrase), "No. That putt, and that opportunity, are my rewards for all the practicing I've done."

Slowing down is often the best way, but there are other possibilities. If the rhythms are complex, set the oboe down and practice just the rhythm until you understand it. If the rhythms are easy but the notes are complex, play with no rhythm at all; play each note, but don't go on to the next note until you know what it is and how you want to get there. You can invent your own exercises to assure correct playing every time.

To understand the process better, we need to learn how the brain functions. The brain commands many complex physical actions in a way that we regard as automatic. Driving a car, tying shoelaces, eating a meal: all are complex actions requiring hundreds or thousands of muscular responses, which we can do almost without thinking because we have repeated them so often. Musical vocabulary must be learned in the same way. Learn it once; learn it well. The difficulty lies in finding the patience to repeat the passage (correctly) often enough. It may take a thousand times or more for something really difficult to become secure. Worse, with this careful method of working, you will very quickly realize just how much work remains—when you are looking at sixteenth notes and playing them as quarter notes, it's hard not to become discouraged. You may lose patience and be tempted to resume the old sloppy way of working. Don't do it. With the accurate method of practicing, you will eventually learn the passage. The other way has only ignorance as its advantage—you will never learn the music well, but you may not know that until the concert. If you never make a mistake, there is no reason to ever make a mistake. Practice may or may not make perfect—no sensible musician would ever assert perfection for his or her performance—but it certainly makes permanent. Whatever is stored will eventually be retrieved.

One reason so many young players suffer from stage fright is the legitimate possibility—the likelihood, even—of failure. Often, the odds of negotiating a difficult passage are fifty-fifty; if the music contains two or three of these passages, the probability of playing the entire piece accurately can shrink to 10 percent or less. No professional would accept these odds; we'd all be retired on account of overstress. Practice well. Never do it wrong. You only get one chance to play it right.

How Much to Practice

How much to practice depends a great deal on the age of the player and his or her goals for the instrument. For a twelve-year-old beginner, thirty or forty minutes a day may well be ample. For a college music major, forty minutes should be the minimum amount of time spent warming up for a practice regimen of between three and five hours daily. Time spent beyond five hours seems to me to be unproductive—the body and mind are too tired. Less than three hours, and improvement slows proportionately. The tipping point seems to be around ninety minutes, assuming that the work is being done carefully, as described above, and that a constructive routine is adhered to, as described below. Ninety minutes is about the right amount of practice time to keep from getting worse. The further beyond ninety minutes the time can be extended, the more improvement will take place.

In studying the topic of expertise, researchers discovered that true experts—champions and geniuses—worked harder for longer periods of time than anyone else. If there is such a thing as talent, perhaps this is the talent: the ability to work for long hours on a daily basis for many years. Anders Ericsson, a professor of psychology at Florida State University, proposes that more than ten thousand hours of solitary practice are required before mastery is achieved: "The critical difference between expert musicians differing in the level of attained solo performance concerned the amounts of time they had spent in solitary practice during their music development, which totaled around 10,000 hours by age 20 for the best experts, around 5,000 hours for the least accomplished expert musicians, and only 2,000 hours for serious amateur pianists."[2]

A little bit of arithmetic reveals that 10,000 hours equates to four hours a day, every day, for seven years.

Split the practice time into several sessions during the day. Take a break of at least ten minutes each hour and go do something else. Talk to friends, read a magazine—but don't rush off to make a reed. Take a break. Your body and mind will thank you.

Two other things are as important as practicing enough: practicing carefully (see above) and practicing every day. In many ways, practicing well is just like going on a diet. You cannot go on a diet three days a week. You cannot go on a diet for just a week or two. After a week or two, you have merely experienced all of the discomfort and irritability of dieting without seeing any of the reward. But after a year, besides having a whole new appearance, you also have a whole new world of good habits that will keep you healthy for the rest of your life.

Students who don't practice enough usually regard practicing as dull work and drudgery. To them, more practice only means more work and more drudgery. Any student who feels this way has never practiced enough to experience the reward. Trust your teacher, do what he or she says, and do it well. After six months improvement is guaranteed. By then you'll be enjoying your progress so much that you'll never go back to muddling through.

After not practicing well for many years, or not practicing enough, many students report that increased practice only makes them sound worse. That can't possibly be true. Instead, increased familiarity with the instrument makes them more aware of how their playing sounds.

---

2. Florida State University Department of Psychology, "Expert Performance and Deliberate Practice."

The ear is improving a little faster than the physical playing. After a few weeks, the imbalance will disappear.

There is no such thing as being too well prepared. You get one chance to play something correctly. At that point, you don't want a 50 percent chance of accuracy; you don't even want a 99 percent chance. You want it to be right, and you want to give the listener the impression that it was easy. In order for it to sound easy, it must be easy. There is no faking this.

We practice for many different reasons with different priorities. The most common reason is to grasp the material and learn to play it correctly and reliably. That is what the preceding section is meant to help with. Of course, we sometimes practice with other goals in mind: to test the efficacy of our breathing plan or to develop an interpretation, for example. These kinds of practice require a different sort of attention and a different set of priorities. In these cases, never doing it wrong might mean that we take each breath in exactly the way we intend, or we pace the crescendo at precisely the right time.

Sometimes, when drilling a technical passage, tone production and quality can take a back seat to accuracy. Some students almost whisper through the instrument when learning passagework. But playing the right notes with a weak tone is not the same as playing the music correctly. Be sure at all times to make a beautiful sound with a healthy production. Don't let the practice-room sound take over. Whatever your immediate priority is, make sure that tone quality always has an almost equal priority.

What to Practice

Practice time should be divided into three periods. One-third should be spent on warm-ups and scales, one-third on etudes and specific technical exercises, and the last portion on solo pieces, ensemble music, and excerpts.

Warm-Ups for Tone and Control

Begin with the slow D major scale shown below in example 6.1.
   There are four goals:

- *Each note should have the most beautiful, easy, resonant sound possible.* Use minimal embouchure tension and no vibrato—all the control should come from the air.
- *Each note should be in tune.* Usually, if the sound is beautiful, the pitch will be accurate also. Use the tuner and strive for the resonance bull's-eye of each note.
- *Each note should connect to the next with the most perfect legato possible.* Move your fingers with great care, keep them close to the oboe,

Example 6.1 Slow D major scale for development of tone and control.

and don't let the air die between notes. The fingers should move just quickly and lightly enough to avoid a smear between the notes. As a preliminary exercise, try slurring between G and F-sharp (and back) so slowly that there is an audible glissando or smear. This will actually be quite difficult and should reveal two things: it will be necessary to pour almost all of your concentration just into that one finger to get it to move with the proper control, and it will be necessary to be very mindful of the air production during the slur to avoid a silence. Once the smear is well controlled, practice moving the finger just quickly enough to avoid smearing, while still paying close attention to the air: push with a little more air between the notes—like slowly driving over a speed bump to the next note. Moving the fingers with crisp authority will always cause an accent, which is not what we want for this exercise. There are many occasions in music where the fingers should move firmly, but most players are already good at that. So for this purpose, move the fingers slowly, smoothly, and the smallest possible distance.

• *Each note should sound like each other note.* Not only should adjacent notes have the same tone color, but the high register and the low register should also match timbre. Adjacent notes can display quite a large discrepancy in tone color if not controlled. Starting from the bottom of the scale, the D usually sounds good, the E is fuzzy, the F-sharp again sounds quite good, the G is loud, the A and B can sound pale, the C-sharp is sharp and airy, and so on. When working to regulate these problems, adopt a strategy of concealment—in other words, don't just muffle the loud notes, but try to get the surrounding notes to sound more brilliant. Then work to get the high and low registers to sound alike. Generally speaking, the oboe's tendency is to sound rich and full in the lower register, thin and squeaky in the upper register. Work to draw the sound of the entire scale from the low D. Of course, as you play higher, you will need more air and more reed in the mouth, but try hard not to allow anything behind the embouchure (especially the vowel shape in the mouth) to change. Changing the vowel shape, or *voicing*, is a very useful way of changing the tone color, but should be avoided for this exercise to make sure that the notes are supported with air, not anything else.

Do this exercise at least three or four times each day or until you are satisfied with the result. Listen carefully and insist on the most perfect execution possible. Besides improving resonance, intonation, and finger control, the main point of this exercise is to illustrate just how difficult it can be to get exactly the sound you want. D major is the natural scale of the oboe—just lift the fingers, and D major comes out—so there are no technical obstacles to hurdle past. And yet, playing a perfect version of this simple slow scale is challenging.

When the D major scale is really beautiful, switch to a D-flat major scale and try to get the same results. Later still, an E-flat harmonic minor scale provides a new challenge by extending the range and introducing a skip into the exercise. Slow arpeggios and other broken chords present another challenge, since they are now all skipwise motion. Or try beginning the scale pianissimo, making a gradual crescendo to fortissimo at the top, and diminuendo back down. The goal of all of these exercises is to make sure that each new sound is prepared perfectly. In real music, this happens much faster, but it is always the same process: produce a sound, evaluate it for quality, make any necessary corrections (all this before any listener knows that anything is wrong), and prepare to produce the next sound.

Long tones are next. The simplest form is shown in example 6.2. Be sure you accomplish the following:

- The beginning and the end should be as soft as possible. My teacher, John de Lancie, likened the attack at the beginning to "a hot knife going into butter," and the release at the end to "smoke rising in the air"—you can't be sure when the smoke ends and the air begins.
- The forte in the middle should be as loud as you can play without forcing.
- There should be no dips, wiggles, or wavers in the sound.
- The pitch must remain constant.
- The long tone needs to be active throughout. Don't start soft, get loud, stay loud, and get soft. It should always be getting gradually louder or softer.
- There should be no vibrato. If a trace of natural vibrato appears at the very top of the crescendo, that's fine.

Example 6.2　Basic long tone.

Example 6.3 More difficult variation on the basic long tone.

Example 6.4 Very difficult variation on the basic long tone.

Again, do this at least three or four times each day, or until you're satisfied with the result.

Examples 6.3 and 6.4 show two variations to try after the steady tone is really good. The first is moderately difficult, the second is extremely difficult.

Again, you can develop many more variations on the exercise, containing as much difficulty as you are willing to confront—try practicing the long tone on low notes, or high notes, or with large, awkward skips in the middle.

Technique

Technical warm-ups are next. I begin with scales: all major and minor scales (all three forms). The range of the scales will differ from individual to individual. I recommend full-range scales (composers rarely oblige by writing them neatly from tonic to tonic). Start from the tonic, go to your highest note, go down to B or B-flat (or C-flat, or A-sharp, whichever note is in the scale), and back to the tonic. Younger students should be able to play with facility to high E-flat. More advanced players need facility up to high G. Use the metronome and set it at a speed at which you can play the scales smoothly, evenly, and cleanly. Never play faster than you can control. Ease and facility will come from well-rehearsed, frequently repeated, correct motions. Speed without control is frightening, whether playing oboe, driving a car, or skiing. I play sixteenth notes at 112 on the metronome (I can play much faster, of course, but that's not the point), but this and other metronome speeds should be regarded as suggestions only. Always maintain a tempo where control and smoothness are possible.

Then, practice major scales in broken thirds. Again, play them full range beginning and ending on the tonic. Play sixteenth notes at 92, followed by major scales in broken fourths (or reverse thirds, which is the same thing), also at 92. Minor scales in broken thirds seldom occur in the repertoire, so those can be practiced as needed, but not necessarily every day.

Then, practice the first two pages of the *Vade Mecum of the Oboist* (or any sequence of exercises that includes all major, minor, and dominant seventh arpeggios).[3] I play them once slowly and once at 116–120, but if you've never learned them, you may have to start at half that speed. Even if you can play these very fast, play them quite slowly now and then to ensure smoothness.

Two other scale patterns occur very often in music and should be practiced: the chromatic scale and fully diminished arpeggios. There are only three fully diminished arpeggios and, of course, only one chromatic scale, so these will not add much to the practice load.

Next, practice articulation. I use an easy scale (F major or G major) and play it through one octave with five (or nine) repetitions on each scale degree. Start at a speed you know you can manage (I start at 112 playing sixteenth notes), and increase one click at a time until you reach your maximum speed. Then (this is important), go back down one click at a time until you're out of the danger zone and can once again play with freedom and relaxation. For variety, use the exercise on page 16 of the *Vade Mecum* and apply the same practice method, changing the speed every four measures. Example 6.5 shows the exercise, which we saw earlier in chapter 4. Here is a good place to integrate it into your practice routine.

After these preparations, you are ready to move to the next part of your practice schedule. You may want to vary the technical routine to suit specific needs: whole-tone scales, pentatonic scales, scales in broken sixths, scales in broken octaves, and so on could be included if your repertoire demands it. Also, there are many good books—Bleuzet, Hewitt, Gillet, Debondue, among others—that include a daunting variety of scale exercises.[4] The majority of these can be avoided: it seems to me inefficient to practice, say, scales in broken ninths regularly when they occur in music only very rarely. But if there is something very difficult in your repertoire, there is often an exercise to help prepare it.

The aim of my warm-up is to be as efficient as possible and to cover the most useful territory in the shortest amount of time. Once the patterns are learned (which takes a while), this whole routine shouldn't take longer than thirty or forty minutes and should prepare you to play well for the rest of the day. I cannot emphasize enough the importance of having a complete command of slow scales, long tones, fast scales, and other scale-derived patterns. These are the foundation of any tech-

3. Andraud, *Vade-Mecum of the Oboist.*
4. Bleuzet, *La technique du hautbois;* Hewitt, *Daily Exercises after Maquarre;* Gillet, *Vingt minutes d'étude;* and Debondue, *Cent exercices pour hautbois*

Example 6.5 Exercise to develop single-tongue articulation speed.

nique, by which I mean both sound production and technical facility. With good technique, you can play anything; without it, you have to learn everything from scratch. Since a large proportion of the music you play is some sort of scale or scale pattern, mastering these is the most efficient way to practice.

Etudes

Do not resist etudes. They are composed with a view toward solving specific technical or musical difficulties. Often the difficulties of the etude are readily apparent, and it is tempting to avoid the problems by playing a little slower, or a little less pianissimo, or with fewer beats on the trills, or some such strategy. Do not avoid the difficulty; meet it head on. Otherwise you will never learn what the etude is meant to teach you. Invent your own exercises to solve specific problems. For example, the F major arpeggio is difficult on the oboe, so make up an exercise to improve it. When you've solved that, make up an exercise to get over the break cleanly. Make up exercises that address specific difficulties in the music you are learning—often there is only one troubling passage in an otherwise playable piece. Isolating that passage and solving it makes your practice much more efficient.

Sight-Reading

Don't forget to spend some time sight-reading. The only way to learn to sight-read is to practice sight-reading. It's not a bad idea to do it for the last ten or fifteen minutes of your practice session. Don't go straight in at maximum tempo; give yourself a chance to play it right the first time. Practice sight-reading every day. Skillful sight-reading is an invaluable professional skill, since performances with one rehearsal (or even none) are not uncommon. Mess up badly enough, and you might not be hired back. Of course, if your scales and technique are in good shape, there is very little real sight-reading—just a process of quickly reassembling things you already know into different combinations.

"I Could Play It at Home," or
How to Prepare a Successful Performance

You couldn't play it at home, either. You just weren't paying attention at home (or you weren't nervous, or you weren't distracted, or something). Most teachers would gladly accept a dollar for every time they've heard this complaint, usually asserted with great sincerity. But if you are well prepared, you can play anything in any situation, not just at home. In all of your preparation, never lose sight of the fact that you are preparing to perform something. Make the practice session as much like the performance as possible. In other words, pay closer attention during your practice; that allows you to relax more during your performances. Remember that the performance is the reward for having done all of that preparation. Prepare so the performance is the easy part. You'll be a lot less nervous if you know what you're doing.

When practicing, you must prepare three aspects of playing: you must prepare the technique, you must prepare your interpretation, and you must prepare the performance. Typically, people are as careful as they can be with their technique, somewhat attentive to the interpretation, and rather hopeful about the performance. But if the performance is not successful, the preparation is not successful either, regardless of how many hours went into it. It is futile to defend the process if the result is not satisfactory. So let's spend some time examining how practicing should include the idea of preparing the performance.

Students typically spend ten, twenty, even fifty hours practicing for every hour spent performing. This lack of performing experience often results in performances that are uncomfortable and stressful, even among skilled players. So what is different in a performance?

1. You have an audience.
2. You do not choose the starting time.
3. You cannot stop.
4. You only get one chance to play it right.
5. You usually do not choose the physical space where the performance is held.

Well, guess what? *Every one of these things can be practiced!* First of all, performers usually do not fear all five of these situations; often, they only fear one or two. Identify what worries you and start overcoming it.

1. *You have an audience.* They are both listening to you and looking at you. If they are adjudicators or teachers, they are also judging you. Different aspects of this disturb people to varying degrees: some don't like being looked at, some are afraid of being judged, some have other concerns. But the actual makeup of the audience is ultimately unimportant; the reality is that they are

present and you have to play for them. So play for people as often as you can. It doesn't matter who they are. Of course it is more stressful to play for people whose judgment you respect, but it will help to play for anyone at all. Family members, friends, fellow musicians, church congregations—all will help you overcome the discomfort of being put on display. And really make it a display, even if it's only for practice. Practice the whole performance: walk out, smile, bow, and take your place onstage. Yes, you will feel foolish doing this in front of your friends, but you will feel nervous in front of the real audience, so the same technique of acting confident and relaxed can be learned. Put yourself in stressful situations as often as possible. Take advantage of any and all performances that come along. Play in churches, for retirement homes, for weddings. It doesn't matter what the surrounding is, or even whether it pays anything; the important thing is to be playing for an audience. Again, it doesn't matter who they are, since you ultimately cannot know who they are. Some audiences are more likely than others to include musical connoisseurs, but you can never really be sure when the ghost of Tabuteau might be present. Regard all audiences as equal; don't decide that playing in church is easy while playing in a concert hall is challenging. If you are actually able to decide that one audience is easy, it should be possible to decide that they are all easy.

2. *You do not choose the starting time.* At first glance, that seems a trivial issue, but it really means you cannot wait until you "feel like it" to play your recital or ensemble concert. This is one very important difference between professionals and nonprofessionals: professionals sound consistently the same whether they want to play or not, whether they like their reed or not, whether they are completely healthy or miserably sick. There will always be considerations that can detract from your energy level or enthusiasm level. Perhaps you don't feel well; perhaps you don't like this piece of music; perhaps there is a family issue distracting your focus. Professionals often arrange concerts months or even years in advance. They cannot predict that six months hence they are definitely going to want to play the Mozart Oboe Concerto, but they can predict that their preparation will carry them through the evening. Again, this can be practiced. You can decide in advance that on Thursday at four o'clock you will play your piece *once only without stopping.* You want a true picture of how well your preparation is progressing, so don't practice the piece during the minutes before four o'clock. Warm up and get physically and mentally ready to play, but try the piece cold. Make a recording while you're at it, and before listening to it jot down a few notes with your impressions of your performance. Then listen to the recording and compare your mental picture of your performance with the reality.

Improvement is sure to result. Remember, you play how you play today, not how you would like the playing to be. If the recording exposes things you don't like, start to work on them.

3. *You cannot stop.* You really, really cannot stop. Do not stop! Paradoxically, this problem is caused, to an extent, by practicing. If there are corrections to be made, we have to stop and correct them. But, after a piece is reasonably well prepared, you should also start to practice it without stopping. At first, "without stopping" might mean that even if you make a mistake, you will stay in the right place no matter what. Skip notes, or beats, or even whole measures to achieve this. Eventually, "without stopping" will mean a continuous performance with no gaps of any kind. Some players stop almost reflexively every time something goes even slightly wrong. Sometimes the pauses are very brief and, after a while, not even noticed. Pauses, or gaps, do allow you to regroup a little, or take a small breath, or reset your embouchure—none of which can occur during the performance. If stopping even briefly is a chronic habit of yours, you may need a teacher or helper to call your attention to how often the stops occur. Some younger students never attempt to play without stopping until the lesson, audition, or concert. Needless to say, this is difficult and unreliable. A performance is a very bad time to try something for the first time.

4. *You only get one chance to play it right.* This circumstance can certainly create fear, since many players know they really can't play it right unless they get lucky, which is regrettably undependable. Here is where all of my previous admonitions about careful practice will help. In order to play it right once, you must be able to play it right every single time. Every example of the music stored in your brain should be admirable and perfect.

The following is a somewhat silly example, but it is an accurate illustration of how the process works. You are running for your life and, to make matters even worse, it is pitch dark, and you have to go to your closet and take out a black jacket. Any other garment will spoil your disguise and result in grievous consequences. How can you be sure to complete this task successfully? The only way of being absolutely sure that you will get a black jacket every time is to have a closet filled with only black jackets. You can try to re-member that the black jackets are at the far end, or that they feel softer than the blue jackets, or that there is only one jacket and all the rest are shirts. But if you are running for your life and you *must* find a black jacket immediately *without fail,* there is no better option than having the whole closet filled with them. As you approach your concerts, the best method is to have your entire mind filled only with correct examples of the music you are about to play.

5. *You usually do not choose the physical space where the performance is held.* Indeed, sometimes you don't even see it until the sound

check an hour before the concert. But you can have a pretty good idea. It is not difficult to find out the seating capacity, the general layout, the basic acoustic, and so on. And you can be quite sure that the performing space will be larger than your practice space. This difference in size, and the resulting difference in tone projection, frequently flusters students: the reed worked perfectly an hour ago, and now nobody can hear it. Take every possible opportunity to spend time practicing in large spaces. Arrive at ensemble rehearsals early and practice in the rehearsal room. It's only a rehearsal room, not Carnegie Hall, but it's bigger than your practice room. Your school will have an auditorium or other performing venues; try to use them when they are available. You may have to do this early in the morning or late at night, but it will be time well spent. Play for the person sitting in the last row. The "practice-room sound" will not work in a performance.

All of these suggestions should help to prepare a more successful performance, and all of them are based on the commonsense idea that a performance is a very bad time to try something for the first time. As far as is possible you want to know everything that is going to happen during the performance, and the only way to know it is to do it many times before the performance.

This still may not completely eliminate nerves, or what is more eloquently described as performance anxiety. Nervousness is a reality, and anyone who declares that he or she no longer gets nervous is not being completely truthful. There is always a different state of awareness during a performance than at any other time. This reaction is very human and is rooted in our most primitive instincts. When confronted with danger, the body reacts by preparing you to respond in an aggressive and forceful manner. Within seconds, you are physically and mentally prepared to kill the bear, or slay your opponent, or run from the avalanche. But instead of having a bear to vanquish, we only have a concert to play. Moreover, the oboe is not a good outlet for pent-up aggression. We need control and calm, not adrenaline and a racing heartbeat.

Other professionals also have to harness this fight-or-flight syndrome —athletes, policemen, soldiers—people who confront very dangerous situations and must respond instantly and appropriately. They have two advantages. The first is that the performance of their duties often gives them a vigorous physical outlet for their anxiety—just the sort of thing that adrenaline is meant for. Their second advantage lies in their training. Whenever they train, they are being supervised and coached. They have weight trainers, marksmanship instructors, drill sergeants, pitching coaches—the list could go on for a very long time. Musicians sit in a room by themselves and practice. They do their best, but I wonder how different it would be if an authority were constantly watching over their shoulder. You have to rely on your training, so be sure that it is very reliable, indeed.

Fortunately, playing concerts is not as dangerous as fighting a battle or making an arrest; indeed, the worst that can happen during a concert is embarrassment, not injury or death. Many concerts are quite pleasurable; some are thrilling. Even so, some players are so distracted by nerves that they seldom play as well as they can.

A good deal of literature exists to help players with performance anxiety. Much of it is based on concepts borrowed from sports psychology, and many of the ideas are extremely helpful to create an optimized state of performance. But no matter how many techniques we study and apply to reduce nervousness, the reality will always remain that we must learn how to play when we are nervous. Familiarity with the situation and very diligent training are the answers. Make sure that nothing you do in a performance is being done for the first time. Highlight that previous sentence in big boldface italics and use it.

Even with the physical distractions of nervousness reduced, we still have to fight the mental confusion that sometimes takes place during a performance. Some players think of almost everything except what they are trying to do ("Was that exit sign blinking yesterday?"); others are almost unable to think at all. In either case, it is helpful to have something useful to think about. So, if your mind is betraying you, bring it back on course by insisting that it focus on two things: making a beautiful sound and staying present in the music. Even if you think about nothing else but these two things, they should help you stay on course and play beautifully.

"I Can Play it Fast, but I Can't Play it Slow"

It should not be necessary to say this, but this statement really means, "I can't play it at all." You should be able to play it fast, slow, in between, in different rhythms, in different articulations, in little chunks, as part of the big picture, and every other way you can think of. That flexibility is not just a practice tool; it has real professional benefits. In orchestral rehearsals, conductors often make suggestions to the players. Sometimes the suggestion is something the player had not thought of until that moment. You must be prepared to change your performance completely and immediately if needed. It is a favorite strategy of audition committees to ask applicants to play an excerpt a little differently, just to see if the player can do it. Anticipate some possible variations and be prepared. Quick is good. Flexible is good.

Metronomes, Tuners, and Other Tools

Incessant use of the metronome is not recommended; the clicks can actually obscure what you are trying to hear. Nevertheless, the metronome, used intelligently, is an essential practice tool. It has two main uses. Most commonly, it is used to restrain your tempo while preparing technical passages. Far from being a tool that whips your tempo forward, it usually ends up being a device that insists you play slowly enough. Most people get ahead of the metronome, not behind. When you use it, make sure that you play *exactly with the clicks*. Many times students who practice constantly with the metronome find they cannot play without it. This shows a failure to play with precision—to play *exactly* with the metronome. Only when that is achieved can the metronome help to transform the clicks into a physical, internal feeling of pulse stability.

Start with the metronome clicking small subdivisions—let's say eighth notes. Be very strict with yourself, and do not allow even the smallest deviation from perfection. If we were to record your practice session and slow the recording down to a crawl, the metronome clicks and your beat should still be together. As the small subdivisions become easier to follow, gradually make the clicks further apart and finally as far apart as possible, leaving you to fill in the gaps. Don't react to the click; instead, accurately predict the arrival of the next one—that is what good rhythm is all about. At first, trying to play exactly with the metronome can be maddening—it can be very difficult to do it for more than a few beats. Slow down the tempo, increase the subdivisions, and try again. Until you can do this, it is irresponsible to proceed.

Once accuracy is established, increase your speed very, very gradually. The metronome can be regulated to increase the speed in barely noticeable increments. The object is to trick your brain into believing that the speed has not changed, so you must be very patient. If you are practicing successfully at 72 beats per minute, do not increase the speed to 88; increase it to at most 76. If you have any physical or mental awareness of a faster tempo, the benefit is lost. If you make mistakes, or get tense, or need a great deal of conscious thought to keep going, you're going too fast. Slow down and take your time. It can be difficult to find the ideal practice tempo—if you play too slowly, you will get bored, and if you play too quickly, you will make mistakes and become tense. So find a tempo that is slow enough to allow you to control everything, but fast enough to require active concentration.

The other use for the metronome is to check any tendency toward wayward tempo. It is useful to play even very familiar pieces with the metronome once in a while. Note where you tend to rush and where you tend to drag. Try to identify any consistent tendencies—whether you tend to rush only articulated passages, for example. Remember to be really vigilant and play exactly with the metronome, or you'll receive no benefit. If you wish to push or pull certain passages for artistic effect, that's wonderful, but you should do it with complete awareness.

Some students complain that the metronome makes everything more difficult and distracting. This may well be true, but that is also a clue for them to use it much more. Always practice the things that are difficult and distracting. Spend as little time as possible doing the things that already work well.

For some repertoire, notably Allegro movements in baroque and classical Viennese-school music, it can be extremely useful to play with the metronome clicking the offbeats. For anyone who has never tried this before, the first half hour will be frustrating, to say the least. But after a while, this way of practicing will yield a whole new relationship to the beat and give much more assurance in tempo stability and rhythmic integrity. If you have any tendency to rush during the first movement of the Mozart concerto, for instance, a few hours spent this way will cure the problem forever.

Tuners are useful for tone and pitch development, but not as critical for oboe as they are for other instruments. The oboe changes daily (actually, the reed changes daily)—usually just slightly, but enough to make things much more complicated than is the case with instruments that stay more or less the same every day. As a result, it is more difficult for us to rely on physical memory to produce a sound: the notes are usually not in quite the same place as they were yesterday. So use the tuner as a means of discovering your pitch tendencies (is your E always sharp?), and especially as a means of learning the relationship between pitch and resonance. We discussed this briefly before: awareness of this relationship is crucial to improving security of pitch and maximizing resonance.

Flat notes, sharp notes, and in-tune notes all have a particular quality of sound that is consistent regardless of register. Sharp notes sound thin and shallow, flat notes sound flabby, and in-tune notes sound resonant and focused (your terminology may be different, but the ideas are the same). Learn to detect these differences in tone color, even minute ones, and your ability to play in tune will be much enhanced. It is easier for most players to hear a small difference in timbre than to hear that the pitch is slightly sharp or flat. If I play a note, talk for a minute, and repeat the same note very slightly sharper, many people would be unable to say which was higher or lower. But almost everyone would be able to say which example sounded better.

Do not use the tuner as a visual aid—in other words, don't just try to get the needle to go straight up and down. That's an easy trick, possible to accomplish consistently without learning anything. Make a determination first—are you sharp, flat, or in tune?—and then glance at the tuner for verification. Observe the change in resonance as you bring the note into tune—this will help you learn the relationship between intonation and tone quality. Pitch and resonance on the oboe are very nearly the same thing. If the note is in tune, chances are that it sounds about as good as it can; if the tone is resonant and full, chances are that the note is also in tune.

Recording devices are time-consuming but can be valuable. Many students are more perceptive about the playing of others than they are about their own. Listening to recordings of their own playing can help to redress this imbalance. If you record every practice session and then listen to it, you have just doubled your practice time, so that may not be productive. But twenty minutes here or there will be very helpful. Don't be afraid to record yourself, fearing that you won't sound good. Within the limitations of the audio equipment, the recording playback will reflect how you play. If you don't like it, identify what you don't like and start working on it.

Further Aspects of Successful Preparation

Advantages of Slow Practice

Apart from the obvious benefit of allowing you to play accurately, slow practice also allows you to play perfectly. It allows you to include nuances and inflections that might be difficult at full speed. It allows you to play really well in tune, with perfect resonance on each note. It allows you to seek a really clean technique with no bloops or sloppiness between any of the notes. And it allows you to control timbre, vibrato, and tone color to match your interpretation. Slow practice lets you really play well. Later, when the music is proceeding at full speed, some of this detail will be lost, but remnants of it will still be there, improving your performance. Never play slowly and bored; play beautifully.

Self-Diagnosis, or How to Practice Productively

Do you get mad when you practice? Frustrated? Do you sometimes reach the end of a practice session feeling like you have accomplished nothing? It's your own fault. Remember that while you are practicing, your task is to be your own teacher. You must do exactly what your teacher does: listen, make a diagnosis, prioritize the problems, and come up with a plan for improvement. Instead, many players merely judge: it's bad, it's pretty bad, it's ugly, it's a mess. If you were unfortunate enough to work with a teacher who was constantly negative, abusive, or vague, you would find another teacher. Don't do the same thing to yourself. Instead, employ a four-step process:

1. *Is something wrong?* Sometimes nothing is wrong. Do not be afraid to give yourself credit for playing well.
2. *What's wrong? Exactly what's wrong?* The more specific the answer to this question can be, the easier it will be to come up with a solution. If multiple things are wrong, start with the one that will improve your presentation the most. Fix one thing at a time. Don't get buried under problems; make them go away.
3. *How do I fix it?* Finding the answer is usually easy if the problem has been identified with precision.

4. *Have my changes and corrections eliminated the problem?* If the remedy is effective, wonderful. Move to the next problem. If there
is no improvement, make a new plan. But don't let defects pass
by without attention.

Many students are only good at the first of these steps—they know
something is wrong without knowing exactly what it is. Work hard to
get to the second step, which is where all the action is. Don't allow
yourself to use meaningless but judgmental words like "it's bad" or "I
sound ugly." Learn to identify a specific issue like "my A-flat to B-flat
is sloppy," or "the last four sixteenth notes of this run are uneven," or
"these three high notes are flat." Learn to hear what is coming from
the instrument. If all you know is that it sounded bad somewhere on
the second line, you are trapped into playing the second line badly once
more to try to focus the problem. If, instead, you know that the third
measure has three awkward notes in a row that you tend to rush when
you don't miss them outright, you can easily develop a method for improvement. Once you know exactly what's wrong, coming up with a
solution usually isn't too difficult. The hard part is figuring out what's
wrong. Work very hard to develop this skill.

Finally, persist with your plan until something changes. Until you
have change, you cannot know if the plan was a good one or a bad one.
At the end of a practice session conducted in this way, you will have
improved *something*. If you improve something every day, you will improve over 700 things in just two years. (Imagine what could happen if
you improve two or three things every day.)

Positive Thinking

Attention during a practice session is usually focused on the elimination
of error—a mindset that is correct and necessary. But often some aspect
of your playing works temporarily much better than usual and more
easily than usual. Every once in a while you will accidentally play really well. One day it might be that your tongue goes faster than normal;
another day you might be able to play for hours without tiring; on yet
another day you may find that you are playing with bewildering accuracy. When this happens, make sure you learn something from the experience. Be as vigilant for really good things as you are for bad things.
Be on the lookout for things that feel really easy: that's how you want
your playing to be all the time. Many breakthroughs occur after happy
accidents of this kind; don't miss them.

The opposite of this idea is important, too. If something doesn't work
today, move on to something else. We all have days where the tongue
doesn't work, the tone doesn't sing, or the fingers feel sluggish. So if you
can't tongue today, stop trying to force it. Practice something legato. If
the tone won't ring, there are plenty of scales that can still be improved

using your dead tone. Eventually, when your focus has shifted far enough away from tone, perhaps it will come and join you anyway.

Mental Practice

You cannot play what you do not understand. For this reason, mental practice—in other words, thinking and studying—is very useful. Imagine how the phrases will sound in your ideal performance. Try them, in your head, in all different ways—without the worry of operating the oboe, you can play any way you choose. While you're at it, study and learn the other parts as well. The oboe is almost always part of something larger, whether a duo with piano or a full symphony orchestra. Make sure you understand the whole and your part in it. After you have done all of this work, you can return to physical practicing with a much clearer idea of what you should work on and how you should proceed. Remember that imagination is the source of improvement. If you cannot imagine the music as more beautiful than you are playing it, you will not improve. Mental practice is part of the answer to this problem.

Spend as little time as possible being perplexed. If there is a rhythm you do not understand, put the oboe down and figure it out. If there's a German word or other foreign term you don't know, get a translation so you know what it means. Make sure that you understand perfectly every single mark on the page and can reproduce it accurately.

Often students prefer practicing fast music to practicing slow music. In preparing fast music, the goal is obvious—learn to play it fast and accurately. In slow music, it can be hard to know what to practice. Mental practice is the answer here, too. Imagine how the music would sound if it were sung by a great singer, played by a great violinist, played by an oboist with no expressive limitations. Then go back to the instrument. Now you've got work to do.

Speed Reading for Musicians

There is another aspect to mental preparation. Remember, you cannot play what you do not understand. Your fingers, tongue, and embouchure will move no faster and no more accurately than your brain commands them to do. If you are playing faster than you are thinking, you will make mistakes. Slow practice and fast thinking can make up some of this deficit, but at some point it will be impossible to think any faster. Usually the music still needs to be played faster, so we need a better plan. The only possible remedy is to find a way to give yourself less to think about. Recognizing patterns and intervals is the answer. Scale practice is useful because much of the music we play is made from a scale or some pattern derived from a scale. Thus, the solution has two parts: the player must be able to execute the scale or pattern, and he or she must be able to recognize it immediately and retrieve it instantly.

Example 6.6   Ferling, *48 Famous Studies*, no. 6.

Let us examine example 6.6, taken from the Ferling *48 Famous Studies*, to get a better idea of what I mean.[5]

Measures 1 and 2 are a G major triad with each chord tone approached from a half step below (the exception is the appoggiatura on the downbeat of the second measure). Knowing this makes it unnecessary to read the lower neighbor notes, including the potentially pesky A-sharp; instead, we will automatically insert a note a half step below the chord tone. Measure 3 is a D major arpeggio. Usually, when I present this idea to students and ask what they see in measure 3, the answer is, "An arpeggio." While correct, that answer is only half of the necessary information; it must be a *D major* arpeggio. Measures 4, 5, 6, 7, and 8 are all a G major scale. It changes direction a couple of times, it has some skipwise motion to break up the stepwise motion, and it has a C-sharp at the very end that is not part of the G major scale. We now have three

5. Ferling, *48 Famous Studies*.

or four things to think about in order to play thirty notes, instead of thirty things. Of course, the other benefit of thinking this way is that students good enough to play this etude should be able to play a G major scale automatically, so this whole first line can almost be sight-read. Measure 9 is a G major arpeggio with one exception—the F-sharp at the end of the bar. Measure 10 is a C major scale; measure 11 is a C major arpeggio. Measure 12 is fully diminished; measure 13 is G major again. Measure 14 is the first measure in which we actually have to read all six of the notes to be sure we have them right. Measure 17 is E minor, measure 18 is B minor, measure 19 is B major, and the next three measures are all E minor.

When analyzing material in this way, make sure to find the exact key so that the relationships are logical and correct. For example, the notes in measure 17 could conceivably fit into quite a few keys—it would not be incorrect to infer C major, A minor, G major, E minor, even D major or B minor. But clearly the function is E minor. The next measure (measure 18) has to be B minor because of the altered A-sharp. The only scale that has A-sharp on the way up and A-natural on the way down is B melodic minor. This is confirmed in the next measure, which is in B major. Why? Why couldn't it be F-sharp major? All the same notes would fit. I hope you see how your music theory studies are necessary here. A progression from E minor to B minor to F-sharp major is not out of the question—in fact, it's common. However, immediately arriving at E minor following the F-sharp major makes little sense. In contrast, the progression E minor–B minor–B major–B minor (measures 20–23) is perfectly smooth and logical.

If you are unused to thinking about music in this way, this analysis may seem like it causes extra headache and trouble. But believe me—every professional player with a good technique looks at music this way. Many gigs are little more than paid sight-reading; there is no time to read all of the notes, let alone practice them. Intervals and patterns are all we see. The music theory aspect—expecting certain chord progressions in preference to others—is basic musical literacy. If I begin a sentence, "I am going to walk through the . . .," there are many sensible ways to finish it: "door," "park," "grocery store," "house," and so on. The literate English speaker would expect one of those words or something similar, but he or she would also have eliminated many other words without thinking: "button," "doughnut," "reed knife," and so forth. Cultivate this way of thinking about reading music; it will eventually give you much less to think about. Ultimately, there will be little real sight-reading, but rather the rapid-fire reassembly of things we already know very well.

Transposing well-known material is a good way of gaining facility in this skill. Take any Barret or Ferling study and transpose it up or down a half step while looking at the same music. Now intervals and patterns become essential information, since the process of reading the note, transposing the note, giving it the right name (E-sharp, not F, for instance), and playing it correctly is much too difficult. Try it with this etude—play it a half step lower by changing the key signature to six flats and reading the music in the way described above. It will be diffi-cult at first, but it should get easier quite quickly.

Summary

- Never do it wrong.
- Practice every day for an appropriate length of time.
- Adhere to a constructive routine designed to be as efficient as possible.
- Practice performing.
- Be your own teacher.
- Be alert for good accidents.
- Practice away from the instrument.
- Learn to recognize and execute common patterns.

7

Extended Techniques

Over the past few decades, music has ventured beyond the traditional arrangement of notes and rhythms into realms of sound requiring new techniques of tone production. Books by Peter Veale, Libby Van Cleve, and Bruno Bartolozzi give a comprehensive picture of the possibilities.[1] I cannot improve on these, but I can offer a few practical suggestions for the novice.

First and foremost, do not regard the special techniques as noise. They should not frighten you, nor should you approach them with the glee of making an amusing sound. Extended techniques are part of a composer's carefully calculated sound picture and must be performed with as much care as any other sound you make. Often, producing the sound or maneuvering from one sound to the next requires a sophisticated flexibility of embouchure and air that will improve all aspects of playing, whether modern or traditional. So take the time to make sure that you can really play the piece at hand and don't have to resort to faking some kind of approximate version. When speaking about new music, even serious musicians are sometimes heard to say, "Nobody can tell the difference if we play this right or not." That is a betrayal of what it means to be a musician. As music professionals, it is not our job to like or dislike a piece; it is our job to present it with as much commitment

---

1. Veale, *Techniques of Oboe Playing;* Van Cleve, *Oboe Unbound;* and Bartolozzi, *New Sounds for Woodwind.*

as we can. Imagine if we were to take the same cavalier attitude toward a Brahms Symphony—we'll play as many notes as we can, guess at some of the more complex rhythms, and not worry if the trickiest ensemble places aren't really together. Played this way, no piece of music would sound convincing.

Of course, some new music is extremely difficult and will take many hours to learn. So, before committing to something, make sure that you have the time and the inclination to really do the music justice. Until nobody on stage is faking his or her part, the piece won't sound right and can't be fairly judged by the players or the listeners.

When performing the effects, especially those that require a distortion of the standard tone (pitch bends or extreme vibrato, for instance), be sure to really present the effect vividly, so the listener is in no doubt of what you are intending. A halfhearted pitch bend might just sound out of tune and poorly focused.

Over the past few decades, the line separating an extended technique from a traditional one has moved considerably: double tonguing and circular breathing used to be avant-garde techniques, while today they are accepted elements of any modern player's technique. Perhaps in future decades there will be no extended techniques, only oboe techniques.

Listed in the following sections are some of the most common extended techniques, along with a few performing suggestions for each.

Monophonic Techniques

"Monophonic" means that only one pitch sounds at a time, as distinct from multiphonics, which produce several pitches at the same time.

Harmonics

Harmonics are produced by fingering a twelfth below the note desired and venting with the appropriate octave key. So the harmonic A shown in example 7.1 is produced by fingering a low D and adding the side octave key (since the side octave is the correct octave key for high A). When a harmonic is required, it is notated by a small circle above the sounding pitch. Harmonic fingerings are also sometimes useful for regular

Example 7.1   Harmonic A, produced by fingering a D and adding the side octave key.

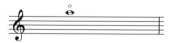

playing—for example, when a very soft note is wanted to blend completely into a chord.

Occasionally, composers will place a small circle above a note that cannot possibly be a harmonic (in other words, a twelfth below the note is beyond the oboe's range). In that case, an alternate fingering is substituted—utilizing an approximate fingering that plays the same pitch but has a different tone color.

Microtones

Most often, these are quarter tones (pitches halfway between two semitones), although eighth tones and others are also possible. Quarter tones are most reliably produced by using a dedicated fingering. Simply lipping a note up or down is not usually secure enough, especially in faster passages. Do not regard quarter tones as being out of tune and therefore free from our constant concern for good intonation. They require their own careful attention to precise intonation so that they can express the pitch inflection the composer intended. Fingerings can be found in the Veale and Van Cleve books or through experimentation, usually by adding fingers lower on the tube of the oboe. Notation is not entirely standardized, though composers almost always provide a key to show you what their symbols mean, and the systems are almost always logical.

Tone-Color Fingerings

Composers often request fingerings that produce the same pitch but have a slightly different tone color. In Luciano Berio's *Sequenza VII*,[2] for example, six different fingerings are needed for B-natural. Sometimes the fingerings are provided, sometimes they must be found through trial and error. Sometimes the suggested fingerings won't work very well and you'll have to find something else. Try hard to find something that only sounds different, not something that audibly raises or lowers the pitch.

Extremely High Notes

Consult the fingering chart in Appendix 2 for suggested fingerings for extremely high notes. With the exception of a few great virtuoso performers, most oboe players do not sound good on notes A and higher, though pitches as high as C-sharp and even D (more than three octaves above middle C) are possible. Many of the fingerings for these notes are produced by experimentation—the Van Cleve book, *Oboe Unbound*, for instance, shows seven fingerings for high A—and many of them require unusual venting techniques or even the direct application of the teeth to the reed.

2. Berio, *Sequenza VII per Oboe Solo*.

Glissandi and Pitch Bends

Pitch bends, especially downward ones, are quite easy on the oboe. Upward pitch bends are more difficult, especially if the reed is stable. Both are achieved by adjusting both embouchure tension and reed placement.

Glissandi are not easy at all, especially downward. As long as the fingers can be gradually peeled off the instrument, all is well, but as soon as we encounter any sort of break in the finger sequence, the glissando will break also. Peter Veale's *The Techniques of Oboe Playing* has an excellent chart showing the various possibilities.

Vibrato

Vibrato is not a special technique, but it can be used in various unusual ways to change the sound. Composers can request very slow vibrato, very wide vibrato, jaw vibrato, or no vibrato at all, among other possibilities. As noted earlier, if a special vibrato is wanted, make it very special, indeed, to make sure that the listener recognizes that the effect is intentional.

Double Trills

These are produced by rapidly alternating two different fingerings for the upper note of the trill. One possibility is shown in example 7.2. With careful coordination, alternating the fingerings in this way should give a trill that is much faster than usual. Obviously, this technique is possible only on a limited selection of pitches. Double trills are notated like normal trills, but with two squiggly lines instead of one. If the requested double trill does not have two fingerings for the upper note, it will be played with two fingers alternating on the same key. For example, a double trill between F-sharp and G can be accomplished in this way. Put the first two fingers of the right hand on the F-sharp plate and alternate trilling with them.

Tremolos

A tremolo is a rapid alternation of two pitches separated by more than a whole step. Many are quite easy on the oboe, and again, both the Van Cleve and Veale books provide very good fingering possibilities. However, some tremolos—usually those spanning large intervals—are quite

Example 7.2 Double trill. Alternate left and right E-flat fingerings as shown.

difficult, and even the best execution still sounds labored. Composers should check with an experienced performer before assuming that any two notes can be rapidly alternated. Some tremolos can only be produced rather slowly.

Multiphonics

A multiphonic produces several pitches simultaneously. These can be notated in various ways, and no one system is the most widespread. Some composers write the stack of pitches they want to hear, some provide an "X" note head with a corresponding fingering, and some provide only the fingering. Most composers will choose the pitch classes very carefully, but different styles of playing and reed making dictate that the results may not be completely reliable. A multiphonic that works perfectly for an Italian player may not work perfectly for an American (sometimes, due to differences in reed construction and/or instrument design, the suggested fingering won't work at all). So in some cases, it may be necessary to find a solution that approximates what the composer asked for. Again, experimentation and reference to good sources will help. Sometimes composers will be satisfied with something rather simple—each sound should be louder and higher, for instance—but sometimes they are extremely precise. If the composer is available, he or she can be a big help. Before giving up on a fingering provided in the music, experiment—some multiphonics are very sensitive to reed placement and air pressure. You may need to take lots of reed, or hardly any. You may need to bite and blow hard or to vary your technique in some other way. The fingering had to work for someone, or it would not have found its way into the music.

Other Effects

Flutter Tonguing

Flutter tonguing can be produced by rolling the tongue while playing. For oboe, neither the Italian "rrr" (produced with the tip of the tongue rolling just behind the front teeth) nor the German "rrr" (produced by rolling the back of the tongue against the soft palate) is ideal. The former interferes with the reed, while the latter does not give quite enough flutter effect. The best result is accomplished by rolling the tongue against the roof of the mouth somewhere between the two extremes. Flutter tonguing is notated by multiple slashes through the note stem, or by writing the word "flutter" or "flutter tongue" above the note. The German term *Flatterzunge*, frequently abbreviated *ftz* or *fltz*, means the same thing.

"Noise" Effects

Many other effects are possible as well—key clicks, playing the oboe without a reed, playing the reed without an oboe, singing while playing, buzzing like a brass player, and others. Most of these are quite easily produced and clearly understandable. Again, commitment and sincerity are the keys to making the composer's intentions come to life.

Conclusion

In many cases, the exact sound the composer wants is not completely apparent. In some cases, it is not really possible exactly as requested. And regrettably, in some cases, it may be something that you personally cannot play. In every case, you should figure out what the composer means if the literal notation—what the composer says—is not clear.

II

REED MAKING

8

Reed Construction

Reed making preoccupies oboe players more than players of any other reed instrument. The complex construction and short life of oboe reeds combine to mandate daily attention to the craft of reed making. The steep learning curve for reed making frustrates oboists of all levels. The following thoughts and comments should help to reduce confusion and open some new doors. If you have never made a reed, find a teacher. Otherwise, continue reading.

Before we begin, it is most important to understand that reed making is a craft governed by fairly consistent principles. It is not a black art; it is not swayed by astrological forecasts; it does not require even the smaller, less severe ritual sacrifices to the reed gods. It is a complex craft, and like anything else that you might wish to master, it will require years of careful work and study. But it will eventually become a consistent, logical activity that functions almost completely under your control.

This notion of craft is important when the going gets tough. Don't give up in frustration—instead, use what you know. You may not know everything; you may not be able to make swift decisions. But even after only one year of reed making, you will know quite a bit. Ask the right questions, and the right answers will usually come. The various scraping operations usually give a similar and predictable result. Think before you scrape, and anticipate the likely result.

Indeed, reed making is the oboist's advantage. We can construct a reed to match our instrument, our embouchure, and our physical capacity. We can even tailor it to the music we're about to play and to the acoustical situation that surrounds us. Few other instrumentalists have this degree of control.

Since most oboists begin playing two or three years before learning to make reeds, the reed making will remain a few years behind the oboe playing for some time. Until this disparity is caught up, reed making will be rather trying for the student. I think it is this uncomfortable time, which can last for five years or longer, that leads to the lifelong obsession with reeds—"if only I had a good reed, I could play well. . . ." This attitude often persists long after it is no longer necessary.

A better reed does not make you a better player. In the sound-producing chain of player–reed–instrument, you, the player, are by far the most important link. Without doubt, a better reed will allow you to play better, just as a Porsche lets you drive faster than a Toyota. But the Porsche does not make you a better driver. To be a better oboe player, you must *become* a better oboe player. There is no shortcut in this process. Do not neglect the basic concerns of practicing all aspects of oboe playing: tone production, finger technique, articulation, and so on. Without real skill in all these areas, a better reed will not help you enough. The legendary quote attributed to Marcel Tabuteau—"any damn fool can play on a good reed"—is usually interpreted to mean that we must learn to make do with inferior reeds. But this quote could also mean that you must learn how to play, how to really play well. Having a "perfect" reed could temporarily lull you into thinking that some of your playing problems are solved. You must master all aspects of oboe playing. Then all of your reeds will work better.

Remember that it will take thousands of hours and many years to become really proficient at reed making (or anything else, for that matter). Along the way, there will be many days where you spend hours working on reeds, only to have nothing useful to show for it. This time is not wasted. It is another step along the way. You have to spend the time. You have to do the work. Worry as much about process as you do about product.

A Few Words of Encouragement for Beginning Reed Makers

As a beginner, you are not making reeds. You are learning to make reeds. There's a big difference.

One day, your teacher says, "We're going to make reeds." An hour later, you are wishing you had four hands, wishing you could complete one or two ties without pieces flying in all directions, hoping that this time the string won't break. As soon as these goals are achieved, the standard is raised. The reed is supposed to be straight, of a particular length, without leaks. The string wraps should go neatly one next to the other, not snarled one on top of the other. Moreover, the reed should have a proper *overlap*. Too many things to control, all long before the knife goes anywhere near the reed. You are now firmly stuck in the deep end of the pool, trying not to drown.

The problem is that there are not enough preparatory exercises to help you build the skills you need to truly make reeds. The only way to learn to make reeds is to do it. The analogous situation would be to go to your first oboe lesson and have the teacher say, "Here's the Strauss Oboe Concerto. We're going to learn this." Possibly, eight years later, you might make a presentable job of the Strauss, but you can imagine the frustration of being so unsuccessful with it for so long.

So you're not making reeds. You're learning to make reeds. There's a big difference. The frustration can be reduced considerably if you can become much more interested in the process than in the product. Do each task as well as you possibly can. Know that you will probably make mistakes, or that you will overlook something because you haven't learned it yet. If the reed plays, great. It was probably an accident. Don't get used to it. Don't think that the battle is won; it isn't even close. Ponder the working reed—you must have done something well, and you'd like to do it every time—then put the working reed aside and start again. Getting a reed is less important than developing skills in knife technique, analysis, and diagnosis.

There is a way to speed up the process and minimize the frustration. Since reed making is something you learn by doing, do it a lot. It will likely take about one thousand reeds (!) before you feel like you know what you're doing. If you make two reeds a week, those thousand reeds will take you ten years to finish. Too long, don't you think? Two reeds a day, and you're down to a year and a half. Much better. After those thousand reeds, you will start to feel like you aren't drowning any more. Then we can proceed to actually swimming.

And there is hope and light at the end of the tunnel. Reed making is not the oboist's curse; it is the oboist's secret weapon. Eventually you will be able to adjust a reed to suit your situation exactly. You will be able to make different reeds for different halls, different repertoire, different size ensembles, and so on. Other instrumentalists need expensive additional equipment to make those changes; you can make them in a few seconds with your reed knife. Get to work.

As your playing improves, so will your reeds. You will demand more function, more resonance, more control. These musical demands are the beginning of improvement. If all you demand is a superior reed without a musical impulse to support it, you may have a perfectly tidy and functional reed, but the soul will be missing. Reed making is only interesting because music making demands that you have a reed.

The remainder of this chapter is a step-by-step guide to constructing the reed from the most basic raw materials. The next chapter will describe how to maximize your reed making time, with lots of general observations, helpful adjustment hints, and a guide to common problems with some suggested solutions.

Gouging, Shaping, and Tying

You cannot make a great reed without a great blank. By the time the reed is tied and ready to scrape, the work is more than half finished, and the fate of the reed is already determined. Make a great blank.

Reed making can be divided into two processes—the construction phase (during which you do the same thing to every reed with the goal of getting it to vibrate), and the finishing phase (when you begin to regard the reed as an individual and to adjust it according to your needs). Over time, the construction phase becomes automatic, even monotonous. Attention can flag; negligence can creep in. If that occurs, the advantages of processing your own cane are lost completely. Be attentive and construct the best reed you can.

Even though the descriptions offered here, together with the figures, should give a clear picture of the process, it will not be enough. If a picture is worth a thousand words, watching a professional do this may be worth a thousand pictures. If you have never processed a batch of cane, find an experienced reed maker to walk and talk you through the process. Then supplement that knowledge with the information that follows.

Here is the process, starting from the very beginning. Along the way, this section will introduce various supplies and pieces of equipment, which are all pictured in figure 8.1.

Cane stalks are sawn into sections and sold by weight (or sometimes by the stick); a pound is the typical measure in the United States. A pound contains between 100 and 140 tubes of cane. Before offering it for sale, vendors sort the cane according to tube diameter, usually in increments of 0.5 mm. Some dealers offer more precise sorting for a surcharge. Oboe cane diameter ranges from 9 mm to 11.5 mm, with most players preferring cane between 10 mm and 11 mm. In theory, the larger the cane diameter, the smaller the finished reed opening, although this relationship does not always hold true; other factors (cane resiliency, gouge, tying, staple dimensions, etc.) can influence the reed opening. Furthermore, cane sorting by most vendors is not very precise —deviations of 1 mm or more (sometimes much more) are common— and the cane tubes themselves are rarely perfectly round. If consistency of diameter is important to you, you will have to sort the cane yourself using a diameter or radius gauge. The simplest gauges resemble rulers with cutouts of various sizes; more precise mechanical measuring devices with dial readouts are also available.

The first task of the reed maker is to split the cane tube into three equal parts. Examine the tube carefully before splitting; most cane tubes are not round, but careful splitting can yield at least some pieces of optimum diameter. When viewed from the end, some tubes have a noticeable "nose" or point; this should not end up in the middle of your reed, so you will have to place the splitter to avoid it. Study the tube to see which sections might give the straightest pieces of cane.

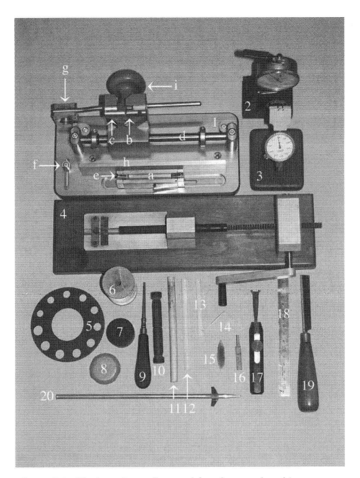

Figure 8.1 Tools and supplies used for oboe reed making.
1—gouging machine (a: cane bed, b: blade, c: guide, d: rod,
e: cane clip, f: cane stop for guillotine, g: guillotine blade, h: rail,
i: handhold). 2—dial indicator. 3—cane diameter gauge (modern). 4—pregouger. 5—cane diameter gauge (traditional).
6—string (or thread). 7—cutting block. 8—beeswax. 9—mandrel.
10—easel. 11—cane in tube form. 12—cane after splitting.
13—gouged cane. 14—shaped cane. 15—plaque. 16—tube
(or staple). 17—shaper handle and tip. 18—ruler. 19—reed
knife. 20—cane splitter.

Splitting is accomplished by using a cane splitter, or by placing cuts
with a razor blade at three equal places on the endgrain and driving a
paintbrush handle or similar tool through the cane. It is no longer necessary to risk life and limb when splitting cane; modern cane splitting
devices are available that keep the blades well away from your hands.

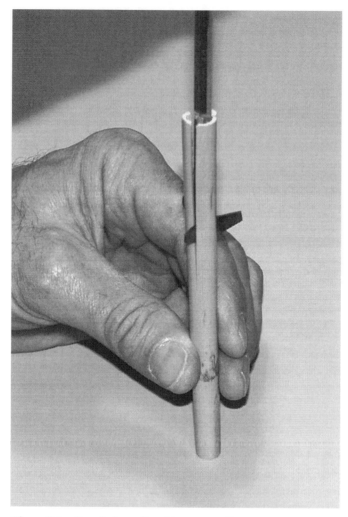

Figure 8.2   Cane being split with a cane splitter.

Splitting is easier and more accurate if the cane is dry, although no harm will result from splitting it wet. Figure 8.2 shows the tool and the procedure.

Since the cane tubes are rarely round and splitting releases internal tensions, the time to check the diameter is right after splitting. Accurate measuring tools are available that will tell you the diameter within a tenth of a millimeter. Ideally, the diameter of the cane should match the blade and bed of your gouger as closely as possible to allow the machine to function as it was designed. However, it seems to me that cane of really good quality is harder to come by than cane with the right diameter, so I tend to be rather permissive when sorting diameters—for me, anything between 10 mm and 11 mm is acceptable if the cane looks good. For some players, the tolerance is very close—not more than a tenth of a millimeter.

In trying to predict the future reed opening, you must learn the characteristics of your particular batch of cane—some cane is very stiff and springy, while some is rather weak. Even with the same diameter, those two pieces of cane will give a different reed opening, at least after a few minutes of playing. The prevailing weather and altitude can have an influence, also. Reed openings tend to collapse more readily in very dry weather and stay open much better in humid climates. Likewise, higher altitudes tend to collapse the opening. Finally, you should consider your recent experience with that particular batch of cane. If your reeds have been consistently too open, you should select larger diameter cane. If they have been too closed, you need a smaller diameter.

At every step of the way, some cane will be rejected because it fails to meet certain standards. With some batches, as much as three-quarters of the cane will be discarded before any reeds are attempted. This seems wasteful and expensive, but it is much better than the wasted time spent making reeds from cane that displays no chance of success. Cane is a natural substance, and perfection is sadly rare. So you, as the customer, end up doing most of the quality control. This is certainly not ideal, but it is reality; so do not mourn the pieces you toss in the trash.

If the cane has not already been soaked, the split sections of cane should now be soaked in warm water for one to two hours. The next step—trimming the cane sections to the correct length—can be performed dry, but small cracks often result, so I prefer to have the cane soaked at this point.

Next you will examine the cane pieces very carefully for straightness. It is not necessary for the entire section of cane to be straight. About three inches is enough; we will trim off the excess in the next step. Sometimes the straight three-inch piece is in the middle of the cane section after both ends have been trimmed.

Cane should be straight in three dimensions: when viewed from the end (sight down the piece of cane like taking aim with a rifle), when viewed from the side (to make sure it is not twisted), and when laid bark side down on a flat surface. For the last test, the cane should lie completely flat along its entire length. It is acceptable for a small amount of light to show at either end of the cane (it will refuse to stay in the gouger bed if it is bent too much), but the cane should be rejected if even the slightest glimmer of light shows underneath the middle of the piece of cane. If the cane is bowed in this way, the distortion will result in looseness of the blades at the tip—a fatal flaw, since for the reed to be stable the two blades have to touch tightly all the way up.

Every reed maker has a different tolerance for bent cane; my own preference is that it be very straight indeed. Very careful sorting can result in a great deal of waste, but if structural problems occur later in the process, I know the integrity of the cane is not to blame. Again, don't worry about the waste of discarding unsuitable cane—the reason for processing cane yourself is to gain control, not to improve yield.

Next, the cane is trimmed to length using a guillotine. Often this is mounted on the same plate with the gouging machine, but sometimes the guillotine must be purchased separately. In the latter case, make sure the cut of the guillotine exactly matches the length of your gouger bed. After identifying the straight section of the cane, feed it through the blade opening, set it firmly against the cane stop, hold it down, and chop. Toss the trimmed cane back in the water. The other portion of the cane is discarded. The pointed guillotine blade supplied with some gougers can result in small cracks that do not appear until later. If your blade is not round, follow the same procedure, but do not hold the cane against the cane stop while chopping. This will result in a slightly uneven appearance, but the defect is cosmetic only and the risk of cracking is reduced. Figure 8.3 shows the cane being chopped.

The cane must now be pregouged. Pregouging trims the top surface of the cane flat and prepares it to fit into the gouger bed. The most common sort of pregouger has a straight blade fitted across the end of a metal cane bed. The operator (you) pushes the cane past the blade with a wooden pusher. More sophisticated devices are also available; these include a second, curved blade which scoops out much of the cane that must otherwise be gouged away. These are expensive but save a remarkable amount of time as well as wear and tear on the gouging blade. See

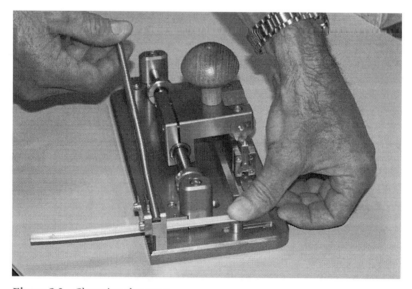

Figure 8.3 Chopping the cane.

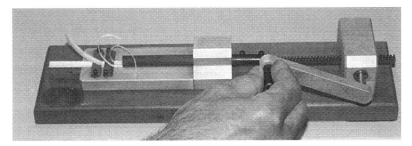

Figure 8.4 Pregouging the cane.

figure 8.4 for a picture of cane being pregouged. After pregouging, remove any debris from the pregouger and place a small drop of oil on the
blade to prevent rust. The cane is now ready for the gouging machine.

Gouging machines follow two basic design technologies. Most have
a blade curvature that is a section of a circle; a few have a curvature that
is a section of an ellipse. The latter has the blade set slightly off center,
giving a gouged piece of cane that already has a small "spine" gouged
into the cane—if viewed from the end and magnified, the gouge would
be slightly W-shaped. Regardless of the design, gouging machines work
their best only if they are kept well adjusted, cleaned, and oiled. The
blade must be kept at optimum sharpness. The cane should come off in
smooth silky curls about 0.05 mm in thickness. If these cane "chips"
come off in mushy stringy shreds, or if the surface of the gouged cane
looks torn rather than cut, there are three possible causes: the cane was
oversoaked (thirty to forty minutes is plenty for pregouged cane), the
cane is too soft, or the blade is too dull. Sharpening the blade once a
year should be often enough with normal use. If the gouger has multiple users (or one very prolific user), more frequent sharpening will
be necessary. Keeping the gouger blade sharp is as important as keeping
the reed knife sharp. (See chapter 11 for a more detailed discussion of
gouging machines.)

Place the gouger on a sturdy table or on your lap, as you prefer. If
your machine is designed with a single radius design (in other words,
the blade curvature is a section of a circle—machines made by Dan Ross,
RDG, Reeds 'n' Stuff, and most others fall into this category), gouge until
no more cane comes off, then reverse the piece in the bed and gouge
once or twice more. Make sure that each swipe of the blade travels from
stop to stop—from one end to the other, in other words. You should
only have to exert mild to moderate pressure until the last couple of
strokes. If you need to press firmly, the blade is probably dull, or else it
has receded too far into the guide.

If you have a dual-radius machine (in other words, the blade curvature is a section of an ellipse—Graf machines and their derivatives

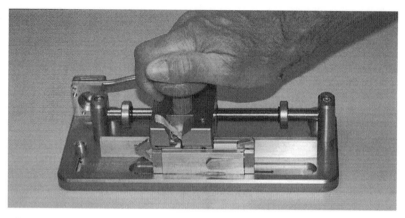

Figure 8.5   Gouging the cane.

fall into this category), reverse the cane in the bed every six strokes or so and continue until no more cane comes off. Note that the large screw knob that extends upward from the blade of many gougers is not a handhold—its purpose is to adjust the amount of blade extension beyond the guide. Find a way to move the carriage without holding on to the knob. Some gougers are more ergonomically friendly than others —those that have a comfortable wooden grip, for example. Figure 8.5 shows the cane being gouged.

After gouging, measure the thickness of each piece of cane carefully with a micrometer or dial indicator. A dial indicator is more reliable, since the pressure applied to the cane does not depend on the skill of the operator. (What's the difference? A micrometer requires you to manually tighten a screw knob until the spindle contacts the cane; a dial indicator does this for you automatically with spring pressure.) The recommended optimum thickness of oboe cane is 0.60 mm in the center of the piece (0.63 mm for oboe d'amore cane and 0.68 mm for English horn cane). If the cane is too thin, discard it; if it is too thick, put it back in the gouger and try to remove more material. Cane is a porous natural material, and measuring devices are not completely consistent, so the same piece of cane measured on three or four different tools will give three or four slightly different results. We are talking about hundredths of millimeters, tolerances that machinists work with, so being intensely picky about cane thickness is not sensible. Harder cane tends to gouge somewhat thinner than softer cane. Placing the measuring tool in different places will also give slightly different results. A useful working range of thickness for oboe cane is between 0.58 mm and 0.61 mm (between 0.65 mm and 0.70 mm for English horn cane). If it deviates from that range, then discard it. But insisting on complete uniformity from piece to piece will be frustrating.

After measuring the center of the cane, also measure the sides. The actual side measurement depends on many factors: the diameter of the cane (and the relationship of the cane diameter to the diameters of the gouger bed and blade), the cane's resiliency, and how far to the side you place the measuring tool. Measure where you imagine the widest part of the shape will be—the cane should be about 0.10 to 0.12 mm thinner there than in the center. The actual measurement is not crucial, but it is essential that the two sides be symmetrical. Be careful to measure in exactly the same place on both sides; moving the tool even one or two grain lines will give a different measurement.

Note that these dimensions are guidelines only: the final test of any setup is to make reeds from it. Consider also that the point of owning a gouging machine is to add consistency, not complexity, to your reed making. If an expert technician set up the machine, and if the reeds are working reasonably well, leave the machine alone.

After gouging, use a small bristle brush to remove any cane debris from the gouger and put a drop of oil on the blade. When not in use, the gouger should be stored with a small piece of cotton in the cane bed underneath the blade to protect the blade from direct metal-to-metal contact. Gouging machines are robust devices, but the blade is made of very hard steel and can chip, so it needs to be protected. The rod will also need to be oiled from time to time. Do this at the first sign of sluggish movement. Use a paper towel to clean off the old oil before applying the new.

The cane is now gouged. It can be stored in this state almost indefinitely given reasonable conditions. Store it indoors in a cool, dark place. Make sure the cane is protected from bugs and other pests. Stored cane can last a remarkably long time—twenty years is certainly not too long, though fifty probably is. However, there is no benefit to aging the cane unless it is clearly immature—too white or too green (see the discussion in the next section). Cane is too old when the interior surface has a brownish-orange color and the scrapings feel more like splinters than shavings, but this takes decades.

Cane Selection

Reed-making yield will increase significantly if careful cane-selection procedures are followed. We have already sorted and selected the cane so that it meets certain physical criteria: the correct diameter, acceptable straightness, and so on. Now we will sort it further to weed out the pieces whose texture and resilience are too strong or too weak.

Making a reed from every single piece of cane you own is a waste of time and effort. Some of the cane will be good, some bad, most in between—even within a batch of supposedly consistent quality and origin. Effective cane selection requires that you discover three things: the qualities that apply to good cane in general, the qualities that apply to your particular batch of cane, and the qualities that help your own personal reed-making style. It is not necessarily always true that hard cane is better than soft cane—everyone has made bad reeds from hard cane and good reeds from soft cane. So, along with learning the general principles, it is still necessary to observe every characteristic of every piece of cane in order to maximize your yield. As you read what follows, bear in mind that my recommendations are empirical—the result of making thousands of reeds over the course of several decades; I do not claim any sort of scientific truth for my statements.

The bark of the cane must be free from physical defects (wormholes, etc.); it should not have dark stains that penetrate through to the cane (superficial mottling is normal, even desirable); it must not be ribbed (like celery); and it should not be very pale in color. White cane has been too recently removed from the bleaching effects of the sun (a normal part of preparing and aging the cane for sale) and will not vibrate well yet. This cane is not defective; it will gain normal coloration and quality after a few months spent in a dark place—a small closed box of some kind. The same is true if the interior of the cane is green. It will not yet make a good reed. Set it aside until the green color fades through aging.

After examining the bark, turn the piece of cane over. On the interior surface of the gouged cane, look for even, unbroken lines. Reject cane with an obvious and excessive grain, especially if it appears soft and pulpy. A strong backlight is helpful for seeing the grain clearly. (Note: Since cane is botanically a grass, not a wood, this "grain" actually consists of vascular bundles. I will use the term "grain" for the sake of simplicity.)

Ideally, the inside surface of the cane will appear almost shiny, it will be very close grained, and the cane will appear smoothly cut by the gouger blade rather than torn.

While gouging the cane, observe the cane quality. Material should come off in smooth, silky shavings. If the gouger blade is sharp and the cane has not been oversoaked, shreddy, soft shavings mean that the cane is of inferior quality. Pay particular attention to the last one or two shavings—they will have more or less the same texture as the tip of your finished reed.

Mechanical devices to measure cane hardness are available—bassoon players use these frequently. They are not yet well suited to oboe cane since they measure hardness by probing the cane and measuring the resulting deflection. Oboe cane is not really thick enough to allow this to work accurately, so for now we must rely on our observations.

After forming a judgment about the hardness and structure of the cane, examine the elasticity of the cane by twisting the gouged piece. It should be springy but not tough. Since this is a "feel" test, experience will show what combination of elasticity and hardness works best. Cane that is too springy and stiff can sometimes make a reed with a large opening that will not respond to repeated attempts to squeeze it shut. At an extreme, these reeds can also display an unpleasant metallic sound that no amount of scraping will remedy. On the other hand, cane that twists too readily is also likely to be too soft and pithy and usually makes a reed with a small opening and weak vibrations. The strength and elasticity of the cane contribute as much to the strength of the reed opening as the original diameter of the cane.

Cane can also be tested by sound. Hold the gouged piece of cane bark side down a few inches above a hard surface. Any solid tabletop will do, but for accurate comparison, it should be the same surface each time. Drop it. The sound on impact varies between a dull thud, a bright ping, and an almost musical tone. All of them will have a pitch. If this pitch is rather close to C (within a half step either way) and the sound has some depth, it is likely to have a good vibration characteristic as well.

Finally, when you're working through your stash of cane, apply the 20 percent rule: it is likely that 20 percent of any batch of cane is going to be bad. The last 20 percent is the cane you've already rejected three times. So, if you gouge fifty pieces and you've got ten or fifteen left, it's time to gouge more. Just toss the rest out.

As I said at the outset, these observations are empirical, not scientific. The important point is that you must observe everything and remember everything. That is when experience becomes useful. Keep notes if necessary.

Shaping

After gouging, the cane must be shaped. The gouged cane is folded over a template called the shaper tip, and the excess material is removed from the edges with a sharp blade. The dimensions of the shaper tip significantly influence the reed's final performance. In general, if the shape is wide, the reed will vibrate more readily and the tone will be richer. The trade-off for this vibrancy is a lack of focus in the sound and difficulty in making a reed with pitch stability. Commercial cane is often shaped wide for beginners to use, since it makes a basic reed rather easily—the reed begins to vibrate long before it is finished, encouraging the neophyte reed maker. Narrow shapes give better tone and pitch focus with better control of the vibration. If the shape is too narrow, however, the tone becomes shallow, the pitch rises, and the reed never vibrates sufficiently. This conflict between stability and vibrancy defines the dichotomy of reed making: it is easy to make a stable reed that won't vibrate, and equally easy to make a vibrant reed that can't hold a pitch. The correct shaper form for you is part of the solution to this equation.

In addition to the width, the other important dimension of the shaper tip is its curve—how does it get from being wide at the top to narrow at the bottom? There are many answers to this question, each with its own peculiar result. The variety of shaper tip choices is daunting to the beginner, who should get a solid recommendation from a teacher or other professional player and use that tip until the student's reed making is stabilized. Don't begin to experiment with different shaper tips until you have enough experience to be certain that the shaper is causing your reed problems. I am always concerned when beginning reed makers talk about changing their shape or already own four tips. The result is more likely to be confusion than progress. Consistency is worth its weight in gold; don't blame equipment when your own lack of skill is the real reason the reeds are problematic.

So, in order to shape the cane, place it on an easel: a wooden cylinder designed to make folding and trimming the cane easier. Make one last check for straightness; the cane should lie flat on the easel. With your reed knife, scrape each end of the cane until it is fairly thin. This provides a smoother appearance when tying and can help prevent leaking. Scrape at least some of the cane as thin as you want your tip to be; this will give insight into the cane's quality at every layer. Cane is always harder close to the bark and softer underneath. After trimming, follow the guide on the middle of the easel with your knife and lightly score the bark of the cane to facilitate folding. Fold the cane over your knife edge and squeeze on the fold to confirm it. Squeeze only on the fold; if you squeeze further down on the cane, it may crack.

It is possible to fold the cane manually without using the easel as a guide. Bend the two ends together and make a fold in the middle. If the cane cracks at this point, be glad. Don't gently pamper the cane during processing; if it's going to crack, it's much better for it to crack now than during a concert. I never mind it when cane cracks, only when finished reeds crack. Throw the cracked piece of cane away and move on. Figure 8.6 shows how to fold the cane.

The edges of the piece of cane need to be narrowed before it will fit on the shaper tip. Remove an equal amount from both edges—about 1 mm—until it fits snugly between the ears of the shaper. Make sure that the fold sits firmly against the top edge of the shaper tip and that the shaper is centered underneath the cane. Hold it up to the light to confirm that an equal amount of cane extends on either side of the shaper and that the cane is straight up and down. When everything looks right, tighten the cane jaws to secure the cane firmly in place. I prefer to use shaper handles that have adjustable jaws, since these can be tightened in many positions rather than having to remain in a single fixed position. Often, the handles with fixed jaws force you to clamp too high on the cane, compressing fibers in a region that will later need to vibrate.

To shape the cane, use a single-edged razor blade or other sharp tool such as an Exacto knife or an old reed knife. Single-edged razor blades can be resharpened and used many times. Set the ear of the shaper firmly against a fixed surface to stabilize it, and cut away the excess cane with the blade, starting at the top of the shaper and cutting toward your body. Be sure to follow the contour of the shape exactly by using firm pres-

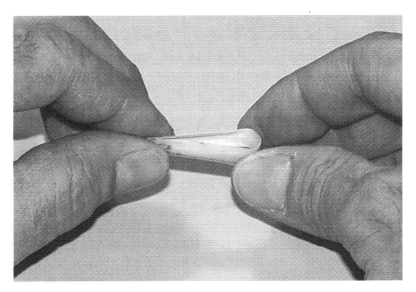

Figure 8.6 Folding the cane.

sure and maintaining a consistent cutting angle. Try not to let the blade get caught by the grain of the cane; insist, with firm pressure and a fairly steep angle, on guiding the blade to follow the contour of the shaper tip. Some reed makers finish the shaping by tilting the razor blade slightly, so that it cuts only one cane blade at a time. Whether you do this or not is optional, but it is important to do the same thing every time. Figure 8.7 shows the cane being shaped.

I prefer not to store shaped cane, but to use it immediately. Once the cane is folded, that fold should be cut open quickly in order to preserve a tight seal at the tip of the reed.

Tying

Fit a staple onto your mandrel. (The words "staple" and "tube" are used interchangeably by reed makers.) The choice of tube is a personal one; there are many different brands of various internal dimensions and, lately, different materials and designs. See chapter 11 for a more complete discussion of the various options.

The standard length in North America is 47 mm, though 45, 46, 46.5, and 48 mm staples are also available. It is preferable for the staples to fit the mandrel exactly, allowing you to judge the dimensions of the staple at a glance. Otherwise, you will have to learn what constitutes a good fit for your particular mandrel. Staples often have inconsistent dimensions, even when they are all the same size and from the same maker.

Reed Making

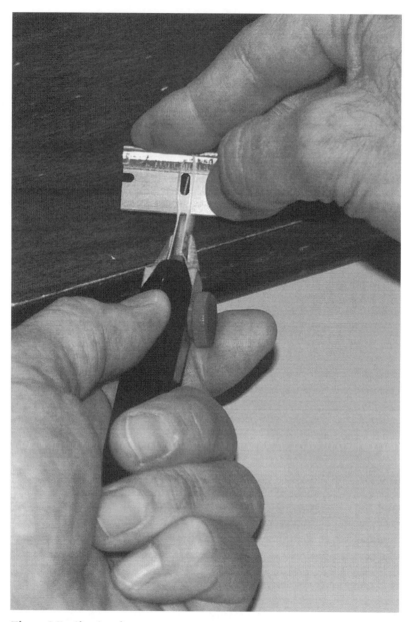

Figure 8.7 Shaping the cane.

Before tying the reed, unless the staple is brand new, clean out its inside. A small brush (a straight mascara brush works very well) and some running water will do a good job.

Hold the mandrel with its staple in your left hand and tie with the right. (Note: this instruction applies whether you are right-handed or left-handed. Holding the mandrel in the right hand and the string in the left hand defeats the manufactured "twist" of the string and causes structural problems later.) Take your spool of reed thread and remove three or four reeds' worth of string—two or three yards—and wind it on to an empty spool or a piece of dowel. (Tying with a full spool of thread is clumsy and snarls the string.) Tie one end of the string to a firm support—a cup hook or C-clamp fastened to a sturdy work surface. Have a very good light available—a solid utilitarian desk lamp with an adjustable shade and arm. Please do not tie onto a music stand, a door-knob, a drawer pull, or some such unstable surface; getting the blank put together perfectly is too important to leave to this sort of chance. I have seen students tying reeds in near darkness, while sitting on the floor, with the string tied to some mysterious point of origin more than a yard away. While this does not assure a poor result, it certainly doesn't help it. Tie under the same well-lit and organized conditions you will use while scraping.

Coat the string with beeswax to seal any small gaps between the string wraps (or paint the string with nail polish after the reed is tied on). Either precaution will seal any small leaks between the string winds and assure that the knots hold tightly.

Before tying, the future overlap of the reed must be established. The front blade of the reed must be displaced slightly to the right of the rear blade when the reed is assembled. The correct overlap allows the string tension to help pull the two blades tightly together. If the over-lap is reversed, the string torque around the reed may cause the blades to pull apart from each other. Displace the blades of the shaped piece of cane in the direction of the overlap by about half the width of the cane and gently squeeze on the hinge to enforce this. In other words, overlap the blades much more than normal to establish the correct be-havior. Then move the blades into a position where they are just barely overlapped—the front blade is just barely to the right of the rear blade. Slide the staple (on the mandrel) into the bottom of the cane, and hold the cane firmly in place on the tube with the thumb and index finger of the left hand. Hold it at the correct tie length (see the following dis-cussion) for your shape and staple. Make the initial wind three or four wraps below the end of the tube, and begin winding upward toward the top of the tube. With one wind remaining, pull tight with both ends of the string. Be careful to keep the cane flat on the tube oval; do not let it torque away from you. Use your mandrel handle as a reference. With luck, the flat of the mandrel handle will align with the flat part of the mandrel shaft, so a glance at the handle will tell you if the cane is still

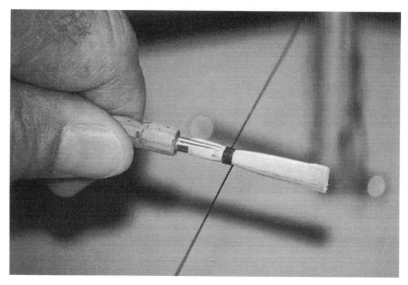

Figure 8.8   Initial winding of the reed.

on straight. (Oddly, many mandrels do not meet this simple requirement.) Figure 8.8 shows the initial winding of the reed before the string crosses over.

The next step will complete the tying process, so now is your last chance to make sure things are correct. You need to check three things. First, the reed should be straight when viewed from any direction. This means that it should not lean to one side or the other, nor to the front or the back. In addition, it should be aligned with the flat part of the staple. Second, it should seal tightly at the bottom of the cane just above the string. A suction test is the only really reliable way to check this—lean down toward the reed and make sure no air can be sucked through the two blades of cane at the point just above the string. Trying to blow air is not as good as the suction test; visually checking for leaks is almost worthless. Don't worry if the blades leak a little near the tip; this should disappear once the reed is opened. Finally, check the overlap. Be sure to look at both edges of the reed; one edge might be set correctly while the other is still reversed. If that occurs, one blade is essentially trapped inside the other, resulting in dangerous structural instability. If any of these three things is not right, relax the string tension slightly and make adjustments. Take plenty of care and time—any problems that remain now cannot be repaired later.

(Note: It is normal for the cane to split underneath the string windings. These cracks cause no harm even if they extend slightly above the string into the reed cane. If they become very deep or extend halfway up the reed, that is cause to discard the reed. Otherwise, only worry about cracks that originate at the tip of the reed.)

The correct tie length for the reed is not absolute ("tie length" is the total length of the reed after tying but before any cane is removed by scraping or clipping). Depending on various factors, the right length could be anywhere between 71 mm and 75 mm (the finished length of the reed, however, is always the same at approximately 70 mm). Here is my rule: the reed should be tied on as long as possible. "As long as possible" means that there are no leaks just above the string, with one wind still possible before reaching the end of the tube. Whether to make the last wind or not is a judgment call—sometimes "one wind" is not exactly 1.0; it might be 0.7 or 1.2. Do not, under any circumstances, wind beyond the end of the staple. Bear in mind that the edge of the reed facing away from you will have the string half a wind higher up than the edge you are looking at.

The tie length arrived at through this method is the ideal one for your setup—your shape, your staple, your gouge. If the reed is tied on too long, meaning without enough cane on the staple, it will leak. If the reed is tied on too short, the cane will be too wide at the bottom of the reed. That will cause the string to pinch the sides of the cane before the staple can support the tension, causing instability and possible looseness at the sides near the tip.

After everything is correct, cross the string over the winds you have already made and wrap toward the cork, pulling tight after each wind. Before the crossover, you should pull on both ends of the string; after crossing over, you can pull only on the length between the reed and your hand, since the other end is now being wrapped underneath. Keep winding until space for two or three winds remains. Make a series of three knots by twisting a loop of the string and pulling it tight (see figures 8.9, 8.10, and 8.11). Be sure that the knots look tight, and always make several knots to ensure that the reed does not fall apart.

You are now ready to begin scraping the reed. If the preceding process has been followed carefully, and the result is exemplary, the reed is already more than half finished. But before taking a rest, you should apply a basic scrape to the reed and cut the tip of the reed open as described in the next section. Do not store a completely unscraped blank; the fold at the top should be opened immediately after tying to prevent any possible spreading of the blades at the tip.

Scraping and Finishing

Carefully trim off the ears remaining from the shaping process. Try to remove them completely, leaving a straight line to the end of the reed. Follow the edge of the reed with your knife until it catches a grain, then just split off the ear from there. Do this before beginning to scrape. It is

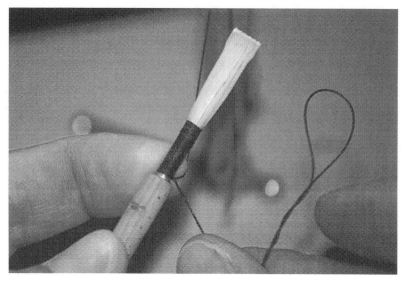

Figure 8.9　To make the knot, first make a loop of string and twist it two or three times.

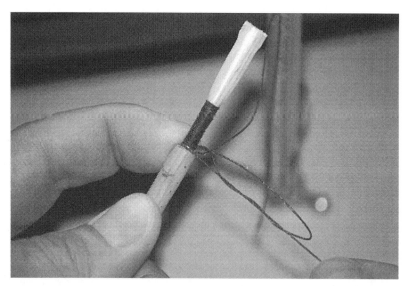

Figure 8.10　Then pass the loop over the reed and align it with the bottom of the string winds.

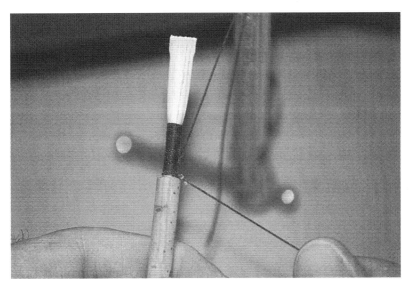

Figure 8.11 Finally, pull the loop tight to create the knot.

tempting to leave the ears intact to provide more room for error, but this makes it more difficult to gain access to the parts of the tip we want to scrape. First, however, before we begin scraping we should learn how to hold and sharpen our knife.

Brief Digression: Knife Technique

Hold the reed in your left hand (if you are left-handed, it makes sense to reverse all of these instructions—my suggestion for standardizing handedness applies only to the tying process). It does not need to be gripped strongly, just enough to make sure the reed will not slip out of the hand. Some players prefer to leave the reed on the mandrel for additional security; this is fine if it helps to keep the hand relaxed. Additionally, some players are unable to bend the thumb backward far enough (the "hitchhiker's thumb") to get enough clearance above the reed to accommodate the knife. These players will also benefit from using the mandrel, since the whole assembly can now be gripped with the third and fourth fingers, relieving the thumb of this duty.

If the reed is held without the mandrel, hold it between the second knuckle of the middle finger and just above the first knuckle of the thumb. Let the other fingers gently curl around the reed and allow the reed tip to rest on the index finger near the first knuckle. Figure 8.12 shows the correct position. Relaxation is crucial here—the reed is light, and the knife pressure will be light (we hope), so there's no reason to grip the reed strongly.

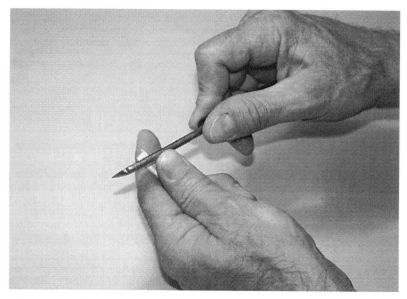

Figure 8.12   The reed and the reed knife held correctly.

Hold the knife in your right hand with the thumb on top of the handle and the index finger almost underneath it. Use the index finger to press the spine of the knife blade against the left thumb, just under the thumbnail. The rest of the fingers of the right hand merely restrain the knife from leaving the hand. In no way does the right hand grip the knife; it merely holds it in place.

The knife is pressed against the tip of the left thumb just underneath the nail. Fairly firm pressure against the thumb is necessary to assure stability. This point of contact acts as a fulcrum or pivot; it will be possible to arrange the knife in many different angles and attitudes from this basic position.

Scrapes should be short in length. The knife works best when used nearly perpendicularly to the cane surface. Long U-shaped scrapes always create a U-shaped result. The thinnest part of the cane will not end up where you intended it to be—it will occur at the bottom of the U-shaped swipe, usually a couple of millimeters behind the spot you are aiming at. So use short scrapes—about 2 mm long—and overlap each one slightly over the previous one. Hold the knife securely in the right hand (hold it, don't grip it) and make the scraping motions by rotating the wrist. Keep the wrist relaxed, or else control and sensitivity will suffer. The movement of the knife stroke should begin and end in the air; if the knife motion starts from the surface of the cane or (especially) if it stops on the cane, nicks will occur that can quickly become ridges. Do not scrape on the return stroke; the scrape takes place on the forward stroke only. Try to avoid scraping in the same direction as the cane fibers—in other words, do not scrape straight up and down the reed, but rather at different angles. This will preserve the remaining cane in much better condition. The pressure of the knife against the cane should be minimal. If the knife edge is sharp, this pressure can be quite light, again preserving the remaining cane in better condition.

For beginners, judging how much knife pressure to apply to the reed is the most troublesome aspect of knife technique. If the pressure is too light, no cane will come off the reed. If it is too heavy, cane will come off in unpredictable quantities, and large chunks of tip may disappear altogether. Maintain a sharp knife edge, and work with as little downward pressure as possible.

Second Digression: Knife Sharpening

In chapter 11, I recommend using Japanese water stones in various grits: coarse, medium, and fine (extra-fine and ultra-fine stones are available, too). This is the procedure I use with those stones, though the basic sequence will work on any stone. The crucial element that must be controlled while sharpening is the angle of the blade to the stone. The precise angle is less important than the consistent use of the same angles.

Start with the coarse stone. You will need a cookie sheet or some sort of shallow tray to catch the water and mess made by sharpening. Some water stones require the stone to be soaked for a time before use. The ones I prefer do not require prior soaking; using a water spray bottle, water can be sprayed onto the surface right before sharpening. Additional water should be sprayed onto the stone whenever the surface is no longer shiny. Use the whole stone for sharpening and move the blade backward *and* forward. Hold the knife with both hands—one hand on the handle, and the thumb and forefinger of the other at the tip of the blade. Pressure should be light—just enough to keep the knife stable on the stone.

Begin with the blade facing away from you (left-handed reed makers will need to reverse these directions). Raise the back of the knife one click above the stone (a click is your own physical idea of what a very small amount is—not any particular angle, just a very small amount. The memory created in this way is physical, not visual, making it much easier to return to the same positions every time). Work the knife back and forth until you can observe a tool mark along the whole blade. This step does not sharpen the knife; it is a maintenance step to create a "relief" and keep the blade thin enough to accept a good edge. The same result can be accomplished by leaving the knife flat on the stone, although that will weaken the spine of the knife over time.

Continue with the blade facing away from you. Now raise it two to four clicks and continue. Sharpen until you see a burr on the side of the blade facing up. You don't have an edge until you see this. The burr will be visibly obvious on the coarse stone, less obvious on the medium (though you can still feel it), and very subtle on the fine.

Now turn the blade toward you. Raise it two to four clicks and work until the burr is visible on the other side (again, on the side of the blade facing up).

Turn the blade away from you again and swipe it once at the two-to-four-click angle, or until the burr is back on the other side. These first few steps may take very little time on a brand new knife, or ten minutes on an older knife that has been inconsistently sharpened. Once the proper geometry is established, each subsequent sharpening will take much less time.

Repeat the identical steps in the same order on each of the finer stones. Be sure to clean the stone (spray with water and scrub with a good paper towel if necessary) before storing it, and be sure to clean the knife blade when you switch stones, too. Even a little of the coarse grit on a finer stone will cause scratches.

When the knife is used, the microscopic burr that scrapes the cane is gradually displaced to the other side of the blade. It has not broken off (although it eventually will), so the knife does not need to be sharpened yet, but the burr needs to be bent back to the correct side of the blade. A nonabrasive knife steel can be used to accomplish this, extending the intervals between actual sharpenings.

Once the knife has a good edge and the proper geometry has been established, it will not be necessary to start with the coarse stone—start with the medium and finish with the fine.

Back to Scraping

The configuration of the basic scrape and the order of the steps that follow differ from player to player. Everyone has a slightly different order of operation for removing enough cane to create a vibrating reed. But each method has the same goal: it creates a feedback system for reed makers so they can evaluate and gauge their progress toward the goal of a playing reed. If you have a system that works and that communicates the reed's progress to you along the way, then by all means continue to use it. I follow the system described because I have more than thirty years experience with it and it is completely familiar to me.

The first scrapes are going to define the future tip. The lower end of the tip should be placed at 65 mm measured up from the bottom of the staple. My initial goals are to construct a tip that is clearly defined and completely symmetrical. It should not yet be thin at all—that's dangerous at this stage; we are concerned with symmetry and clear definition. Figure 8.13 shows the reed following this step.

Next, I scrape the bark from the rest of the reed in two narrow channels. I am careful to leave distinct rails up both sides and a heavy spine down the middle. This structure must be preserved throughout

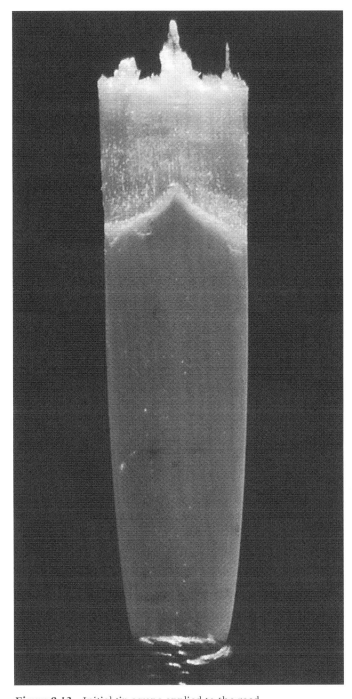

Figure 8.13 Initial tip scrape applied to the reed.

the entire reed-making process. The following chapter has more discussion of structure.

After the bark is removed from the future back and heart regions, I clip the reed open. Make the initial clip just a little longer than the finished reed will be. If your finished reeds are usually 70 mm, then make the first clip to 70.5 mm or so. If you leave the reed longer than that, you will be scraping on a very long tip. Later, half of it will be clipped away. Furthermore, when the reed starts to vibrate with that very long tip, it will give wild feedback that is impossible to analyze. Clipping is accomplished by holding the reed firmly on the cutting block and rolling the knife blade back and forth across the tip of the reed. So clip the reed open, examine the tip to see that the scraping is tidy and symmetrical (sometimes the plaque makes this easier to observe), make any necessary corrections to the tip symmetry, then soak the reed for a few minutes to encourage a good opening. Before setting the reed aside for the day or continuing to work on it, perform two simple checks. First, gently squeeze on the tip opening to confirm that it closes symmetrically. Don't try to squeeze it all the way shut—the reed is still too thick for that—but make sure that the sides compress first, and that it looks like it will close symmetrically toward the middle from there. We are not checking for cracks; this test is to reveal structural defects in the cane—some reeds close toward one edge or the other, making them very unstable. If your reed fails this test, discard it now. Second, examine the tip for any looseness at its edges. The reed should grip a plaque firmly almost as soon as it is inserted. If the sides are slightly loose, they might eventually collapse with scraping, but it is likely that the reed will always have some structural instability. If they are visibly loose, there is nothing to be done. Discard the reed.

The reed now has what I call the basic scrape. Any reed, once tied on, should be scraped to this point before being stored. Now I set the reed aside for a day before working on it further. Figure 8.14 shows the reed at this stage.

Final Digression: How Quickly Should a Reed Be Finished?

I prefer to work on a reed over the course of several days, allowing it to dry in between sessions. This gives the cane more time to adapt to its new surroundings and produces a reed that lasts longer than one made all at once, with better stability and consistency. The first few times the cane is soaked, the fibers raise above its surface just a little, often causing the reed to feel somewhat heavier each time it is soaked. After a few days, the grain no longer raises, and the reed is structurally stable. So an advantage of my approach is that the reed is finished and broken in at about the same time.

The first day's procedure can be summarized: apply the basic scrape, clip the tip open, soak the reed, make sure the tip is symmetrical and

Figure 8.14 Reed with basic scrape applied and tip cut open.
Scrape the reed to this stage before storing it.

tight, and set the reed aside. On a second day, scrape the reed until it crows. On a third day, scrape the reed until it plays somewhat roughly. Then, the following days allow for final adjustments of the reed. The sessions don't literally have to be one day apart: "day" in this context means, "Let the reed dry out completely before soaking it again and resuming work."

It is entirely possible to make a finished reed in one sitting and get a good result, but the inevitable changes in its playing characteristics during the first few days often mandate that the reed is only useful for a short time. The next day it must be replaced with another. There is nothing wrong with this—oboists have to work on reeds daily regardless of the strategy used. I prefer to work slowly because I would rather have reeds that have been tested for a length of time—two or three good practice sessions and a rehearsal or two—before depending on them for a concert.

More Scraping

The opened reed can be stored in this rough-scraped state, but the opening is more stable if the reed is finished within the next few days.

After the basic scrape is applied and the reed clipped open, the back is separated from the heart. Scrape the back starting at the top of it (at 61 mm measured up from the bottom of the tube), and with short overlapping scrapes, work your way down to the bottom. Stop about 5 mm above the string. The first 4 or 5 mm above the string will remain as bark. Be sure to leave the spine down the middle and the rails up both edges as strong as you can. I aim my knife blade to scrape just to the inside of the rail; this assures that the rail is preserved, and that the spine is not accidentally scraped off. If this structure is frequently destroyed in your reed making, a dull knife is to blame. A dull knife will require firmer pressure against the cane; this increased pressure will flatten the arc of the cane, which will result in removal of a wider path of material. Remember that "dull" in this context is a relative term—even if the knife still seems sharp by household standards, it can be quite unsuitable for reed making. A good knife for reed making has an intensely sharp edge that is resharpened every few minutes.

After scraping the back, remove about half that amount of cane from the heart. If any bark remains in the spine region of the heart, remove that as well, but stop scraping as soon as the bark layer is gone. After this step, scraping the heart is the same procedure as scraping the back: avoid the center and avoid the edges. The rails and spine should continue all the way up to the tip.

Repeat this procedure twice more. Scrape from the back, then scrape about half that amount from the heart. Each time the back is revisited, proportionally more cane should be removed from the upper half of the back and less from the lower part; the lower part of the back needs to remain stronger and gradually blend toward the bark at the bottom. Always follow the rule of thumb: whatever amount is scraped from the back, half that much should come from the heart.

Then, I go back to the tip. It should have been thinned enough initially that its location is still clearly visible, but it should in no way be thin. Scraping the tip too thin too soon forces you to readjust the balance of the whole reed. So, when scraping the tip at this time, listen to the sound that the knife makes as it leaves the tip and hits the plaque—there will be a little clicking sound each time. As the tip gets thinner, the clicking sound will gradually get quieter. As soon as you notice that it is beginning to quiet down, stop scraping. Don't keep going until the sound disappears completely; stop when it just begins to quiet down. For now, the tip is thin enough—leave it alone until you make the final adjustments. You will get the reed to vibrate by scraping the heart and the back and clipping whenever the crow threatens to drop below B. Then return to the tip as your final adjustment.

The tip needs to be thinnest at its extremities—edges and corners—and stronger elsewhere to give the vibrations an orderly path into the reed. At all stages of the reed-making process, the tip is always scraped toward the corner of the reed, never along the grain of the cane, but always toward the left or the right. Also angle the knife slightly so that it makes contact with the edge of the reed tip only, not its center. Careful plaque placement is necessary to accomplish this accurately—the plaque needs to be slipped to the side you aren't scraping, allowing the knife access to the edge of the tip. Apply this scraping technique anytime you work on the tip, not just when finishing the reed.

At this point, you have completed the construction phase of the reed making. All of the previous steps should be performed on every reed, with the primary goal of getting the reed to vibrate. Now we begin the adjustment phase of reed making, where the reed is regarded as a unique specimen, requiring analysis and diagnosis to reach its full potential. After completing the procedure described, the reed should vibrate fairly well; it will be coarse and unrefined, but it should not be strenuously difficult to blow. If it is, take another layer of cane from the back and heart and test it again. Figure 8.15 shows the reed at the completion of the construction phase, and figure 8.16 shows the finished reed.

When differentiating between the construction phase of reed making and the adjustment phase, I do not mean that reeds are ever made in a mechanical fashion, nor without constantly gathering evidence. While constructing the reed, you should already have learned many things about the quality of the piece of cane, its vibration characteristics, and its structure. These observations will help determine the course of the next steps.

As you read the following chapter with its many suggestions and tips, keep one thought in mind: reed making follows logical processes most of the time if you are analytical enough with your method and

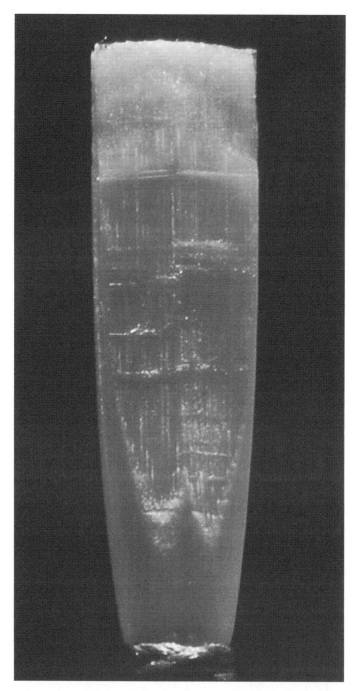

Figure 8.15 The reed with the back separated from the heart. Note that the tip definition has faded somewhat owing to the thinning of the heart. Next the tip will be scraped to restore the definition.

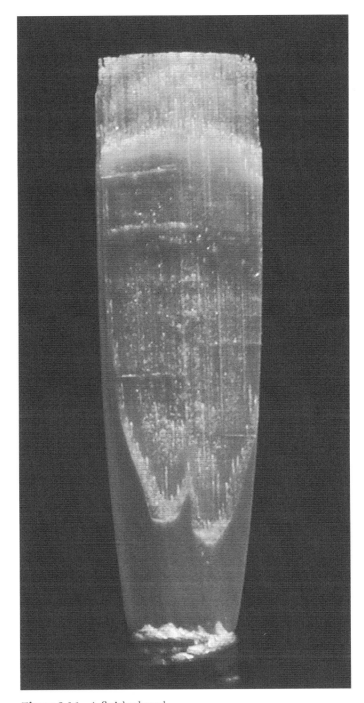

Figure 8.16 A finished reed.

precise enough with your actions. If your reed-making process feels as though it never reacts in a logical way, check three very important considerations: balance, structure, and symmetry.

Balance means that every spot on a reed occurs four times—twice on each blade. Each of these four spots needs to be the same thickness. Structure means that the rails and the spine are strong, that the heart is not too thin, and that there are a few millimeters of bark above the string. Symmetry means that the tip is the same length at all four edges, that the back comes up the same distance in every place, and that the reed is scraped onto the center of the blade—not slightly displaced to the left or the right. If balance, structure, and symmetry are not good, correct them before proceeding to any more detailed diagnostic process. If one or more of these aspects cannot be corrected (if the spine is completely scraped away, for instance), expect the reed to behave unpredictably, and expect to have to begin another reed.

9

Reed Evaluation and Adjustment

There are at least two, and maybe three, golden rules of oboe reed making. The two 24-karat ones are: Sharpen your knife. Don't make any mistakes.

Early in my career, I remember reading a statement by Ray Still asserting that it takes thirty years to learn how to make reeds.[1] Of course, I devoutly hoped he was mistaken—that there was some possible shortcut that he had overlooked—but it turned out that he was nearly correct. After twenty years or so, I started to feel like I could make a reed whenever I needed one. I could make reeds in the interim, too, but it did take about twenty years for the process to become reliable and consistent. So I reflected: what had I learned? Apart from the experience of making thousands of reeds, which counts for a lot, the only things I had really learned, taken to heart, and become slightly obsessive about (unusual for me), were the two statements listed earlier.

Sharpen your knife. And I mean really sharp. You can still remove cane with a dullish knife, just as you can fix your bicycle with a pair of vise-grip pliers, but it won't do exactly what you want, and it will rule out neat and efficient work. If you can't sharpen your knife, let your teacher sharpen it. If your teacher can't sharpen it, get a new one (a new knife, I mean, not a new teacher). Reed making doesn't have to be a matter of luck—get a good knife and keep it sharp. Chapter 8 includes a detailed discussion of sharpening technique.

1. Gorner, "Virtuoso Ray Still."

Don't make any mistakes. This suggestion includes serious mistakes like removing big chunks of the tip or tying past the end of the tube, but it also means that you must avoid doing slightly foolish things in the hope that they won't affect the final result. Choose your cane carefully, gouge it carefully, and shape it carefully. Tie it on with care. Use good materials. Use good tools in proper repair. Get the overlap right. A well-made blank from decent cane will make a decent reed almost every time (see the previous chapter). Of course, scrape carefully (with your sharp knife).

That leaves out the experience factor. But experience is the result of time, thought, and observation. So while you're spending time making reeds, think and observe, and file everything away in your brain (or your notes) for future reference. Observe everything, from the appearance of the cane to the result of a certain scraping operation. Don't make twenty reeds in the hope that one will work. Remember that reed making is not a black art; removing wood from a certain area will usually give a predictable result if the reed has structure, balance, and symmetry. Think about what you are doing, and be able to defend it if questioned. Most students already know enough to make reeds successfully if they are disciplined, analytical, and methodical in their approach. Experience allows the reed maker to assemble facts and reach a conclusion quickly, almost automatically, but students should try to assemble them, also.

Ultimately, when you finish a reed and it still doesn't work, poor cane quality should be the only reason it didn't turn out. With enough observation of cane characteristics—choosing what works best for you—even that problem can be minimized.

In addition to the two golden rules already discussed, there is a third almost golden rule. as early as possible in your reed-making career, try to introduce complete consistency into your reed-making process. Try to acquire equipment that works, cane that works, dimensions that are standardized, a process that is consistent, tools and supplies that work, and so on. Having the same things to work with every time is essential to consistent success. Only make changes to your equipment or your technique if you are sure that the change is necessary, and then change only one thing at a time.

Reed Adjustment Guide

Writing about reed making is similar to writing about food or wine: ten seconds worth of hands-on experience is probably worth more than ten paragraphs of text. Similar difficulties of terminology appear—does wine really taste of leather or pencil lead, or are these terms arcane references to experiences only familiar to wine connoisseurs? Some difficulty of description is inevitable, but the primary goal of the following section is to show how careful, logical thought can be imposed on the process of adjusting reeds. Your specific terminology and desired outcomes may differ from mine; the important idea is that you can expect relatively consistent results when you apply enough analysis and method to the diagnosis of problems and the setting of goals.

You must have a goal for the reed that is more specific than just making it "better." You must first determine that you would like to do something precisely defined: "I want to improve the response without affecting the stability," for example, or "I want to increase the resistance without changing the response." With a specific goal, you can devise a specific method. Without a goal, you are left to depend on luck and chance.

Diagnostic Procedure

The performance of a reed can be analyzed by observing four basic characteristics. These are, in order of importance, response, stability, resistance, and tone quality. It may be a surprise that tone quality is listed last, but it is the least important consideration when adjusting reeds and its control is the least predictable. We can control the other factors: it is easy to develop a strategy that improves response, makes the reed more stable, or lightens the resistance. But the sound quality is largely predetermined by the genetics of the cane and is not readily adjustable. So your priority must be to make a reed that works—one that responds, plays in tune, and feels comfortable for you to blow on. Then the sound quality of that reliable, comfortable, reed will be close to its maximum potential.

Here is a more detailed consideration of the four main considerations when evaluating a reed's performance.

- *Response*. Response refers to the readiness of the reed to make a sound at the moment the player demands it. The reed should speak freely at all dynamic levels—it should speak easily at the softest possible dynamic while maintaining a true sound, and it should speak cleanly at a loud dynamic without splattering or spreading. These characteristics should be found consistently in all registers. Response is the most essential of the reed's functions. If the tone is beautiful but the note fails to speak on time, then the beautiful sound doesn't matter. When the conductor points at you, he or she wants to hear a sound.
- *Stability*. Stability refers both to the reed's overall pitch level—flat or sharp—as well as its ability to maintain that pitch. Reeds can manifest a confusing variety of combinations: flat and stable, flat and wild, sharp and wild, sharp and dull, and so on. Some of these problems have no ready solution and should cause you to reject the reed (although really crazy things shouldn't happen if the reed is well structured, has good balance and symmetry, and

is made from a good blank). A good reed will play in tune and hold its pitch at any dynamic, any level of air pressure, and any reasonable variation of embouchure tension or reed placement in the mouth. Again, when the conductor points to you, he or she wants to hear a sound, and that sound should be in tune. If your response and pitch are consistent and reliable, most conductors will already be very pleased with you.

- *Resistance.* Resistance refers to the amount of air pressure required to make the reed vibrate with a full tone. When you are blowing with your comfortable maximum effort, the reed should also be vibrating fully. Any mismatch here will result in fatigue—if you are blowing as firmly as you want to, but the reed still has more capacity, you will get tired. Conversely, if the reed is vibrating as much as it can, yet you can still blow harder without discomfort, fatigue will again follow quickly. Having a reed that matches your physical capacity is essential to efficient playing.

  Here's a good test to determine the reed's overall resistance level: with the reed in the oboe, blow gently through it with a neutral embouchure—do not try to influence the tone color or the dynamic—and make a very gentle breath attack. At first, the only sound should be air passing through the reed. Gradually increase the air pressure until the reed speaks by itself. The resulting dynamic should be mezzo piano or very close to it. If it is too loud, the reed will require too much embouchure intervention to play quietly; if it is too soft, the reed will feel limited.

  In addition, we can describe another aspect of resistance: hardness. This refers to the amount of embouchure tension (preferably minimal) needed to control the reed. Before making a judgment about the reed's hardness (and possibly tuning it), confirm that the tip opening is not too large. Before scraping, squeeze the opening to the proper size and test the reed again.

  Finally, the last characteristic that falls under this heading is dynamic range. Ideally, the reed will play loudly when you blow with energy and fade to nothing on demand. Occasionally factors beyond your control can cause some deviation from this ideal. Otherwise good reeds may have an opening that is slightly too small or too large, or a change in humidity or altitude can alter the reed's performance. If this happens, consider that the dynamic *range* of the reed probably hasn't changed; it has just moved to a different part of the dynamic spectrum. So if you can't play very loudly, chances are that you can play more softly than usual. Conversely, if the reed fails to function at the very softest limit, perhaps it has more capacity at the loud end. If the reed just won't play any dynamics at all, then don't play it in public. You have to practice scales on something.

· *Tone Quality.* The actual timbre of the sound is a personal matter and is not important here. It is important to get a good balance between low and high partials, allowing the sound to be as complex and rich as possible. A reed that has only the lower partials will sound dull, lack brilliance, and project poorly. (Do not confuse this with a dark sound.) A reed that has only the higher partials will sound shrill and thin.

I repeat: tone quality should never be the paramount consideration in reed adjustment. It is much more important to make a reed that works. If the reed's function is inferior, even if the sound is beautiful, you may miss attacks, you may play out of tune, and you may tire quickly—playing flaws that any listener can hear. Response and pitch security are the most important considerations in finishing a reed, since a defect in either of these will make you sound incompetent.

Oboists are justly concerned with beauty of sound; the distinctive tone of the oboe is what defines the instrument for many listeners. Reeds must sound beautiful. But it is not worth giving up aspects of function to gain a bit more beauty of tone, which is, after all, a subjective quality. The only listeners who can distinguish your excellent tone from your very good tone are other oboists. If you doubt this, assess how confident you feel when evaluating the tone quality of other instrumentalists. Can you really tell when a clarinet player's tone is a little less good than usual? Probably not. Most likely your clarinetist colleague sounds about the same to you every day, and chances are you sound about the same to them, too. Unless your reed doesn't work.

However, anything we do to the reed will also affect the tone quality. So if you know you need to remove wood from somewhere but can't decide quite where, the tone quality can come to your aid. Do you want the reed to vibrate more or vibrate less? Is it too shallow or too noisy? Does the reed need more flexibility or more stability? Answering these questions can help guide you to a successful scraping strategy.

Any reed adjustment will change all four of the basic characteristics described earlier. You will seldom cure one problem without affecting another. Success in the diagnostic process consists of finding a solution that solves the most problems and creates the fewest new ones. Think before you scrape! Keep notes if necessary. Most young reed makers are quite successful at getting their intended result, but they fail to anticipate the unintended effects, which cause most of the puzzlement. Reed making need not be mysterious if you think it through. Everything about a reed—not just the aspect you are trying to change—will be affected by anything you do to it.

Eventually, the best reed making will feel purely intuitive, and you'll just know what to do. But that's only the way it feels. It isn't really intuition, but rapidly compiled and applied knowledge. This knowledge is the result of experience. That is the best teacher—but the teacher cannot help unless the pupil pays constant and diligent attention.

Common Actions and Their Effects

This section is partly informational, and partly meant to illustrate that there are not as many complicated options as beginning reed makers imagine. There are really only about half a dozen operations that can sensibly be performed on a reed in progress. The suggestions presume that the reed is already mostly finished and that it performs basically correctly. If it is still in the primitive stages, scrape the reed until it vibrates.

Gradually, as reed makers develop more experience and skill, they progress to more specific strategies for making small changes in the reed, but these are highly detailed and depend on the entire organic construction of the reed. Do not be tempted to integrate Mr. Smith's little trick for making the spine narrower into your reed making without making Mr. Smith's whole concept of a reed. Start by making a fundamentally correct reed before developing your own "tricks." So, to some, this section will seem like an oversimplification. But simple is a good place to start.

Results of Thinning the Whole Surface of the Tip
- Easier, faster response.
- Slightly lower pitch and decreased stability.
- Lower resistance.
  Lighter, somewhat shallower, sound.

If the reed is nearly finished, scraping the whole tip is seldom a good idea. It tends to make the reed chirpy and shrill because it emphasizes the tip vibrations too much by isolating them from the rest of the reed. In the case of an unvibrant reed, it is usually better to try to get more vibrations some other way—scraping the heart a bit, for instance—and then finishing the sides and corners of the tip. Scraping the tip will make the tip vibrate better; it may not necessarily make the reed vibrate better. If the tip is overscraped, it will make the heart thicker by comparison and actually cause the reed to feel thicker and stuffier.

Make sure that the tip has a good internal balance. It must be thinnest at the extremities—the edges and corners—and a little heavier toward the center and toward the heart. This will give the vibrations a nice smooth entry into the reed. However, if the reed needs just that last little bit of brightening up, scraping lightly from the whole tip accomplishes that without compromising the reed's stability very much.

Results of Scraping the Extremities (Sides and Corners) of the Tip
- Somewhat faster response.
- Negligible effect on stability.
- Somewhat lower resistance.
- More focused, refined sound.

   If done carefully, this procedure should improve stability and tone focus without lowering the pitch. Often, finishing the tip will unify all the elements of the reed after everything else looks correct. It should be among the last things you do to a reed, and you should always do it with your sharpest knife. Work with the lightest possible knife pressure —twenty or more scrapes might be necessary to remove a few wisps of cane. Your technique should feel like you are gently brushing dust from the tip surface, not scraping. Refining the edges and corners of the tip can also help with a reed that just needs to vibrate ever so slightly more quietly but does not need clipping.

Results of Clipping the Tip
- More sluggish response.
- Sharper pitch and improved stability.
- Higher resistance.
- Duller, shallower, less vibrant sound.

   Before clipping the tip, be sure it really needs clipping. A good candidate for clipping will be a reed that is slightly (or noticeably) flat and noisy. Reeds that are not flat should not be clipped. Don't clip just to change the tone! Clipping a bright, sharp reed that doesn't vibrate well to make it "darker" won't help it a bit—it will be even sharper and shallower after the clip. Always clip off the tiniest possible amount; it's better to clip a reed three times to get what you want than to overclip it once. Overclipping will require the entire balance of the reed to be restructured. Before clipping, confirm that the opening is small by squeezing it down if necessary. A swollen opening can make a huge change in the pitch of the crow and cause you to misjudge the amount to clip. Reeds in progress often have openings that are too large, and inattention to this large opening can result in a serious mistake. If the reed is still too stiff to squeeze, don't clip yet. Continue with the basic scraping until the reed is pliable enough to allow squeezing down to the proper size of opening.
   If a nearly finished reed is a little flat, you must clip it. Clip it to get it in tune, even if you feel you might not like it afterward. It has to be in tune first, before you adjust it to meet the rest of your needs.
   Some players clip the reed so that one blade is slightly longer than the other. This is said to assist with response, but I have never noticed that it makes much difference unless you forget which blade to set on

top. If you would like to try this, clip in the normal way but do not chop straight down at the reed—angle the knife blade so that it cuts away from you.

Results of Scraping the Heart
- Somewhat improved response.
- Noticeably lower pitch and decreased stability.
- Lower resistance.
- Noisier, more raucous, and more vibrant sound.

This is the cure for a stodgy, wooden reed that refuses to vibrate freely. Stay away from the center and the edges of the heart—scrape it like the back, with a spine down the center and thin rails up the sides. Think of the heart as a control valve that regulates the passage of the tip vibrations to the rest of the reed. If the heart is too thick, it has the effect of isolating the tip and preventing the rest of the reed from vibrating enough. The reed will seem shallow, stuffy, and resistant. If the heart is too thin, it has the effect of making the tip longer. There will be plenty of vibrations, but the reed will be wild and noisy. Of all the scraping operations, scraping from the heart has by far the most damaging effect on the reed's stability, so test frequently. But do not be afraid to scrape from the heart. Remember the rule of thumb from the previous chapter: whatever amount comes off the back, take half that amount from the heart until the reed dictates a different approach.

Results of Scraping the Back (Top Half)
- Slightly more sluggish response.
- Moderately flatter pitch and decreased stability.
  Lower resistance.
- Warmer, less brilliant sound.

The outcome of this operation depends very much on the balance of the reed before scraping but will usually give the results listed. It is a useful way of getting deeper vibrations in the reed and a bit more warmth in the tone. Usually, scraping the back should be followed by a few scrapes from the heart as well, to make sure the whole reed is permitted to vibrate. During the adjustment phase of reed making, wood should mostly be removed from the top of the back, blending into the bark as you get closer to the string. For me, thinning the whole length of the back equally weakens the reed too much. Avoid having too much of a hump between the top of the back and the heart—blend it in smoothly.

Possible Cures for Common Problems

Note that all of these conditions can occur at some stage during the normal reed-making process. Whether or not they are problems depends on how close the reed is to being finished. If you are observant about your reed and sensitive to early manifestations of these issues, they should never become troublesome for you.

Reed Too Flat   There are several factors that can cause a reed to sound flat: the opening is too big, the reed is well made but needs clipping, the overlap is too slight, or too much wood has been removed from the reed. It can also be a combination of these things. In some extreme cases, flatness that refuses to improve is a sign of a structural defect. These defects include an asymmetrical tip closure or looseness of the sides near the tip, both mentioned in the previous chapter. Those reeds should be discarded. Sometimes persistent flatness is caused by the back opening's being too large—the internal dimension of the reed just above the string is too big. There is no remedy for this, so those reeds can be discarded also.

Flatness in the early stages of reed making is not unusual and can usually be corrected by clipping. The only fatal combination is a reed that is almost playable, still too hard, and already flat. In that situation, squeeze the opening down and hope for an improvement. If none is forthcoming, discard the reed.

If the opening seems too large, take care of that first by soaking the reed for a few minutes and, with the plaque inserted, squeezing gently just behind the tip, holding the reed between your thumb and index finger. If it doesn't crack, squeeze harder. Then gradually squeeze a little closer to the string—your fingers should be right on top of the heart. Twist the tube back and forth a little to weaken the reed further. If it cracks now, don't worry too much; it would have cracked eventually. (Better now than during the concert.) This is the only effective way to make the opening smaller. Weakening the reed by scraping is not effective enough. The next time you soak the reed, the opening will probably be too large again. Repeat the squeezing procedure, and after a few days it should settle down. Reeds that never develop a stable opening are rare. Do not attempt the squeezing procedure until the reed is nearly playable. If you use it in the early stages, it will almost certainly cause cracking.

If the reed seems to play well but is just a bit flat, it needs to be clipped. Be careful to clip only the tiniest amount at a time and to test the reed after each clip. Remember to correct the opening before deciding how much to clip.

You can raise the pitch slightly by increasing the amount of overlap. Gently slip the blades a little further apart. Note that this will also make the tone shallower and less vibrant. And this is at best a temporary solution. The blades tend to settle back to their original relationship after a few minutes.

If the reed is flat because too much wood has been removed, it may be difficult to remake. Usually, this happens if the back or the heart (or both) have been scraped too thin. Try clipping it a little. If the pitch improves, try clipping a little more. Eventually, the tip will be so short that you will have to abandon further clipping. Be prepared to give up and make a new reed without making the same mistakes.

Don't overlook the possibility that you have chosen the wrong tie length or too wide a shape. If the reed has these structural problems—if it is tied too short or shaped too wide—these can be very difficult to correct even with skillful scraping.

The general order of operation in the case of a flat but otherwise well-made reed is to clip it until it crows C, scrape it to free the vibrations if necessary, clip again if necessary, and keep repeating the process until you get the result you want. The closer you get to an acceptable result, the smaller the adjustments should be. Test the reed after every (tiny) clip and after every (tiny) scraping procedure. Don't get caught in the vicious cycle of scraping too much, then clipping too much, then scraping too much, and so on. That process will leave you with a tiny stub of a reed.

Reed Too Sharp   If the reed is sharp it might be that the opening is too small, the reed is too short, the overlap is too large, or too much wood has been left on the reed. Again, structural issues such as a shape that is too narrow can be a factor, but this is something that novices should not try to work out on their own; reliable input from an experienced teacher is essential. Sharpness will usually be accompanied by a shallow, somewhat shrill tone. In the earlier stages of reed making, sharpness is actually desirable since removing wood (which you have to do anyway) will usually cure it.

If the opening is too small, there is usually no remedy. Try soaking the reed for a longer time than usual (fifteen to twenty minutes) and see if it improves. Squeezing it open gently with your fingers is a temporary solution. Some players recommend changing the shape of the tube with pliers to adjust the opening. While this can be effective, it damages the tube and has imprecise results. If you get consistently small openings, try using cane with a smaller diameter and/or a wider shaper tip, and take care to select cane with more springiness. Some players also recommend modifying the opening by altering the tie length. While this is logical from a geometric point of view (a longer tie length should theoretically give a larger opening), changing the tie length is hazardous to the reed's basic structure and not something we want to tinker with.

If the reed is clipped too short, it's probably hopeless. Often, this is the result of carelessly clipping too much and then scraping too much, clipping, scraping, and so on. Be more careful, and make sure to squeeze the opening before clipping. One of the most dangerous things that can happen to a reed is one careless too-large clip. Suddenly the whole reed needs to be made over since everything is now out of balance. It is much better to clip too little five times than too much once. I know I've already said this multiple times, but doing it wrong creates nasty problems.

The overlap can be reduced by coaxing the blades, creating a larger resonance chamber. This will also make the tone more vibrant. The result is seldom permanent, but it can be helpful for a few minutes if you're desperate to get through that solo coming up in a few measures.

If the reed is sharp because it's still too thick, scrape more off. Usually the heart is too heavy, preventing the tip vibrations from reaching the whole reed. This is normal in the early stages of reed making.

Reed Won't Vibrate   This condition is also normal in the early stages of scraping the reed. The difficulty comes in determining where to remove wood. As we discussed earlier, the tone quality of the reed, while it will be quite unrefined at this stage, can help you to decide where to scrape. For all of my insistence that tone quality is less important than other considerations, here is a situation where tone quality is very useful as a diagnostic device. You have to scrape somewhere; scraping will change both the tone quality and the function of the reed. Why not try to find a scraping procedure that will improve everything? Taking note of the tone quality and selecting a scraping procedure accordingly is good practice.

Reeds that lack vibration will be either dull and wooden or thin and shrill. In both cases, wood should be removed from all areas, but observation of the tone quality will help determine your scraping priority.

If it's dull and wooden, removing wood from the heart usually fixes the problem. Note that this will make the reed flatter. If the reed is dull and wooden and flat, it will never work and should be discarded.

If it's shrill, take more wood from the back. Continue scraping until the sound gets a little better, then balance the heart and tip to what you've done. This will also make it flatter, but most shrill reeds are sharp, so you're OK. Shrieking reeds that tend toward extreme shrillness rarely turn out well. Observe the qualities of that particular piece of cane and avoid any others with the same characteristics.

If the sound is basically good (though tough) and the reed crows a C, or close to it, that is a sign that the reed is well balanced but just too thick. Take a layer off the entire reed and try it again.

Reed Vibrates Too Much (Raucous)   This is often a good thing in the early stages, particularly with English horn reeds. Usually the reed is well balanced but just not finished. If this is the case, scrape equally from the tip, the heart, and the top of the back and try it again. Sometimes, raucousness in a nearly finished reed is the result of the opening's being too large. If that's the case, squeeze it down before doing anything else. Usually the reed will play completely differently with the correct opening. By "raucous," I mean a potentially good reed that vibrates with some firmness in the crow and in the tone. Really trashy, noisy-sounding reeds are usually unstable as well, and difficult to refine.

If the problem is rather slight, refine the edges and corners of the tip and try again. This can also help if the crow contains unwanted extra noise—fourths and fifths instead of the desired octave C's.

When working through the diagnostic process, be sure to have the right goals in mind. Reeds can display superficially similar defects for completely different reasons. One reed might be thin and tight and shrill; another might be loud and noisy and shrill. Often the player's only reaction is "shrill," with no notice taken of the underlying cause. The two reeds will require completely different strategies—one needs to vibrate more, the other needs to vibrate less—yet inexperienced reed makers rarely realize that some shrill reeds are not yet vibrating enough. Always pay attention to everything, think things through, and take nothing for granted.

General Observations

What follows are some general thoughts for healthy reed making, in no particular order of importance. The suggestions presume that the reed is made with the standard American long scrape illustrated in the diagram shown at the end of this chapter. The suggestions also assume that the gouging equipment is working well and that the shape is well matched to the gouge dimensions. Players who do not gouge or shape their own cane are starting from a significant disadvantage.

- The reed should crow a C. I crow the reed with my lips partly on the string and partly on the bark with light lip pressure until the reed is nearly finished. For final adjustments, I relax the lip pressure. Begin by blowing gently: there should be a single peep of C. Then, as the air pressure increases, the sound will become more complex. The additional sounds should be recognizable as further lower octaves of C, up to a maximum of three. Although the complexity of the crow will increase with increased air pressure, it is essential that the pitch remain the same. How much rattle the crow contains is a matter of personal preference—I prefer only two of the possible three octaves. Experience will teach just how complex a sound is optimal for you.

  Some players are comfortable with a crow slightly lower or higher than C. These are individual preferences, developed after years of experimentation and practice, so the student should start from the standard, which is C. Just because so-and-so's reeds crow C-sharp doesn't mean that yours should.

  The pitch of the crow in the construction phase of reed making is not so important; wait until the adjustment phase before monitoring it carefully. After that, do not allow the pitch of the crow to drop below B, or you may have very serious problems recovering the pitch. Remember to confirm that the opening is small before testing.

- Balance the reed. Every spot on the reed occurs four times— twice on each blade. All four should be exactly the same thickness. Do whatever you have to: count scrapes, use a good backlight, measure with a micrometer, and so on. Oboe reeds are small. Even small mistakes in symmetry and balance can cause serious problems that will compromise the diagnostic process.

· Gouge and shape your own cane. Even if you know nothing about the effects of the gouging process on reed quality and must depend entirely on professionals to maintain your machine, the resulting consistency in reed quality is well worth it. The vendor who is selling you shaped cane is interested partly in your customer satisfaction and partly in selling the maximum number of pieces per pound. Some inferior cane will slip through that the careful reed maker would reject.

· Before testing the reed, always confirm that the opening is small. An opening that is too large will give very misleading information. I know I've already said this many times. It's important.

· When testing reeds, there are two things that are very important. First, do not try to make the reed sound good. Just play it. Even though it may be possible for you to sound beautiful on the reed for ten seconds, or even for ten minutes, that is not why you are testing it. When testing the reed, you should be much more interested in how bad it can sound than how good you can make it sound. If it can sound bad, it eventually will. Getting rid of a bad quality in a reed is equivalent to adding a desirable one.

The second important thing when testing is to play at least a few seconds at the reed's maximum capacity. Many students play the reed at about half power and then determine that it is too hard and too loud. But they never play it with a completely full effort, and thus they don't learn exactly how much too hard and too loud the reed is. This information is essential to correct adjustment.

· Many students test the reed in the oboe much too early. You may find yourself saying, "My reed sounds terrible." Well, yes, it does, but only because it's half finished. Learn to work on the reed by testing the crow (see the earlier discussion) and judging the resistance of the reed while crowing. Most students have tested enough decent reeds to know how they feel without the oboe. The reed should be relatively easy to blow through, and it should crow a C. Until the reed you're working on approaches those qualities, putting it in the oboe will be disappointing.

· Don't judge the progress of your reed by how much time you have invested in it, nor by how much cane you think you have scraped from it, nor by how thin it looks when you hold it against a backlight. If the reed is too hard, there is still too much cane on it. Simple.

· Don't be misled by the occasional professional reed you might see that looks sloppily made but plays well. It would have played better if it had been carefully made.

- Make a reed a day. Every day. More is better; remember the beginner's goal of making a thousand reeds before becoming proficient. Reed making responds to the reed maker's being in shape, just as playing does. You cannot make reeds only once a week any more than you can practice only once a week.
- Because the American style of reed has wood removed from most of its surface, it is essential to maintain a skeleton of structural elements to give strength to the reed. We have four structural elements that must be preserved at all costs: the bark at the bottom of the reed, the spine up the center, the rails up the sides, and the heart.

  The bark at the bottom should extend for a few millimeters above the string, perhaps four or five. Too much bark, and the reed is shallow; too little, and the reed can become weak. The spine must be visible all the way up the reed. It doesn't have to be a wall of cane, but it must be present all the way to the top of the reed, including the tip (the spine at the tip might not be visible, but it should be measurable). The rails should be visible all the way up to the tip—they don't have to be very wide, just present. The better we can preserve the structure, the more wood we can remove from the rest of the reed without losing pitch and tone focus. Improved structure always gives improved function, control, and tone. Reeds without spine and rails collapse quickly, making it very difficult to maintain pitch and tone focus.
- Don't deliberately remove wood from the center of the reed. Enough comes off anyway, no matter how carefully we try to avoid it.
- Try to analyze the tone characteristics of the reed without using the words "bright" and "dark." I think these words are largely meaningless—people use "dark" to describe a tone they like and "bright" to describe a tone they don't like. Being more specific ("dull," "shrill," "rough," "stuffy," "glassy," etc.) will improve your ear and your reed-making skill. We have already seen how two different reeds, both of which could have been described as "bright," needed completely different strategies.
- Make the extreme tip (corners and sides) as thin as you can. Measurements show that many reeds have tips that are 0.01 millimeter thick (that's 0.00039 inch—$\frac{4}{10,000}$ of an inch).
- Learn to anticipate the unintended effects of what you are about to do. Most scraping operations will give you the intended effect, along with two or three others you may not have thought about. When less experienced reed makers get into trouble, this is usually the reason. Think before you scrape.
- Try the reed after each operation. Don't decide you need to scrape the back, finish the tip, and then clip it. Results are sometimes unpredictable. Do one thing at a time, and always test the reed before proceeding.

- If you have a plan for improving the reed, persist with that plan until you note some change. Many times students will scrape a little, find no difference, and conclude that they had the wrong idea. Scrape until something changes. Otherwise you will never know whether you were right or not.

- Almost every scraping operation will cause the pitch to drop, sometimes significantly. Scraping the tip causes the least disturbance; scraping the heart can drop it dramatically; scraping the back usually drops the pitch moderately. The entire conflict of reed making is balancing stability with vibrancy. It is easy to make a stable reed that won't vibrate, or a vibrant reed that has no stability. Getting the proper balance between the two is the difficult part. So every scraping operation has to consider the reed's stability. Will the reed still be stable enough after I do this? If it loses a little too much pitch, is there enough tip length to allow a clip? It is better to do too little than too much where stability is concerned: scrape a little, clip a little. Sneak up on the final result. The cycle of clipping too much and then scraping too much is almost always fatal.

- Resist the temptation to completely finish a reed, especially at the first sitting. The reed will be different tomorrow. Work on the reed until it is reasonably comfortable to blow, and practice on it for twenty or thirty minutes. Then put it away, let it dry out, and revisit it the next day. It will require a different strategy from the one you were considering the day before.

- The sides of the reed must hold tightly together all the way to the tip. If the sides are at all loose, the reed should be discarded. It will not work, and no amount of optimism will be rewarded. The blades of the reed must be tight enough to grip the plaque even when it is inserted only a short distance. Some players adjust loose sides by bending the staple with pliers. This can work if the problem is mild, although I do not recommend it—it's usually better to make a new reed.

    Looseness at the tip is most commonly caused by warped cane—the gouged piece will show space under its middle when laid on a flat surface. Other causes can be careless tying—if the reed is tied too short, the string will bite into the cane before the staple picks up the tension, resulting in a tip that springs open. Likewise, overtying the reed past the end of the tube can cause looseness. Sometimes the reed is loose only on one side, in which case it is likely that the cane is not tied in alignment with the flat part of the tube. Sight through the bottom end of the tube and verify that the reed's tip opening bisects the oval of the tube. There is no scraping operation that can correct looseness at the tip. Make diligent efforts to minimize the problem. Tie cane immediately after shaping it. Apply a basic scrape immediately after tying the reed and cut the tip open. Before storing the reed, soak

Reed Making

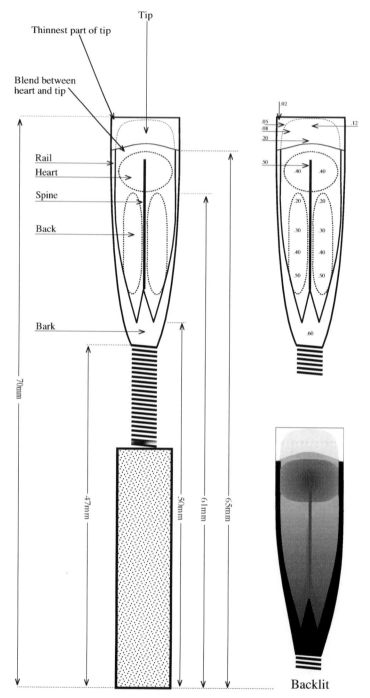

Figure 9.1 The oboe reed.

it for a few minutes to stabilize its shape and structure. Do not work on the reed dry with the plaque jammed down to the string. Soak it frequently and insert the plaque only a short distance.

· Remember the three essentials of reed construction: balance, structure, and symmetry. If you observe a shortcoming in any of these, even a small one, make the correction before proceeding to a more detailed diagnosis. Sadly, if the structure is deficient, you may have to make a new reed without the same mistake.

· The diagrams in figure 9.1 show the appearance of my oboe reeds. These are basic reference pictures; individual reeds can and should differ in response to different circumstances. But when trouble strikes, trying to make a good-looking reed that "looks like the picture" can be a starting point for fixing problems. If the diagnostic process yields only problems, not solutions, focusing on making a really handsome reed can be the beginning of restoring order.

English Horn Reeds

English horn reeds differ from oboe reeds in two important ways: they are not quite as "finished" as oboe reeds, and they generally carry a wire.

Many oboe reeds have extremely thin tips and a rather thin back, especially just below the heart. If you make an English horn reed this way, it will sound small and dull, and it may well be flat. Instead, for English horn, make a reed that works well and is well balanced but has less contrast between the three main areas—in other words, slightly thicker tip, slightly thinner heart, and slightly thicker back. In addition, the difference in thickness between the top of the back and the lower portions is not as pronounced. If you want to think in terms of oboe reeds, make a reed that plays well but is not refined.

Many English horn players put wire around the reed near the bottom. The wire is not used to control the opening of the reed. If the opening is wrong, the wire may control its size, but the reed will still have the problems associated with openings of the wrong size: reeds with small basic openings will feel limited, while reeds with large openings will feel unwieldy. The wire stabilizes and focuses the tone of the notes above the staff—the range between G and C. Often this allows you to remove more wood from a reed that was sagging slightly before the wire.

I add the wire after the reed begins to vibrate. When the crow becomes pretty free and rather louder and less controlled than we want, it's time to add the wire. Or, to say it another way: if you feel that you will not scrape from the bottom of the back anymore, it's time to add the wire. Use #24 gauge brass wire from the hardware store or hobby store, wound round the reed twice and tightened by twisting with pliers. The stuff called "reed wire" is the same thing, but "reed wire" usually costs more than plain "wire." Don't twist it on so tightly that it grips all the way around the reed; stop tightening the pliers as soon as you feel the wire gripping the sides. When it's tight enough, you will see the tip of the reed start to spread apart a little. Stop twisting and restore the correct tip opening by squeezing closed on the wire. Don't put it up too high on the reed—5–6 mm from the string (in other words, just into the beginning of the scraped area) is high enough. The wire will usually slide around when the reed is dry but return to its proper position when the reed is soaked.

I am aware that the use of the wire is a matter of some dispute: some players insist that reeds should never have a wire, some apply it to the unscraped blank, while some wind it around the bark at the very bottom. You can find almost as many opinions about wiring as you can find English horn players. My use of the wire allows for better support of the upper notes and a clearer tone focus to correspond with my concept of sound. If you do not use wire but feel that it is difficult to make reeds that "sit up" well, try a wire. Conversely, if you use one but feel your reeds are too shallow and limited, take it off and see what happens. This is very much a matter of doing what works. I use a wire because it helps me.

English horn cane is gouged to 0.68 mm in the center, with a 0.10–0.12 mm drop-off at the side. Just as for oboe reeds, the "side" is measured at the widest point of the shape. Since cane is a natural material and results within a hundredth of a millimeter cannot really be expected, any thickness between 0.65 mm and 0.70 mm is acceptable. After shaping, the reed is tied on just like an oboe reed—in other words, as long as possible. If that length is more than 59 or 60 mm, consider using a narrower shape. The finished length of the reed should be 55 mm.

English horn reeds should crow a C-sharp. English horn reeds are the opposite of oboe reeds in this regard: oboe reeds with a crow higher than C almost never work for me, while English horn reeds with a crow lower than C rarely play.

Summary

- Sharpen your knife.
- Make no mistakes.
- Be consistent.
- Think through what you intend to do.
- Adjust function first, not tone.

III

EQUIPMENT AND ITS CARE

10

Instrument Selection, Care, and Adjustment

Buying an oboe or English horn is a little different from making a major domestic purchase like an appliance, and even a little different from buying a more popular wind instrument like a saxophone or a clarinet. Before moving to more specific tips for buying an oboe, let me make a few points right at the outset. If you only read the rest of this section, you'll already do well with your selection and purchase.

Include your teacher in the purchase process. Unless you are an experienced oboist, you should never buy an instrument without advice from a teacher or professional player. In my experience, every time a young student (or a well-meaning parent buying a Christmas gift) has bought an instrument without seeking advice, they did not find the best instrument at the best price. Include your teacher in the purchase process. If you don't have a teacher, get advice from an oboe professional.

Some experienced consumers feel confident in their research capabilities and think that they can make a wise oboe purchase based on their investigations alone. While this will almost certainly work when purchasing an automobile or a television, oboes have a musical component which only oboists are qualified to evaluate. Find a trustworthy professional and then trust his or her advice.

Deal with specialists in double-reed instruments. There might not be any in your town, but don't worry. All of them are equipped to do business through the mail with complete efficiency. Most will send you an instrument to try for a week or so if you give them a credit card number. You will also have to pay for shipping, though often the shipping is free if you buy the instrument. Shipping costs can mount quickly when trying multiple instruments, so remember to get advice from your teacher before you waste too much money trying instruments you don't like. General music stores are, with rare exceptions, not good places to buy oboes—they cannot afford to keep a large selection of oboes on hand, and the staff is not usually well trained in double-reed instruments.

You get what you pay for. Good dealers service instruments before sending them out for trial (even new instruments need service) and will provide excellent support to you afterward. These services cost money, and they are worth paying for. Good makers will spend money improving the musical qualities of their oboes and may have to economize on providing extra keys or features. These are considerations that are difficult for the layman to evaluate, hence the need for professional advice.

Why Does It Cost So Much?

Oboes and English horns are expensive. Even the least expensive oboe costs about $1,000 in today's market; the most expensive can cost nearly ten times that amount. Since oboes sell much more slowly than drums or guitars, never mind refrigerators or cars, the advantages of mass production are limited and don't affect cost. (A caution on pricing: beware of "list price." No one ever pays list price, so it can safely be ignored. Do not be impressed by vendors who offer you a big discount from list price; everyone else does, too.)

If you spend more, you get more, but what do you get? Three things: quality of construction, additional keywork, and refinement of tone. The cheapest oboes are made of molded plastic (injected into a mold and left to cool) and supplied with keys made of inexpensive material. These keys can bend rather easily and can even break right off if abused. Moreover, beginner oboes will have fewer keys than more advanced instruments—enough to play most of the notes (sometimes the low B-flat is left off), but not enough to play the oboe with facility. Intonation and tone quality will range from acceptable to unplayable depending on the make of the instrument.

Better oboes have more keys, with only one or two trill keys omitted; they're made of better plastic (machined using cutting and drilling tools, not molded); and they have a more sophisticated bore, allowing a more refined tone with better pitch security. This category includes most of the popular mid-range "student" instruments such as the Fox Renard. These instruments are handmade to a significant extent by experienced craftsmen.

The professional-level oboes are constructed from grenadilla wood (or other rare hardwood such as rosewood or cocobolo) and are supplied with a complete assortment of keys made of extremely durable material. The interior construction of the bore will be very complex, resulting in an instrument with a distinct personality. Almost everything on the instrument will be handmade by master craftsmen and checked by an artist.

Plastic or Wood?

It is not true that all wood oboes are better than all synthetic oboes. The world supply of grenadilla wood is shrinking. High-quality wood is expensive. Buying an inexpensive wooden oboe from a budget maker offers no benefit whatsoever. The wood will be cheap along with the rest of the instrument.

The advantages of wood are simple: it sounds a little better and has a more complex personality. That's why professional players choose it. The disadvantages of wood are many: it reacts to changes in humidity, it cracks, it wears out. It simply doesn't make sense to buy a student-quality oboe made of wood. The difference in tone will not be noticeable (at least not until the student's reeds and playing skill have outgrown the instrument), but the extra maintenance hassles will certainly be perceived. That's why schools routinely buy plastic instruments: they don't have money to spend on regular professional service. Unless you're in the market for a professional-quality instrument, or something close to it, stick to plastic.

This rather definitive statement assumes that you are a youngster looking for an instrument to use until you can afford something better. If the student-quality instrument is not a stepping-stone—if it's the instrument you want to keep and live with until it wears out—then by all means consider a wooden instrument. But in the cheaper price ranges, wood can be more of an image feature than a functional one.

What to Buy?

There are three things to consider: the amount of money the buyer is able to spend, the player's level of commitment, and the length of time the instrument is intended to serve. Discuss all of these points with your teacher to ensure that the money is well spent and the instrument gives satisfaction.

In making the following suggestions, I have avoided giving exact prices since they are apt to change. The proportions will likely remain the same, however—it is probable that a sturdy student oboe will always cost two to three times as much as the very cheapest instrument available. A professional oboe will probably always cost two or three times as much as the student oboe. I have also avoided making specific recommendations, since there are many good brands and the market changes frequently.

Let's consider the options, starting with the cheapest. I should say "least expensive," since owning an oboe is never cheap. I'll make a blanket statement to begin: the very cheapest oboes you can find are not worth the money. This category includes most rental instruments—

they're acceptable only while a student is deciding whether he or she likes playing oboe, but they're not worth buying. Remember, you get what you pay for. Resist the encouragement you will receive from the music store to buy the instrument being rented.

So, instead of buying the very cheapest thing available, look to spend two or three times that amount. This will give you a good basic oboe with solid construction that will endure years of use (not abuse) with regular care and maintenance. Some of the better student instruments are really advanced amateur instruments and will perform well for almost all nonprofessional players. If the initial cash outlay seems hard to swallow, you can take comfort in the fact that most well-made oboes have terrific resale value if they are kept in top condition. It is not unusual for a player to keep an instrument for several years and then sell it for more than it cost when new. The key considerations are initial quality and regular maintenance.

To keep costs down, some keys or trill mechanisms will have been omitted on most oboes that are not professional quality. The only mechanism that is not really essential is the split-D key for the right hand; it gives better intonation to the D-sharp to E trill. You do need a left F key, a forked F resonance key, a low B to C-sharp trill key, and an A-flat to B-flat trill mechanism. You don't really need a low B-flat resonance key or a third octave key, though both are useful. An oboe with every key and trill mechanism will be called "full conservatory." Mindful of the lure of the word "conservatory," makers are now providing "modified conservatory" or "simple conservatory" oboes. These have keys missing, sometimes rather essential keys. Do not be impressed by the word "conservatory" unless it is preceded by the word "full."

If you're contemplating the purchase of a professional-quality instrument, you probably don't need my advice. But recognize that there are many high-quality brands with excellent musical potential. Expand your search beyond what everyone else is playing. It is not true that you must play a certain brand to get a job: an oboe is a small black stick— nobody can tell from a distance who made yours. It is wrong to say that brand X is the best and all the others are inferior, although players enjoy having these discussions. Find the oboe that makes your sound and enjoy it. Buy the oboe, not the brand.

Used Instruments

One of the comforting aspects of buying a new oboe is its resale value. If you buy a quality instrument and maintain it well, you probably won't lose money on it, even after several years. That's the good news; the bad news is that the price of used instruments rises steadily as new instruments get more expensive. Still, you can save a meaningful sum of money by buying a used instrument instead of a new one. Since there's nothing like the stereotypical used-car salesman in the oboe business, you can buy confidently from well-known vendors, who will always service a used instrument before selling it to make sure it's in good playing shape. That, again, is the good news. The bad news is that you won't save as much as you might hope. Let us say that the cost of a new professional instrument is $6,000. In that market, a good used instrument will be about $5,000. For $3,000, the used professional instrument will be about twenty-five years old. It may still be a good instrument, but it may not be as good as a new $3,000 instrument of lesser provenance. As always, get good advice and involve your teacher in the buying process. For those people who have an old oboe in the garage (not a good place to keep it) and wonder how much it might be worth, be aware that oboes very rarely have any value as antiques. Unless it's the first Lorée ever made or the oboe that Tabuteau made all his recordings on, the only criterion is the instrument's playing condition.

Very old oboes have a few adherents in the business. You will find some vendors selling instruments more than fifty years old, claiming "they don't make them like they used to." In my opinion, oboes older than ten or fifteen years are no longer suited for top-level playing, oboes older than twenty or thirty years present a risky repair proposition, and very old oboes are almost certainly not worth the trouble unless you want to build an interesting collection. Certainly, makers produced far fewer oboes many years ago, so they were able to select better quality wood and age it longer. But these advantages are offset by the inherent instability of wood and the inevitable wear of the mechanism. Mechanisms can be restored indefinitely (if parts are still available, which they frequently are not) but may or may not be worth it. Professionals usually play new or nearly new instruments, since they require a precision of sound, response, and technique that older instruments may no longer possess.

Experts disagree whether oboes "blow out" or not. After years of use, the wood will suffer small dimensional changes from age and wear. ("Old," to me, is an oboe more than fifteen years old.) A blown-out oboe will have inferior pitch security and distorted tone focus resulting from these minute dimensional changes. Some repair technicians have measured old oboes, observed no measurable signs of wear, and determined that blown-out oboes are a myth. But those of us who play every day and need an oboe to make a living can attest that oboes do indeed wear out and need to be replaced regularly. The evidence may not be scientific, but the empirical evidence is convincing. New oboes have secure intonation, good tone focus, and a precise mechanism that older instruments cannot duplicate. Some players change oboes every year, some every two or three years, some a little longer. It is rare to find a professional player using an oboe more than ten years old.

What does this mean for students? First, it means that they might find a good supply of instruments buying castoffs from professionals— a good five-year-old oboe that's been well maintained can still serve a student very well. And it means that a brand new second-tier instrument is probably a better bet than a twenty-year-old top-quality horn, which will have lost much of its original sound quality.

The recent increase in Internet sales and marketing has given rise to a whole new problem. It's true that there are no "used-car salesmen" in the oboe trade. But there are still individuals selling inferior instruments through online auctions to poorly informed buyers. You can avoid all of this risk by following a simple rule: do not pay any money for anything that you haven't personally inspected and tested. Occasionally you may miss out on an apparent bargain by being cautious. But the rule "you get what you pay for" continues to apply. If it's really cheap, there is something wrong with it.

If you have an oboe you want to sell, the usual channels (word of mouth, newspaper classifieds, etc.) will probably not be very effective unless you live in an area teeming with oboists. Your best bet is to work with one of the many oboe vendors who sell instruments on consignment. Typically, you and the vendor will agree on a price for your instrument in advance, after he or she has inspected it. This is the sum you will receive, not the amount the vendor will charge the customer. The dealer will add his profit and a reasonable charge for servicing your instrument. Expect the selling price to be 10 to 20 percent higher than what you're getting. Some dealers just charge a straight commission, typically 15 to 20 percent of the sale price. These charges will affect your bottom line, but you will only have to ship the instrument once, and you will assume none of the financial risk of sending the oboe to strangers.

When shipping the instrument, make sure that it is secure inside its case and cannot move around when the case is shaken a little. Fill any gaps with paper towels until the case holds the instrument firmly. Pack it in a new cardboard box with 2–3 inches of space all around the instrument case. Fill that space with packaging material until nothing moves inside the closed box when it is shaken. Shippers usually require that a musical instrument be double boxed for shipment. If the instrument is packed in its own hard case, that counts as one of the boxes. Select one of the faster shipping options; you don't want your oboe to be sitting in harsh climate conditions waiting for the next leg of the journey. Insure it for its replacement value unless you already have an all-risk policy covering your instrument against loss or damage.

On the topic of insurance, most household insurance policies do not cover musical instruments used professionally. Professionally in this case means that the instrument has been used by an owner who got paid for playing it. It doesn't mean that you have to be a full-time professional musician. It is best to get specific musical instrument insurance from a company experienced in this business. They will cover the instrument against nearly any eventuality anywhere in the world for a reasonable premium. Any musical professional organization such as the International Double Reed Society will have a relationship with one of these insurers.

Instrument Maintenance

If you have purchased a new wooden oboe or a wooden instrument that has not been played for some time, you will need to break it in. This break-in period acclimates the wood to the stress caused by moisture on the inside of the instrument while the outside remains dry. Done carefully, it can help to reduce the chance of cracking. Read that sentence again: it can *help* to *reduce* the chance of cracking. Oboes crack. It's usually not the player's fault. And unless the crack is huge, it can be repaired without any damage to the playing characteristics of the instrument. But to minimize this risk, you should break your instrument in carefully. At first, play it for a maximum of ten minutes at a time separated by two-hour rest periods. Before each playing session, make sure the instrument has been warmed to near body temperature; this will reduce moisture condensation. After each playing session, swab it out carefully and make sure all of the tone holes are free of moisture. Check for water in keys that you might not have used during that playing session, such as the third octave key or the C-sharp and D trill keys. Put the instrument in its case and close it. Increase the playing time by five minutes a week until you reach an hour or so. After that, you should be able to use the instrument regularly. If the oboe is going to crack, it will usually do so within the first year, but maintain careful habits all the same. Instruments should be stored in very moderate conditions: neither excessive heat nor excessive cold is good for them. If you live in a dry climate, put a little humidifier in your case. If you live in a cold climate, carry the instrument in an insulated or lined case cover.

Although you should have your instrument professionally serviced every year or two, there are things you can do to prolong its life. Learn how to perform your own adjustments. I have provided a basic guide. Then, learn how to take your instrument apart and put it back together. By learning these two things, you will also learn enough about your instrument to differentiate a genuine repair crisis that requires professional services from something minor you can fix yourself, often in just a few minutes.

Instrument Disassembly and Reassembly

Taking an instrument apart is not as daunting as it sounds. If you have never done it before, find someone experienced to help you, or keep a fully assembled oboe nearby for reference. Do one joint at a time to avoid too much confusion. You will need a supply of paper towels, a silver polishing cloth (nothing abrasive), a screwdriver, a pair of needle-nose pliers to pull the rods out, oil (any oil suitable for sewing machines or clocks will work, though most professionals use Nye's Clock Oil), a few cotton swabs, and a small brush to remove the dirt and dust from the wood. You should also have a container or a system for storing the parts while they are off the oboe. Many of the parts are tiny and will be difficult to find if dropped on the floor.

While the long rods are easy to distinguish from each other, some of the shorter ones all look about the same length. So, if you have any doubt, after removing the key, slide the rod back in its place and leave it there until it is time to reassemble the instrument. After the keys have been removed, brush all the dust and dirt from the wood and around the posts. Use a fairly stiff-bristled brush to make sure all the dirt comes off. Then take a cotton swab and tease it until it comes to a point. Moisten it very lightly with a bit of oil and clean out each tone hole. Be sure to remove any oil that stays on the surface of the tone hole—oil will spoil cork pads. Put a very light layer of oil on the springs. Inspect the springs carefully for any rust. Now, clean the keys. Using a silver polishing cloth, clean any dirt, dust, and tarnish off each key. Be careful not to dislodge the small bumper corks. If any of these corks is damaged or missing, replace it. You will need a supply of thin sheet cork (0.40 mm, or approximately ⅟₆₄ inch). Repair technicians all have a favorite method for adhering the cork to the instrument; for our amateur purposes, a very small amount of superglue works just fine.

The bumper corks reduce mechanical noise by preventing direct metal-to-metal contact. Some oboes instead have small Teflon tips on all of the adjustment screws. These are marginally noisier but much more stable in terms of adjustment, since they will not compress over time.

After all the keys are polished, reassembly can begin. Clean the old oil from each rod with a paper towel, apply a thin layer of fresh oil, and put the instrument back together. You will have no trouble if you think about two things. First, do not force anything. Good oboes have very fine tolerances, so if a piece will not go back in, it's because the angle of approach is slightly wrong. Try again. When you have it right, the piece will slide into place very smoothly. Second, refer to your assembled oboe for help with the order of reassembly. For example, on the lower joint, the F key has to go on first. If you put anything else back before it, the F key will be blocked and you will have to start again. If you don't have an assembled oboe to refer to, be prepared to start over a few times.

The springs can be reattached to their little notches either by picking them up with the key while coaxing it back into its position, or by gently pushing the spring back into place with a spring hook or screwdriver after the key has been reattached to the instrument. Be very careful not to distort the curve of the spring. Never bend it; just return it to its place. If you have replaced any of the bumper corks, the instrument will need to be readjusted.

If you have never done this before, be prepared to spend an entire weekend. With practice, it will take only a few hours and save you money on repairs while contributing to the longevity and performance of your instrument.

After the oboe is in top condition, the following routine will keep it that way:

- After each playing session: Wipe the keys with a soft cloth.
- Every week: Brush the dust off the wood, especially under the rods. Small brushes, such as those intended for cleaning camera lenses or electric shavers, work well.
- Every month (or more often if needed): Check the adjustment.
- Every three months: Oil the mechanism. Get a needle oiler and put a small drop of clock oil or sewing machine oil at every joint along the mechanism (there will be about eighty spots in all). Don't get any oil on the pads. Wipe off any oil you get on the wood.
- Twice a year: Take the whole thing apart as described earlier, clean everything (including tone holes and octave key inserts), replace bumper corks as needed, oil the mechanism, and put it back together.

Some people recommend oiling the bore, defending the practice quite passionately and stating with emphasis that oil is the lifeblood of the wood. I've never noticed that this does any good at all, since the oil barely penetrates the surface and is probably removed the next time you swab. Some instrument makers feel that oiling the wood can actually increase the chance of cracking, since it creates a stress between the surface layer, which the oil penetrates, and the rest of the wood, which is dry. So don't bother. Oil does repel water, however, so if you have persistent issues with water gurgling in tone holes, perhaps a thin layer of oil in the bore can help. If you choose to oil the bore, do so very lightly. Put a drop or two of almond oil inside the bottom of the joint and distribute it with a turkey feather.

Adjustment of the Mechanism

What follows is a practical guide to oboe adjustment. It is not intended to be exhaustive, nor is it meant as a guide for the budding professional repairperson. But it will take care of most day-to-day problems and keep your oboe working well, assuming there are no structural problems such as bent keys, faulty pads, or cracks in the wood. A few notes are necessary before starting.

- Record the exact position of any adjustment screw before moving it. Look at the slot in the screw head, regard it like you would a clock face, and assign a time of day to what you see. If your adjustment fails to give the desired result, you can at least put it back to where it was when you started.

- Before beginning the adjustment process, make sure that none of the rods—the ones that hold the instrument together—are loose. Tighten these securely, and the instrument will be much more stable mechanically. Be careful to differentiate between the rods and the adjustment screws. The rods are parallel to the instrument body; the adjustment screws face outward.
- When making an adjustment, unless you are very sure of how far to turn the screw, move it no more than a sixteenth of a turn at a time. Fine adjustments sometimes feel more like you are leaning on the screwdriver than actually turning the screw.
- Take note of any sloppy adjustment screws. Screws should exhibit a moderate amount of drag when turning them. Loose screws will rotate on their own and go out of adjustment constantly. If you find a loose screw, adjust it to its correct position and then hold it in place with a small drop of clear nail polish. The polish will chip off easily the next time you want to move the screw. A better remedy is to remove the screw entirely, wind a little bit of dental floss or plumber's Teflon tape around it, and return it to its housing. Those with more mechanical savvy could use a modern threadlocking adhesive like Loctite. Whatever the method, make sure that all of your adjustment screws are stable.
- By tightening an adjustment screw, you are either loosening or obstructing something else. So, if a little tight is good, very tight will not be better. Be gentle.
- When one of the main fingered keys is responsible for closing another key, the nonfingered key should close slightly less tightly than the main key. For example, pressing the A key (middle finger of the left hand) should close the C vent. The C vent should be slightly less tight than the A key. In any relationship of this kind, the fingered key (the A key in this example) is referred to as "primary," while the linked key (the C vent) is referred to as "secondary."
- Even without detailed instructions, it is relatively simple to determine the task of any given adjustment screw by applying a kneebone-connects-to-the-thighbone analysis. If you look at the screw and follow the motion of that piece of keywork to its destination, the function of the screw should be apparent.
- When keys are named, they refer to the lowest key that is pressed while that note sounds. Thus, the A key is the key pressed with the middle finger of the left hand.
- When the instruction says to hold a key closed with your finger, do not use more than the normal finger pressure you would apply while playing.
- Only very simple tools are required. You will need a screwdriver of the correct size and with an undamaged blade (the inexpensive screwdriver supplied with the instrument will suffice for

most jobs) and a triangle of cigarette paper about 5 cm long and 2 mm wide at the narrow end. This will function as your feeler gauge.

· The cigarette paper will be placed under the farthest part of each pad—that is, the point farthest away from the pivot that attaches the key to the instrument. Place the cigarette paper under the pad, close the key with normal finger pressure, and withdraw the paper. It will take some practice to learn the appropriate amount of drag for the various keys; have a teacher or other professional give you a demonstration. Cork pads are relatively easy to learn; the pads made of skin or leather grip the paper very lightly even when correctly adjusted, requiring much more experience.

· Oboes have different configurations of adjustment screws. Not all oboes will match the illustrations (figures), but I have discussed the most common adjustments.

Refer to figure 10.1. Screws no. 1 and no. 2 regulate the relative heights of the octave keys. If you want your octave keys to open further (or less far), these will do the job. But it is almost never necessary to move these, and they are best left alone.

Screw no. 3 adjusts the opening height of the third octave key if your instrument has one. The third octave key should just barely open. You should be able to see that it moves, but it should not open far enough to slide a piece of cigarette paper underneath.

Screw no. 4 adjusts the opening height of the half-hole plate. Properly adjusted, the plate will open much less than the other two fingered keys on the top joint, so don't be alarmed if it seems rather close to the wood. Turning screw no. 4 clockwise will move the plate closer to the wood; turning it counterclockwise will move it further away. Finding the correct adjustment requires a playing test. Slur up to high D (two ledger lines), lifting the finger off of the half-hole completely to assist the slur. As the plate is adjusted closer to the wood, these slurs will improve. However, as the plate is adjusted closer to the wood, ascending slurs to high C-sharp will gradually fail to respond and the sound of the C-sharp will become stuffy. Keep moving the plate closer until the response and sound of the C-sharp fail, and then back it off just enough to restore good results. At this point, the plate may be only one or two millimeters above the wood, which is correct.

Screws no. 5, no. 6, no. 7, and no. 8 should be considered as a group. If there are response issues on the oboe, especially if the low register feels tight, this group is almost always one of the culprits. Assemble the lower joint to the top joint before beginning. Begin with screw no. 7. This adjusts the opening height of the B-flat and C vents and controls the amount of play felt at the right-hand index finger (the F-sharp key). Turning the screw clockwise increases the amount of play; turning it counterclockwise reduces it. For best results, adjust the screw so that the

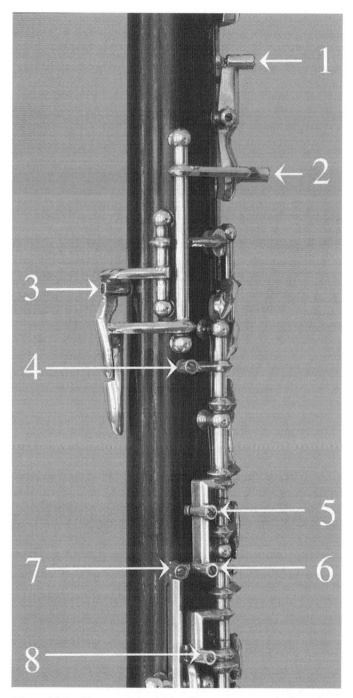

Figure 10.1 Oboe top joint with adjustment screws indicated.

F-sharp key has barely any play. It should move only very slightly before engaging the linkage to the top joint.

Then go to screw no. 6. Screw no. 6 regulates the balance between the B-flat and C vents when they are being held closed with spring tension only. Turning the screw clockwise tightens the C vent and loosens the B-flat vent; turning it counterclockwise tightens the B-flat vent and loosens the C vent. Using the cigarette paper, test the tension of the B-flat and C vent keys and compare the two; they should have equal tension.

Screw no. 5 is next. This adjusts the relationship between the A key and the C vent. Turning it clockwise tightens the C vent; turning it counterclockwise loosens the C vent. Turning it too far clockwise will prevent the A key from closing. To test, place the triangle of cigarette paper under the C vent, hold the A key closed, press the F-sharp key (now the A key is holding the vent closed, since pressing the F-sharp key releases the spring closure), and remove the cigarette paper. It should have some drag, but not as much as you get when you test the A key—the A key should be stronger.

Finally, we adjust screw no. 8. This performs the same task as no. 5 but for a different pair of keys, in this case regulating the relationship between the G key and the B-flat vent. Turning the screw clockwise will tighten the B-flat vent, while turning it counterclockwise will loosen the B-flat vent. Turning it too far clockwise will prevent the G key from closing. Place your cigarette-paper triangle under the B-flat vent, hold the G key closed, hold the F-sharp key open, and test the tension. If the preceding paragraphs seem confusing, a quick visual demonstration from someone who has done it before will clear things up immediately—it's actually not very difficult.

We are almost done with the top joint; only no. 9 remains. Screw no. 9 does not appear in the photograph. It's too small and hidden to show up, and different oboes have it in different places. But if you follow the linkage between the A-flat key and the A key, you will find it somewhere in that connection. Pressing the A-flat key should completely close the A key; this screw allows us to adjust that relationship. Turning it clockwise will close the A key more tightly and lower the opening height of the A-flat key; turning it counterclockwise will loosen the A key and raise the height of the A-flat key. If the A key does not close completely, the A-flat to B-flat trill will have a very sharp B-flat; if the screw is overtightened, the A-flat key will not open far enough. So tighten no. 9 just enough to ensure that the A key closes when the A-flat key is pressed, and stop.

Figures 10.2(a) and 10.2(b) show the adjustment screws on the bottom joint of the oboe. Screw no. 10 is another play test. Its task is to ensure that pressing the F-sharp key holds the A-flat key closed. Turning it clockwise will close the A-flat key more firmly; turning it counterclockwise will close it less firmly. If screw no. 10 it is too loose, the G-flat

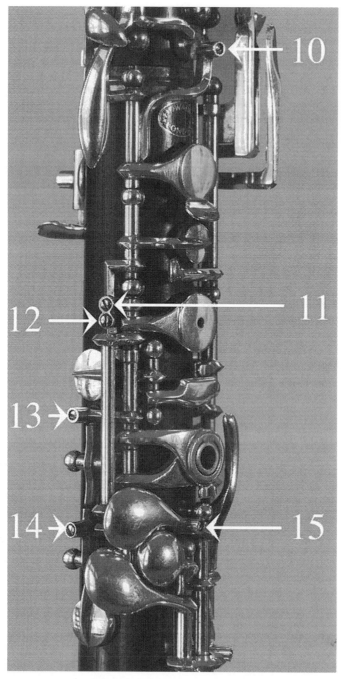

Figures 10.2 (a) and (b). Two views of the lower joint, with adjustment screws indicated.

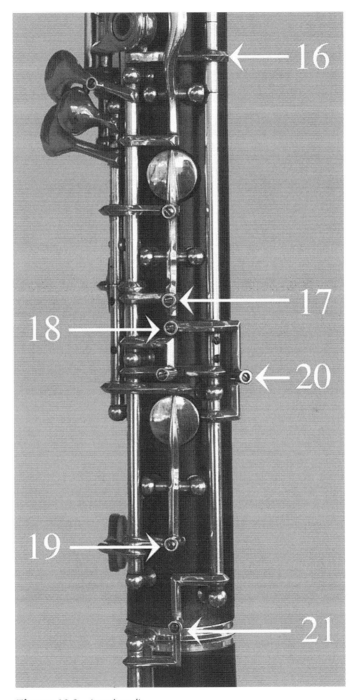

Figures 10.2   (*continued*)

to A-flat trill will not work. If it is too tight, the F-sharp key is prevented from closing and the whole lower register will not work. Begin by loosening the screw to make absolutely sure it is not too tight, perhaps a quarter of a turn. Then play a low C and, while holding it, press and release the A-flat key several times. There should be an audible wah-wah sort of sound. If it is absent and the sound of the C stays steady, loosen the screw another quarter turn and repeat. Once the wah-wah sound is heard, gradually tighten screw no. 10 until the wah-wah disappears and the low C sounds the same whether the A-flat key is pressed or not. Adjust by very small increments as you approach the correct result. Even a little bit of overtightening can make the low register more difficult. This adjustment can be affected by external factors: the alignment of the top joint to the middle joint must be the same every time the instrument is assembled, the arm holding screw no. 10 must not be bent, and the little leather bumper pad on the A-flat key must be intact and firmly attached (if your oboe has Teflon-tipped adjustment screws, it won't have this pad).

Screws no. 11 and no. 12 both affect the closure of the small F-sharp vent above the E key. Before checking these adjustments, first confirm that screw no. 14 is not too tight: finger a forked F, slide your feeler gauge under the forked F resonance key, then finger a D and pull the paper out. If the tension is too firm—if the paper won't pull out—loosen screw no. 14 about half a turn. Don't forget to return to it after these next two adjustments are completed.

Screw no. 11 regulates the relationship between the E key and the F-sharp vent. Turning it clockwise will tighten the F-sharp vent; turning it counterclockwise will loosen it. Turning the screw too far clockwise will prevent the E key from closing. With your cigarette-paper triangle, check the tension of the F-sharp vent with the E key closed. It should be slightly less tight than the E key itself.

Screw no. 12 controls the relationship between the D key and the same small F-sharp vent. Turning the screw clockwise tightens the F-sharp vent; turning it counterclockwise loosens it. Turning it too far clockwise will prevent the D key from closing. Make sure that the D key has a little more tension than the F-sharp vent. When the lower register is working poorly, screws no. 11 and no. 12 are often the problem, together with the group of screws no. 5, no. 6, no. 7, and no. 8.

Screw no. 13 adjusts the height of the D key opening. Turning it clockwise lowers the D key; turning it counterclockwise raises it. If your E is sharp or shrill, lowering the D key can help.

Screw no. 14 is the last of the likely culprits when the lower register fails to sound easily. It adjusts the closure of the forked F resonance key. Turning screw no. 14 clockwise will close the resonance key more tightly: turning it counterclockwise will reduce the closure. Turning it too far clockwise will prevent the E key from closing. To test, finger a forked F, slide the paper underneath the resonance key, then finger a

D. The key will close, and you can withdraw the paper. There should be moderate drag. If it is too light, tighten the screw. If the paper is hard to withdraw, loosen the screw.

Screw no. 15 adjusts the relationship between the low C key and the E key. Pressing the C key should close the E key completely but not tightly, allowing air to escape only through the small pinhole. If screw no. 15 is too loose, the high C-sharp will be significantly sharp and the screw should be turned clockwise; if it is too tight, the low C pad will not close adequately and the screw should be turned counterclockwise. Tighten the screw just enough to close the E key and no further.

Screw no. 16 (not all oboes have this screw) adjusts the closure of the split-D ring when the left E-flat is pressed. Turning the screw clockwise closes the D ring; turning the screw counterclockwise raises it. Screw no. 16 should be adjusted so that pressing the left E-flat key closes the split-D ring but no further. If you tighten it further, observe that the height of the E-flat pad gradually lowers. This is the screw to adjust if you hear a difference in pitch between the left and right E-flat fingerings.

Screw no. 17 is another play test. First make sure the screw is not too tight by loosening it a quarter turn or so. Play a low C and press and release the left E-flat. You will hear the wah-wah sound we encountered earlier with the A-flat trill adjustment. Tighten the screw gently until the problem goes away.

Screw no. 18 rarely needs to be used unless something is bent. If it is too loose, there will be excessive play when operating the left E-flat. If it is too tight, it may cause the low B-flat vent key (on the bell) to stand open.

Screw no. 19 is the last of our play tests. Again, first loosen it a bit to make sure it is not too tight. Then play a low B-flat and wiggle your right-hand little finger on and off the C-sharp key. Tighten until the wah-wah sound disappears.

Screws no. 20 and no. 21 both do the same thing—they adjust the relationship between the closure of the low B and that of the low B-flat. Not all oboes have screw no. 21. Turning either screw clockwise will tighten the B-flat key and loosen the B key; turning either screw counterclockwise will tighten the B key and loosen the B-flat key. The drag on the cigarette paper should be equal between the B and the B-flat keys when low B-flat is fingered. Many oboes have skin or leather pads on these lower keys, making the drag on the cigarette paper hard to judge. So a visual check can be helpful to confirm your impressions. Slowly press the B-flat key and watch the two keys close. They should both make contact with the wood at the same time.

11

Selection and Care of Tools and Equipment

In this chapter, I will describe basic standards for the oboist's tool kit, along with some recommendations for care and feeding of these often expensive and fragile items. I will not make recommendations favoring specific brands; this would be unfair to the many other makers who also provide quality items. Nor will I mention specific dollar figures, as these fluctuate (mostly upward) pretty regularly. Since the oboe market is small, nobody will sell enough of anything to get rich. And there is no luxury market of oboe goods, where makers justify very high prices by maintaining a certain prestige for their merchandise. In other words, you almost always get what you pay for. Costlier items are better than cheaper ones. But they may not be better in a way that matters to you, so be smart in your purchases. If you have never made reeds before, buying expensive gold-plated staples individually machined to very close tolerances won't make any difference to your results yet. I do suggest avoiding the least expensive of anything, not because I think the vendor wants to cheat his customers, but because there has to be a reason for the very low cost.

Equipment preferences are a fascinating topic of conversation, a subject that occupies oboists quite happily for hours. Most players have distinct favorites and will often defend these passionately. My view is that equipment is the least important aspect of playing. It is very rare that spending money will make you sound better without a similar investment in time and thought. I use the equipment I use because I'm accustomed to it and it works properly. I would rather continue on a consistent path than risk confusion and inconsistency. You will not sound like me, and I will not sound like you, even if we both collect the exact same inventory of tools and instruments.

Of course, less experienced players will have to experiment to find what suits them best. But they should consider that consistency is by far their biggest ally. If they choose to change to a different tool or material, they should change only one thing at a time and give it time to show whether it makes an improvement.

Tools and Supplies

Reed-Making Kit

I've listed this first because I believe that it is the only thing available from many vendors that is simply not worth the money. The kit always has a discounted price, meaning that it is cheaper than the same items bought separately. But the selection of the items is not always what a reed maker needs—sometimes the quality is too low, sometimes the quantity is too large or too small (six pieces of shaped cane?), sometimes they include items just to say they did (a sharpening stone the size of my thumb?). The beginner is usually better off buying carefully selected materials individually, even though it may cost two or three times as much. There is no reason for a beginning reed maker to buy flimsy items that will need to be replaced a year or two later. Many of the basic reed-making tools can last a very long time—a sharpening stone or a mandrel can be used for years—so it is worth buying good ones to start with.

Staples

There are many different styles and kinds. Tubes are traditionally made of heavy sheet metal—either brass or nickel silver—covered with a layer of cork to assure an airtight seal in the oboe's reed well. The standard length is 47 mm, although other lengths—45, 46, 46.5, and 48 mm—are available. I have never noticed a difference in sound or response between the brass and the nickel silver tubes, so I have always opted for the cheaper brass tubes. The brass is also softer and therefore better suited for players who like to alter the tube with pliers, a practice I do not advocate.

I advise here and with all equipment that you start with something standard and learn to use it. After you are very sure that you need to make a change, go ahead and make it. But never experiment recklessly, and always make changes based on good reasons. The good reason in this case is that the staple represents an extension of the oboe bore at the most crucial point—the very top. So using a staple with a different dimension can give a noticeably different result. Other materials—gold and silver plating, for example—are also available. And recently, investigation of the physics of energy transfer has resulted in tubes that are not covered in the usual cork, but rather transmit the vibration directly through the metal with minimum interference. So experimentation is certainly justified. But, as with all things reed related, try to regain consistency as quickly as possible.

Many young reed makers, mindful of expense, scavenge their staples from reeds they have purchased in the past. This collection is often a motley assortment of reeds from many different sources, most of which were made using the least expensive staple available, with little thought for its longevity. However, if a few selection criteria are observed, some of these can be reused. First, discard any tubes that are physically damaged—if the cork is chipped at the bottom or if the metal is dented. A little cork damage near the top is only a cosmetic concern. Then, measure each tube to make sure it is 47 mm long and discard the ones that are not. Finally, set each tube on your mandrel. The top of the staple should sit flush with the end of the mandrel. Reject the ones that deviate by more than a millimeter and the ones that allow the mandrel to twist freely inside the tube. By now, probably half or more of the tubes are gone, but you can use the rest with confidence until they wear out. "Worn out" means that the cork has crumbled away from the metal or that the metal itself is dented, even slightly.

Even if you are a beginning reed maker, having fewer than ten or so staples is frustrating, since old reeds have to be dismantled before new ones can be begun. Most professional players have dozens and dozens of tubes and purchase new ones regularly.

String

FF nylon string is standard. "FF" is a designation of thread thickness, and therefore strength as well. A 200-yard spool of thread lasts a long time, so there is no real reason to have many of these. Still, players like a variety of color for decorative reasons or to keep different batches of cane separate, so most oboists end up with a dozen or more spools of string. Naturally, sellers have not failed to note this, so 50-yard spools are now available as well. Silk string is also usable for oboe reeds, though it tends to break more easily than nylon. Some see this as a virtue, claiming that if you break silk string, you are pulling too hard.

Beeswax

Beeswax is used to coat the string before tying the reed. The resulting tackiness fills in any small gaps between the string winds and helps to hold the knots together. Beeswax can be readily purchased from double-reed vendors in small cakes that last a long time. Avoid the product sold in fabric stores, which is too hard for our purposes. As an alternative to beeswax, some players paint the string with nail polish after the reed is assembled. Tying the reed without somehow coating the string is not recommended. The knots will likely come apart—a very frightening experience when it happens to your good reed during the concert.

Mandrel

The mandrel holds the staple while tying and, for some players, while scraping also. The mandrel should match the preferred brand of staple, allowing quick and easy judgment about the dimensions of the staple itself. Many staples, though carefully made, are not completely consistent; seeing how they fit the mandrel allows for quick evaluation of their size and shape. The mandrel should also be straight, meaning that the flat part of the mandrel shaft should align with the flat part of the handle. While that seems a simple requirement, many mandrels do not meet it, so choose carefully.

Easel

An easel is a round, smooth, dowellike piece of wood, usually rosewood. It is used for support while trimming the ends of the gouged piece of cane, and it provides a guide for scoring the piece of cane for folding. The easel is a convenience, and many players like using it, but it is not an essential piece of equipment. Reeds can be made successfully without one.

Cutting Block

This is a small, round block of wood used to support the reed while clipping the tip. These are available in different sizes and different materials. It makes sense to get the larger size in the hardest possible material. The plastic ones are almost useless; rosewood, the most commonly available material, is much better; grenadilla is best of all if you can find one. With use, the criss-cross of hundreds of knife marks eventually makes the surface of the block too uneven to provide a clean cut. At that point, the block could be sanded smooth again or replaced. Do not try to clip the reed on any other surface: cutting blocks made for oboe reeds are gently domed on top, making a clean cut easy to achieve. A flat surface will make precise clipping very difficult.

Knife

A sharp knife is the foundation of every reed-making effort. Without a very sharp knife, great cane, a perfect gouge, and years of experience are wasted. There are reed knives for every budget and preference. The quality of the steel ranges from very soft indeed to incredibly hard. Blade shapes range from light razorlike blades to large cudgels. Handles are rounded, square, and everything in between. The cost ranges from very reasonable to exorbitantly expensive. As a good starting place, try a medium-soft steel double-hollow-ground knife in the middle of the price range. Experience will tell you what you eventually want to use. But this is one place where it is definitely worth spending money to get what you want. High-quality steel is costly, and low-quality steel is difficult to work with. Time spent working on a reed with a dull knife is time wasted, so find something that fits your hand comfortably and that you can sharpen reliably.

Sharpening Stones

A good sharpening stone must be at least two inches by six inches. Larger stones are available, but do not try to use anything smaller. The stone must be absolutely flat. It should not be too rough, because we want a polished edge to the knife, not a jagged one, but it must be abrasive enough to remove metal fairly quickly. This ideal stone doesn't really exist, so it is advisable to have more than one for different purposes. Technology in this area has improved immensely—we can now buy synthetic stones with almost any imaginable grit size held in a completely stable binder. Players of previous generations were limited to natural stones (quarried from the earth) or synthetic stones that were too coarse. For today's reed maker, I would suggest three stones: a coarse, a medium, and a fine. The coarse should be quite coarse, indeed—a grit size of 200–300. Grit size refers to particle size, not particle density. So a grit size of 1,000 means that 1,000 particles of abrasive *could* fit into a square inch, but not necessarily that the stone bears that many particles in each square inch. Particle density is one of the things we pay for when purchasing higher quality stones.

The medium stone should have a grit size of 1,000 or 1,500, and the fine should be around 5,000. Most of the stones sold for all-purpose sharpening are in the range of 1,000 to 1,500. This is neither coarse enough to reshape a blade that has been mishandled, nor fine enough to create the really smooth scratch pattern that we need for ultimately sharp reed making. So, even though having a selection of stones is expensive, it will pay off in more consistent reed making and more reliable technique.

Types of Sharpening Stones
- *India stone*. This is the standard, usually sold with fine grit on one side and medium on the other. The fine is used to polish the edge, and the medium, to restore it when it has been damaged by poor sharpening. India stones are cleaned with oil, which is then removed with lighter fluid. Do not use oil on the stone while sharpening—use it dry, and clean as necessary. In my experience, even the fine side of the India stone is too rough to give a refined edge. Advantage: low cost, easy availability. Disadvantage: too rough for ultimate edge refinement.

• *Ceramic stone.* Sapphire dust is held in a ceramic binder. These stones are offered in a variety of grits; the fine and extra fine are good for oboe knives. The stone is used dry. Some makers say to use the stone with water, but it doesn't seem to work any better, and the water is messy. The water does prevent the stone from loading up with metal as quickly, so make sure to clean it regularly. It can be cleaned with any abrasive household scouring powder like Ajax or Comet and water. The same technology also exists in pencil-thin sticks, which are provided with a mounting platform that holds them at the correct angle in a V shape, making accurate sharpening almost easy. Advantage: low cost, relatively large size (two inches by eight inches) for the money. Disadvantage: sometimes the stones are not completely flat, though the sticks don't have this problem.

• *Diamond stone.* Diamond stones are not stones at all; they usually consist of a steel plate coated in diamond dust. The diamond dust is very sharp and cuts very fast, which is both the advantage and the disadvantage (if you aren't perfect with maintaining a consistent angle). Some diamond stones are made of steel mesh applied to a plastic base. These are excellent for travel, since the base is light, but it is also delicate. Just a few minor accidents and the top of the "stone" is no longer true. The fine and the extra fine are suitable for oboe knives. The fine is actually quite coarse and can remove a lot of material quickly.

• *Water stones.* There are many brands, many of them made in Japan, and right now these represent the ultimate in knife sharpening. They are available from very coarse (110 grit) up to almost ridiculously fine (30,000), with many choices in between. Some need to be soaked in water for a time before using; the best ones can be used with water sprayed on the surface before sharpening, with no need for prior soaking. The water, and the resulting slurry, makes using these somewhat messy, so you will need to set up some sort of basin (a cookie sheet works just fine) to catch the mess. The cost ranges from quite reasonable for the coarser grits to unaffordable for the very finest. But a selection of three or four of these should put an end to anyone's knife-sharpening misery. Advantages: works better than anything else. Disadvantages: relatively high cost, messy to use. See chapter 8 for instructions on knife sharpening.

Plaque

The plaque is used to support the blades of the reed while scraping, particularly on the tip. Plaques are available in steel, wood, or plastic, and can be purchased either contoured or flat. I prefer the flat blue steel version with either rounded or pointed ends. They are slim and cheap and work just fine. I prefer them to the contoured plaques, which spread the blades of the reed too far apart, deforming it. However, the contoured plaques will not dull the knife as quickly, since they are made of plastic or wood, not metal. Again, buy a quantity of plaques: half a dozen or so. They tend to get lost with maddening frequency. Make sure not to use them for too long. You can get a very good indication of how tip thickness and contour are coming along by observing the dark blue plaque color shining through the cane. When the plaque loses its dark blue color or becomes unevenly worn, with lots of shiny silver patches, it becomes a much less useful guide.

Something to Seal Leaks in Reeds

Reeds will occasionally leak at the bottom of the cane just above the string. (If a reed leaks higher up, the cane was warped or carelessly shaped. Those reeds should be discarded.) The traditional product for sealing leaks in reeds is fishskin, which has nothing to do with fish, but is the lining from a cow's intestine. It is sold in sheets usually about a foot square that last quite a while. You cut it into narrow strips as needed, moisten it, and wind it around the reed three or four times. It does a reasonable job of sealing leaks, especially if it is very thin, but it tends to float off whenever the reed is soaked. Painting it with nail polish holds it in place better, but the polish adds a fair amount of mass to the reed.

My preference is to use Teflon tape, also called plumber's tape. This is easy to obtain, easy to use, and stays put indefinitely. Just cut off an inch or so and wind it around the reed. It will look somewhat unsightly —the reed will look bandaged—but it works.

Ruler

You cannot make reeds without an accurate ruler. It should be calibrated in millimeters, and it should be made of metal. Plastic rulers have thicker lines painted on them and are a bit less precise as a result. I have seen inaccurate rulers that were wrongly calibrated by as much as five percent—a big difference on a 70 mm oboe reed—so it's probably better not to buy your ruler from the clearance bin.

Work Light

A good light to make reeds by is almost as essential as a sharp knife. A simple sturdy desk lamp will do. It needs to have a dark shade in order to throw a focused beam of light down on to the reed being scraped. Good reeds can only be made with bright lighting.

Gouging Machine

Gouging machines are made by many different vendors in two basic designs. A single-radius machine has a blade that is set to travel down the middle of the cane, removing material equally from both sides. The curvature of the blade is a section of a circle (hence the single radius), and the diameter of the circle is larger than the diameter of the cane, ensuring that the sides of the cane will be thinner than the center. The cane is gouged until no more comes off, then flipped once to assure symmetrical results.

The blade curvature of a dual-radius machine is a section of the narrower end of an ellipse (hence the dual radius), and the curve is somewhat smaller than the diameter of the cane. This blade is offset slightly to travel down the side of the cane, requiring the user to flip the cane every five or six strokes until the gouging is finished. This process leaves a small W in the middle of the cane.

The dual-radius design is traditional in the United States. It allows the reed maker more flexibility, since more parameters can be adjusted. It also introduces more variables, most of which cannot be modified independently, so unless the user is very experienced, the adjustment process can quickly disintegrate into a confusing mess of conflicting factors. For this reason, it is more straightforward to work with the single-radius concept. It is true that the dual-radius design leaves a small spine down the inside of the cane, but whether that spine is on the inside or the outside of the cane has never made a difference to me. The majority of machines available follow the single-radius design.

Few topics engross expert oboists more than the design and manufacture of gouging machines—"What gouge are you using?" Everyone who has made reeds for years has had one glorious week where everything seemed to function with perfect synchronicity. Reeds made themselves almost automatically and revealed a depth and ease of sound never approached before (or since). This desirable state can be maintained, but at a cost. In order to have a perfect gouging machine, you, the player, must learn an enormous amount about things that have little to do with music making and everything to do with machining, geometry, and materials. It is one of the wonderful things about oboe playing that it can engross the player in so many different ways, but most of us would probably agree that we did not become musicians because we like tools.

However, you should learn the most basic adjustments, and you must know what constitutes normal behavior for the machine. The most frequent adjustment is to the thickness of the gouged cane, which is accomplished quite easily on all machines. Make sure to keep each adjustment small—as with adjustment screws on the oboe, a sixteenth of a turn can make a meaningful difference. Have several pieces of sacrificial cane ready to gouge, since you will likely have to fine-tune the adjustment a few times. Other adjustments may be necessary: for instance, dual-radius machines allow the relationship between the sides and the center to be altered. All machines allow you to adjust the chip thickness—the thickness of the cane sliver that is removed. It is also very useful to be able to remove and reset the blade.

It is perfectly all right if all of these operations frighten you, especially if you have access to a good professional technician who can perform the adjustments for you. So, if you feel mechanically helpless and unable to service the machine yourself, be prepared to measure your cane carefully and observe the behavior of the machine closely in case something changes. A normal machine will remove material in thin (about 0.05 mm thick) shavings without needing much downward pressure; it will yield cane that is 0.58 mm to 0.61 mm in thickness in the center of the gouged piece; the sides of the cane will be symmetrical, as will any measurements from corner to corner; and the cane will stay still in the gouger bed and not push out to one side or the other. Any deviation from this performance, and the machine needs to be serviced.

If you are more mechanically adept, learn to perform the adjustments just discussed. If you are a relentless tinkerer and don't mind having four or five machines with only one of them working correctly, that is also fine. Have fun. But you could be practicing.

Reed Case

A reed case is an essential piece of equipment. It should be one of the very first things that students buy, no matter how young they are. Storing reeds in anything but a purpose-made reed case is dangerous. It may be tempting to use the small container the purchased reeds are delivered in, but those rarely allow air to circulate and often present a risk of physical damage to the reed.

There is a huge variety of cases available. Capacity ranges from three reeds to a hundred or more; materials range from cheap molded plastic to exotic woods and leathers; cost ranges from quite reasonable to very expensive. For a start, a young player should get a case that holds six or eight reeds. It doesn't have to be expensive (though no reed case could be considered cheap), but it does have to meet certain minimum requirements. Reeds stored next to each other should not be able to touch each other, and whatever mechanism is used to hold the reeds—either small pegs or a ribbon formed to carry reeds—should hold them firmly and give them little chance to become dislodged during normal transport. The latch and hinges should look like they will be reasonably durable. These are the weak part of any case and almost always fail eventually, but they should last at least a year or two. Try not to buy a case just because it looks really attractive—it will be much more satisfying to have something durable and protective. Then, care for it as you would something rare and precious. It holds your reeds, after all.

Swabs

All swabs have their advantages and disadvantages. The primary considerations are: do they remove moisture effectively, do they shed inside

the instrument, and is it possible to get the swab stuck? The main con-
tenders for swab champion are:

- *Silk pull-through swabs.* These do a decent job of absorbing moisture and don't shed very much, but it is very easy for them to get
  stuck. Before even thinking about using one, pull it through your
  fist to feel if there are any knots, even very small ones. Then pull
  it through slowly. If the swab is whipped through quickly, it can
  double back on itself and become knotted while inside the oboe.
  If you do happen to get one stuck, stop pulling immediately—
  there isn't any hope of getting it to go through—none. Then,
  take it to a repairperson. Most repair people hate silk swabs, but I
  suspect it has nothing to do with the quality of the swab; they're
  just tired of removing them. If you really want to be sure that it
  will never get stuck, feed the string through the top of the oboe
  and out the bottom. Some silk swabs have a cord at both ends,
  allowing you to remove the stuck swab yourself. Silk swabs are
  very light and don't do much to clean the lower joint.
- *Cotton swabs.* These remove moisture very well, shed moderately,
  and can't really get stuck. They will leave lint in the tone holes,
  and the temptation is to pull them too firmly, risking some bore
  wear. If you have one, use it gently; don't keep pulling until it
  feels tight.
- *Feathers.* These don't really remove moisture at all, they shed into
  the tone holes, and they can't possibly get stuck. Feathers spread
  the moisture around rather than removing it. Adherents say that
  this preserves the oboe in a "warmed up" state, rather than removing all of the moisture that playing has left there. The little
  feather barbs will break off and lodge in tone holes, requiring
  regular cleaning.
- *Mops of various kinds.* These remove moisture very well, don't get
  stuck, and will shed. They are usually sized for the joint they are
  meant to clean, so they will apply the appropriate amount of pressure themselves, relieving you of worrying about using them too
  hard.

So all swabs have advantages and disadvantages. Use whatever you
prefer, but use it carefully.

English Horn Bocals

English horn bocals affect almost every aspect of English horn playing:
pitch, response, tone quality, and projection. Some of these matters are
subjective and should be determined by the individual player. But just
like a good reed, a good bocal should work. It should respond, play in
tune, and create a feeling of resistance that is comfortable for the player.

If you have a high-quality instrument, the bocals supplied with it
are probably quite good. If the instrument is newly purchased and your
English horn experience is limited, I recommend that you use the included bocals for at least the first few months until you are sure that your
playing would be improved by having something different.

Bocals are supplied in various lengths—the usual designations are
no. 1, no. 2, and no. 3, with no. 1 being the shortest and no. 3, the longest.
They also come in different bore configurations; these are individual to
the manufacturer, so you will have to rely on his or her descriptions. In
addition, bocals are made of different materials. The most common are
silver and brass, with some brass bocals carrying silver or gold plating.
I have also tried bocals made of copper and other metals. The standard
is a no. 2 bocal made of silver or silver-plated brass of a medium bore.
Makers will claim certain properties for different bore configurations—
one bocal might have a darker sound (who doesn't want that?), while
another might have better high-note projection (can't I have both?).
In my experience, these distinctions are overwhelmed by differences in
instruments, players, and reeds. So your task is to find the right bocal for
you and your instrument, not the one recommended to you as "best."

Besides affecting the subjective matters of tone quality and projection, a good bocal will play with an even sound throughout the registers.
It will allow a diminuendo on C (in the middle of the staff) down to silence without sagging. A bad bocal will fail this test completely—it will
sag no matter what sort of intervention the player exerts. A good bocal
will allow the G-sharp above the staff to sit up firmly in tune. A bad
bocal will barely sound any different when the G-sharp key is added to
the G. A good bocal will support the tone and pitch of the troublesome
notes above the staff between G and C. A bad one will lack focus and
pitch security on most notes, but those in particular.

Bocals also have slightly different curves. This will present the reed
to you at somewhat different angles, so it is important to make sure
that this relationship is comfortable.

Try a few bocals from different makers to get a general feel for the
playing field, and gradually focus your selection as your preferences
develop. Fortunately, bocals are not ruinously expensive and can usually be sold for only a small loss if you change your mind after a few
months. Professional English horn players often have a dozen or more
(sometimes many more) bocals they have collected over the years.

Conclusion

The oboe is charming in its very low-tech-ness. Look at illustrations of
reed-making tools from the mid-nineteenth century—do they look familiar? How about a photograph of an oboe from 1910? Not much has
changed, has it? Of course, the materials have improved, and the process
of manufacture is much more precise; we have computer-guided tools

and very accurate machining working on sturdier materials with better capabilities. But the fundamental design has not changed in a hundred years or more.

Part of this, probably much of it, is due to the natural conservatism of musicians. While many musicians would regard themselves as free spirits and creative people, and while some would be surprised at my characterization of them as conservative, where equipment is concerned this has always been true and remains true today. People are not going to discard something they have spent a lifetime learning in favor of something new but as yet unproven. This was as true in the nineteenth century as it is today. When new oboe systems and key additions began appearing quickly in the 1820s and 1830s, some older players rejected almost all of them and continued to play on the instrument they had studied in their youth.

Another issue, probably as important, is the low volume of oboe manufacture. The largest maker of professional-quality oboes in the world today is the F. Lorée company in France. In a typical year, they make in the neighborhood of 1,500 instruments. While that is a lot of professional-quality oboes and English horns, it is a tiny number of items when compared with other things in the music industry like microphone cables or drumsticks. When we compare it to televisions and bicycles and such, the number fades into insignificance. Limited editions of artwork are produced in greater numbers than oboes. So, since oboe makers have little money left over for anything beyond normal business expenses— rent, salaries, insurance, tooling, materials, and so on—research and development takes place largely as a process of evolution derived from trial and error. When applied to something like a gouging machine, which is produced in even smaller quantities, research and development is usually one person with a bright idea working hard to bring it to reality in his or her small machine shop.

So here is my thought. If the oboe gouging machine were a piece of medical equipment, it would cost at least $100,000. It would be as big as a small car, but by golly, it would work. You would dump a load of tube cane in one end, punch a few entries on the computer touch pad, and go to lunch. Then, when you returned a couple of hours later, a neat pile of perfectly gouged cane would reside in the out tray, already sorted according to diameter, hardness, and resilience, with the waste material ground up and converted to ethanol.

The difference is stark. With enough economic incentive, huge advances are possible in any field. It is naive (and probably foolish) to hope that millions of people will decide to play oboe, but I would love to see more involvement from the scientific community. Surely, cane can be studied precisely enough for us to know which qualities yield optimum results. For now, most reed makers find these for themselves. Gouging machines are made by oboe players with machine-tool experience (or sometimes by machinists with some oboe knowledge). Elite machinists, for very good business reasons, are not interested in making a few dozen or a few hundred of something incredibly precise. If we could order ten million copies, a dozen companies would already be lined up to submit bids.

So my hope is that some small number of crazy, good-natured people come along and try to find a way to apply all of the enormous recent advances in technology to the equipment used every day by oboe players. It would require some unusual collaborations: botanists, mathematicians, acousticians, machinists, and other scientists and tradespeople would have to work together with practicing musicians and business-people to explore the possibilities of making something better. Even universities, the very institutions that are supposed to facilitate this sort of exploration, are not exempt from commercial considerations. The science professors want grant money, not gratitude from musicians. The musicians have little scientific training and are soon left behind in any discussion of advanced concepts. Businesspeople are interested in funding projects where they can discern a huge future payoff. The bigger the potential payoff, the bigger the risk they are prepared to take. The oboe is at an obvious disadvantage in all of these scenarios.

So, it is entirely possible that the oboe of a hundred years hence will still look a lot like the oboe of today (and of a hundred years ago). That is not a terrible thing, of course, since today's oboe sounds beautiful and still meets the needs of today's music and musicians. But I have long wondered what form the next generation of oboe will take. Will it take advantage of all of the latest developments in semiconductors and microcircuitry? Will it be programmable in some way? And will the ancillary activity of reed making and its related equipment benefit in some way from truly advanced technology?

Or is none of this necessary? Is symphonic music—Western art music—satisfactory as a museum piece? Certainly, many people visit art museums and other institutions to experience a profound connection with the culture the world has developed over the past hundreds and thousands of years. But when living, breathing people are involved daily in the performance of an art, it might be better to find a way for that art to reflect the life that these people live.

IV

PROFESSIONAL AND PERFORMANCE CONSIDERATIONS

12

Professional Behavior and Deportment

Music is a difficult business. Many players compete for a small number of positions. Yet, this circumstance does not and should not deter legions of young people every year from applying to music schools for study. Each of these young people has a dream—usually to play in a professional symphony orchestra—that will probably not be realized. But it is not such an unlikely dream—it is not like dreaming of walking on the moon; it is like wanting to play major league baseball or to sing on Broadway. These are ambitious goals, but hundreds of people do sing on Broadway and hundreds do play in the major leagues. So the difference between the music profession and many other professions is that the music profession really only has room for good people. The student's job is to become one of those good people.

When focusing on becoming good, the student usually works on two aspects of playing—artistry and virtuosity—that they imagine are highly rewarded in the profession. And certainly these things *are* rewarded in the profession, although they may not be within the reach of everyone. However, there are three other things that are also highly rewarded, and these are accessible to anyone who is prepared to work. The first two of these can even be done by anyone, immediately and without any exertion.

Professionalism, Collegiality, and Competence

There is a saying in baseball: "It doesn't take any talent to hustle." And it doesn't take any talent to do something that is rewarded richly in the music profession, and that is to act professionally. First and foremost, this means that you are always on time for everything, no matter what. Let me provide some emphasis—you are *always* on time for *everything*, **no matter what.** There is no acceptable excuse, short of catastrophe, for being late or absent. Everyone else also has alarm clocks that don't work, traffic hassles, parking problems, sick friends, emergency phone calls, family issues, and so on. If there are eighty people in an orchestra and one oboist is absent, the concert cannot start. Seventy-nine musicians and hundreds of audience members are inconvenienced. There is no acceptable excuse, short of catastrophe, for being late or absent. Make sure you have a contact number for the personnel manager or contractor in case you really are involved in a car accident or suffer a mechanical failure. Anticipate the worst. Learn how to change a tire on your car. Have a list of numbers to call if you need help. Perhaps a colleague is traveling the same way as you and can take you to the performance. Extend this fixation for punctuality to your entire life, not just to professional musical engagements. Be on time for lessons, classes, medical appointments, everything. Punctuality should be a fixation for all musicians; it is a basic requirement for professional success.

Do not rely on your memory to keep track of your appointments. Get a date book, enter every one of your scheduled events in it, and read it every morning before leaving home. If your schedule is computer based, keep a regular back-up.

Playing a reed instrument really requires that you arrive at a job thirty minutes early to allow for enough warm-up time to stabilize your pitch. Then, when you arrive, you must have all of your equipment: reeds, music, tools, and instruments. This is obvious, but dumb things happen easily. Most performers have at least one story to relate about arriving at a service with no reeds, or no music, or even no instrument. Perform an idiot check every time you leave home. Ask yourself what you need today to do everything on your schedule—clothes, instruments, reeds, music, and so on. Look at the schedule one more time to make sure you haven't forgotten anything. Do not arrive at the service unprepared. It may be the last one you perform for that employer. When musicians are fired (or not rehired), it is rarely because they cannot play well; it is almost always for reasons of unreliability or unpleasantness. Contractors have no way to impress their employers except through the quality of the musicians they hire. They have a lot of work to do; they want to call you once and have you show up without fail and play well. They cannot afford to have any problems, or it could be their job security that is affected along with yours. Make their lives easy.

Of course, many musicians have colorful personalities and unusual means of self-expression. But the successful ones do not bring this to work; they are able to flip a switch and be completely professional for the two or three hours required. Think of yourself as a small business with yourself as the product. People are buying you—not just your oboe tone, but the whole package. Since many employers are businesspeople and may be only marginally knowledgeable about oboe, they may not even be able to judge your oboe tone. But, they can judge whether you are neat, punctual, and easy to be with. They are consumers, and they have lots of choices. Make the choice easy. Be professional.

Sadly, there is no room for error in these suggestions. If you are on time a thousand times, you will be appreciated but not praised. If you are late just a few times, you will not be hired next time. We all know people who have reputations for being eccentric or unreliable, sometimes quite endearingly so. If they are still working, they will not continue much longer. And often this reputation was earned with only a few transgressions. There is no excuse for anything short of perfection in this arena. It's easy to do it well and very damaging to do it poorly.

The next thing you must do is be nice. In addition to being reliable, you must be collegial. You should be easy to talk to, easy to play with, and easy to work with. You must present a good attitude, and you must be considerate and respectful of those you are working with. It is a fact of human nature that we are more inclined to help people if we like them. Some, usually the bad-tempered ones, feel that this is "favoritism" of some kind, that sometimes less qualified people are given opportunities. It is usually nothing of the kind. Nobody wants to be around you if you're miserable, mean, and difficult; a big part of being a professional is being able to get along with the people you work with. This is hard to overstate: be nice. Don't gossip about colleagues; don't talk about them behind their backs; and don't say bad things, especially if they aren't true. If you are a student, never say anything bad about any professional; you don't know what is involved in being a professional so you aren't yet qualified to judge. These suggestions aren't just for social reasons; as I said earlier, we help those we like. And some people can hold a grudge for a very long time, so it seldom pays to make anyone angry with you. Students are particularly at risk in this arena: since you have no real idea which of your fellow students are going to become influential and important later, it really doesn't pay to be unpopular or difficult.

None of this is to suggest that you should be a pushover. You can be confident and persuasive without being aggressive or nasty.

The third thing that is richly rewarded in the music profession is competence. This is difficult to achieve, but it also does not require any special abilities beyond persistence, diligence, and years of hard work. The word "competent" in this context does not mean merely that you are ordinary and able to carry out duties in a reasonable manner. It means that you can reliably make the right sound at the right time without exception. Doing that requires a very high level of skill—a competent player will make entrances consistently, play with good rhythm, play in tune in various situations, not miss notes, play with a pleasing tone, and employ phrasing governed by a high level of musical intelligence.

All of these things are difficult to achieve, but they can be taught, and they can be learned. To be a competent instrumentalist is a very high distinction. Indeed, competence is the main criterion for success in orchestra auditions, and incompetence is the leading reason for rejection. Orchestra auditions reward applicants who play with good rhythm, have good pitch, and sound like they've heard the piece before. Even with only this bare-minimum standard enforced, the majority of applicants to professional orchestras do not measure up. Achieve competence, be professional and agreeable, and you will be in demand.

Early in their careers, musicians are often in the position of having to freelance; in other words, they have to apply for jobs over and over again rather than winning a single position. (Be glad you aren't a singer; many of them have to do this for their whole career.) In this regard, certain personality traits succeed better than others. Quick is better than slow. High performance is better than low performance. Low maintenance is better than high maintenance. A thick skin is better than a thin skin. Strong and healthy is better than fragile and illness-prone. A cheerful and even temperament is better than a combative or gloomy one. High energy is better than low energy. Actions speak much louder than words. Complainers, of whom there are many, are not really appreciated. Enterprise and initiative are much better than apathy and resignation. If you don't feel cheerful or energetic or healthy, fake it. Other people have their own problems.

Orchestral Etiquette

An orchestra is not a democracy. It is a strictly disciplined system with a time-honored chain of command. The conductor is the boss, and whatever he or she wants to see and hear is what the players should do. The principal players are the conductor's deputies, responsible for the sound and quality of their individual sections. This system is well established and routine in professional orchestras, where everyone has had the same role for many years, even decades. It is much more problematic in student ensembles, with less experienced players who may rotate parts from concert to concert, or even from piece to piece within the same concert. In this case, the players must be prepared to change roles, chameleonlike, from one piece to the next. The principal player is still in charge of the section, but may be the second player an hour later. Personal issues often intrude and can overwhelm professional efficiency. Every player must learn what is expected and perform that role with professionalism, good humor, and competence.

The principal player leads the section in matters of dynamics, note lengths, articulation, and interpretation when the conductor does not make specific requests. The second player, and the third if there is one, follow these directions. Even better, they listen closely to the principal and copy what they hear without being told. The second player should never play louder or with more presence than the principal unless asked to do so. The principal players consult with each other to ensure unanimity throughout the woodwind section. When there is a question for the conductor, it should be raised by a single-part player, or the section principal when there are multiple players on the part. In no case should any musician argue with the conductor or contradict him or her. This can be difficult—conductors are not infallible and do make mistakes. The players need to do what the conductor means, not necessarily what he or she says. "Oboes, you're sharp" really means, "Oboes, you are out of tune." Do not respond, "No, we aren't. The clarinets are flat." Just fix the problem.

Sometimes conductors think they can play your instrument and will make specific technical suggestions. These are not always quite right, so again the players must do what the conductor means. Thus, "Timpani, use harder sticks" means, "Timpani, I need more articulation." Usually the timpanist sets down his pair of sticks on the stick tray, picks up the exact same pair of sticks, and plays with more articulation. Everyone is happy.

If there is a need, as there often is, to have a conversation with the conductor about a point of interpretation, or to have a polite disagreement, the time for that is outside of the rehearsal, not in public. The conductor is the boss and must be allowed to be the boss. Once again: the orchestra is not a democracy.

Just as composers can do nothing more than write their creation on a piece of paper using symbols, conductors are likewise at the mercy of the performers. They cannot make a sound; they are limited to conveying their wishes through facial expressions and gestures. So do the conductor a favor: watch. Maintain eye contact as much as possible. It may improve your performance, and it will certainly improve your status with the conductor.

Be agreeable. If the conductor makes a suggestion to you, nod. Agree with the suggestion even if you haven't the slightest intention of changing anything about your performance. The conductor will usually move on to the next item in the rehearsal. Do not discuss, and do not ever ask "Is that better?" or "How did that sound?" Questions of that sort betray potential weakness, which some conductors are willing to exploit.

It is the job of each individual to do his or her very best to make the ensemble sound wonderful. Often the layers of authority in the orchestra can diminish personal responsibility too much—players, especially the nonsoloists, become too passive and think that if nobody is picking on them, they are doing well. This is not true. You should play your second-oboe part as though it were your recital. Bring the same preparation to your technique, your reeds, your listening skill, and your alertness, and you will be a good member of the ensemble.

Rehearsals, whether orchestral or chamber music, are not socialized practice. Do not learn your part in the rehearsal; learn it in advance.

Learn more than your part; learn all of the other parts, too. Study the score; listen to recordings.

Intonation in the orchestra, while based on an absolute standard, is not absolute. The chord is in tune if it sounds good; it is out of tune if it doesn't. Pointing to the tuner as proof of your rightness does not make you right—in fact, it's annoying and unprofessional. Use the tuner to establish the pitch at the beginning of the rehearsal, and then use your ears.

Pitch will generally rise during a rehearsal or a concert, and it is pointless to resist this. But as oboists, it is our responsibility to help minimize the problem. The principal should make sure to establish a consistently correct A every time the orchestra tunes. This is worth practicing; nothing destroys the authority of the oboist quicker than one or two squeamish-sounding A's. When pitch rises, oboes often feel it first, since the reed is limited in its capacity to play sharp. It is the job of the principal oboist or the concertmaster to request a retuning from the conductor. Conductors are usually happy to oblige. In the concert, sometimes there is no opportunity for retuning, and the problem can be more acute. If it is consistently very bad in your orchestra, have a little conference with the concertmaster and the conductor to find a solution. Perhaps an extra tuning note between movements will help reestablish the proper pitch. (For those players receiving the A rather than giving it, please tune carefully but quickly; do not actually play, just tune.)

The oboists should resolve intonation problems within the oboe section during rehearsal breaks. The principals are responsible for unifying the pitch among the various sections, so rehearsal breaks in professional orchestras always have various duos and trios huddled together around the stage testing treacherous passages. There is not enough rehearsal time to solve every problem.

In summary, your job is to make the maximum contribution to the ensemble while causing a minimum of distraction. If you are not playing, sit quietly and listen to the progress of the rehearsal. You will probably learn something. Conductors do not enjoy making a request of the violins and then telling the oboes the same thing when they have the same music a page later. Do not talk unless the dialogue is essential to the progress of the rehearsal. Do not do paperwork. Do not make reeds unless the conductor permits it. Do not sharpen your knife; it makes noise. Do not read unless you can do so completely unobtrusively. A magazine on the stand is fine for very long rests; a newspaper on your lap is not. Never blow water out of your instrument; it is much too loud. Swab it out, blot it up quietly, or strike the oboe against the palm of your hand to shake it loose. But do not blow it out.

While playing, do not lead with your body unless you are a leader. Do not tap your foot. Do not finger along while the principal plays a solo. Definitely do not warm up on the solo unless you are performing it. Bring a pencil to every service and use it quietly—do not drop it on the music stand. Do not turn around to look at a player performing a solo. Never wear perfume or after-shave or any other artificial scent on-stage. It makes some people ill.

All of these cautions (and there could be plenty more) are really just common sense. But if you look around your band or orchestra—whether it is a student, amateur, or professional ensemble—you will always see people who are not doing their best, and some people who are not even doing their part. Don't let that affect you. Keep quiet, play well, lead and follow as appropriate, and be courteous and respectful in your interactions. It will make you popular with everyone except the slackers.

Small-Ensemble Etiquette

In complete contrast to the orchestra, small ensembles are entirely democratic. For the ensemble to function successfully, every voice must be heard and every option explored. Everyone must be able to speak without causing offense and to hear without taking offense. Everyone must contribute. The final result must be a consensus, not the view of the loudest or bossiest individual.

Intonation in the ensemble, as in the orchestra, is relative. Use the tuner only as a reference, never as a means of settling an argument. It can be useful to spend time tuning chords, but persistent intonation problems will only be solved by improved tone production. Most good wind players play in tune. Most bad wind players do not. As tone production and reed making and concept improve, so will intonation.

Every suggestion made by a player must be tested. Even ideas that seem unworkable might contribute something useful to the finished product. So any suggestion made by a member of the ensemble should be tried. If it doesn't work the first time, try it a couple more times until it produces a change in the performance. A consensus will develop as the effectiveness of the suggestion becomes more (or less) apparent.

Eye contact between members is essential. Even if no cues are given, just looking at someone promotes an awareness of what he or she is doing. There is no such thing as a good chamber group whose players do not look at each other.

Do not be afraid to rehearse slowly. Everyone utilizes slow practice in his or her individual practice sessions. Why not rehearse slowly as a group? This will give everyone a chance to hear what the piece should sound like when it's perfectly correct.

A chamber-music rehearsal is a professional event. Although only a few people are involved, it is not a social event. Personal issues are irrelevant during the rehearsal. Whether the players are friends or not should make no difference. Observations about another's playing should not be meant personally and should not be taken personally. If someone says you are sharp, they are hearing a discrepancy, and it is the collective responsibility of the group to make an adjustment. It may not even mean that you are sharp, only that something is not in tune. In addition, the rehearsal is not an opportunity to catch up on personal matters. Rehearse first, talk later.

Rules of Professional Success

In no particular order, here are three thoughts that will improve your professional success and the enjoyment of your musical life.

1. *Do what you say.* This is an extension of professional behavior just outlined, and it should reach every area of life. Say what you mean and mean what you say. If you say you will call me tomorrow, call me tomorrow. If you say you will be here at eight o'clock, be here. This is not that hard. The corollary is actually much harder to learn—that is, if you don't want to do something, say no. Once you say you will do it, you have to do it.

Musicians have a disease: they fear that if they ever say no to anyone, then everyone will stop calling immediately and permanently. That isn't really true, and people usually understand and respect "no." So, before agreeing to something, stop and think: is this really something I want to be part of? If not, say no. You will be much happier.

This rule also means that you must be accountable. We all know people who constantly have terrible things happen to them, without any of it ever being their fault. Agreeing to do one thing often means that you have agreed to many other things: if you decide to attend music school, you have also agreed to follow that school's curriculum, some of which may not be to your liking. If you sign a contract for a season, you have agreed to perform every service during that season, even the ones that have no apparently valid artistic reason. Do not blame anyone for this; you agreed to it.

Do not blame others for things that are really your fault. Do not blame your reed or your instrument for your failures. You made the reed, and you should have maintained or replaced the instrument. Do not blame colleagues for your mistakes—you also make mistakes and sometimes mislead colleagues who mistakenly followed you. You would appreciate their generous sympathy in that case. Everything that comes out of your instrument is because of something you did. Take responsibility for it.

2. *Never lower your standards.* Your usual job is to play what someone else thinks the audience wants to hear. They may be right or wrong, and sometimes it isn't what you want to play. Let's add a couple more inconveniences. Perhaps the concert is very early in the morning, perhaps the venue is freezing, perhaps the audience

is made up entirely of fourth graders—and it becomes easy to give up and play less than your best. Never do this. If you begin to allow yourself to play less than your best, you will allow it more and more often. It is the beginning of a slippery slope toward apathy and boredom that ends in a severe erosion of skill, when you can no longer play well even if you want to. Every professional orchestra has people like this; when they finally encounter a conductor they respect (or fear), or find a piece of music that excites them, they spend the first few hours scrambling for little forgotten bits of technique they should never have lost in the first place.

3. *Love music.* The business of music is exactly that—a business. It is no more and no less pretty than any other kind of business, with the unpleasant difference that there is usually less money involved. Naturally, when the scraps are smaller, people tend to fight harder for them. So love music. When everyone else is squabbling about the temperature onstage, the number of minutes of overtime, or how much the dinner per diem should be, remember that you are first and foremost a musician.

Somewhere during many lives, a curious transition takes place. Musicians begin as starry-eyed dreamers, eager to learn and practice and improve. Every music school has dozens of them. Somehow, thirty years later, too many of these same people are cynical, jaded music robots who hate life, orchestra, and each other. Somewhere along the way they forgot to love music, they forgot why they wanted to be part of this profession, and they became unhappy. So love music; it will sustain you even when the business of music is hard to love.

13

Career Development

The first step in developing a career is to decide how you will pursue your advanced study. The first part of this chapter gives advice for the young student wishing to be a college music major. Later, we will discuss how the advanced student can prepare for the music profession. Preparing for college can be confusing, stressful, and filled with doubt, especially if the goal is to study oboe. Do you want to find the best law school in your state? There are guides to help you. The same applies for many other disciplines, but not oboe. While this section is written for an American high school student wishing to be an oboe major in college, anyone looking for a place to study should find some useful ideas here.

First, prepare yourself. I find that college freshmen are initially stressed by reed making, by music theory, and by piano. Each of these requires time to study and practice, and each of these can be learned in high school. If they are not, they will each require an hour or two every day during the first semester of college, making that semester almost unbearable.

A lot of lesson time in high school is spent preparing the student for the next concert, audition, or contest. When you are a music major in college, the emphasis shifts to teaching the student how to play. This transition can be difficult and stressful for the unprepared. So here are a few hints that will help to get you ready.

- *Take piano lessons.* It will help your musical development a great deal. It is not necessary to be a virtuoso, but a few years of lessons can help tremendously, since piano shows the spatial aspect of music in a way that oboe cannot. Piano skill improves music reading and ear training and promotes awareness of harmony.

- *Take private oboe lessons from the best teacher you can find.* If there is no one in your town, it is worth driving several hours to get lessons, even if they cannot take place every week. Oboe is very hard to learn on your own and even harder to unlearn later, when the bad habits have to be corrected. The earlier the lessons can begin, the better.
- *As soon as you can afford one, get a good instrument.* College music majors need to have a professional-quality instrument. If that is not possible before college, make sure that what you have is of solid construction and in good repair.
- *If your school offers it, take a music theory class (including ear training) before you graduate from high school.* If your school has nothing of the kind, ask your piano or oboe instructor for advice. Do not come to college with no experience in these areas.
- *Don't waste your summers.* Find a music camp or festival to attend. Ask your teacher for advice. This can be a valuable way to inform yourself about potential teachers and to meet other students. Attend a conference of the International Double Reed Society.
- *As you get closer to graduation (your junior year onward), slim down and focus your schedule so you have time to practice.* Many high school students maintain a schedule that is too stressful and too scattered to be productive. Music schools are more impressed if you play really well than if you have dozens of extracurricular activities on your résumé. If you have definitely decided that you want to pursue oboe, eliminate everything that does not directly improve your qualifications as an oboist. You can try to be a jack-of-all-trades, but make sure you are a master of one.
- *Learn to make reeds before college.* They don't have to be beautiful, but you should have a good command of the basic techniques. Your sophomore year is a good time to start learning.
- *Learn your scales and other technical patterns very well.* These are the basis of any good technique and are by far the most efficient way to acquire good technique.
- *Before you start applying to schools, work with your teacher or your parents to develop a really professional presentation for yourself.* Put together a résumé and print it on good-quality paper. Get a professional-sounding e-mail address and reserve your cute one for your friends. Learn to be confident and intelligent in your interactions.

One of the most stressful questions for any high school student is "What do I want to be when I grow up?" I have always felt that high school students are pressured too intensely in this area; it is better to make the right decision late than the wrong decision early. And students should be aware that a music degree is among the most difficult courses of study. It will involve thousands of hours of work with no certain reward at the end. People should be musicians only if they cannot imagine being anything else. If music is part of who you are, if you wake up thinking about it and go to sleep thinking about it, and that makes you happy, then please come and study music. If music is something you like to do, but you also have an interest in journalism or business or mathematics, then you should probably pursue one of those interests. But if you have decided that music will be the major field of study, it still remains to decide what degree program to pursue.

At many schools, the various degree programs have pretty much identical curricula the first year or two, so if you change your mind there will be little or no penalty. After that, the different courses become much more specialized. Some schools offer all of the degree possibilities listed here (as well as some others such as music composition, arts administration, or music technology); other schools will offer only one or two. Almost all schools are better at some of these degrees than others, which you will find out during your research. For instance, a department may have a strong commitment to music education, with most of their students following that degree program. If you know you are not interested in music education, that school will not support your ambitions as well as you would like, and you should probably eliminate it from consideration. Here are the most common types of music degree programs.

- *Music performance.* Performance degrees have the most emphasis on, well, performance. Typically, two degree recitals are required, and advanced music history and theory classes are included in the curriculum. For the student who really wants to learn to play and who is willing to commit a lifetime of work, this is the right course. Its disadvantage is that it is not a professional degree—in other words, you will not receive any certification; you will have only your playing as your representative.
- *Music education.* This is a professional degree resulting in certification to teach in the public schools. It has less emphasis on performance and more emphasis on education classes, and it requires a semester of student teaching. This should not be a refuge for music students who feel unsure of their performance abilities. Students should sincerely want to teach in the public schools and should have strong performance skills.
- *Music therapy.* This is another professional program offered by some schools. Music therapy is more about therapy than music; it would be good for students who have interest in the healing arts as well as music.
- *Some kind of liberal arts degree with an emphasis in music.* This can be called a Bachelor of Arts in Music or something similar. Typically,

the performance element is less demanding, and the advanced music classes are not required. The time thus released from performance or education classes is spent taking various liberal arts courses. This could be a good program for a student with a strong interest in music, but without a strong interest in becoming a music professional. Upon graduation, the student will not have any professional credential, but should have a clearer idea of an appropriate specialty to pursue during graduate study.

As I said earlier, none of these options (or any others that some schools may offer) is going to trap you into a lifetime of that pursuit exclusively. Undergraduate degrees from universities are meant to give you a good general education with plenty of opportunity to find other interests that might possibly fascinate you more than you imagined. The exceptions are some of the conservatories (see the following paragraphs), which can be intensely focused on music performance.

Having decided to study music and chosen a major, you will need to choose the school itself. To find a list of potential colleges, you need information. Unfortunately, reliable sources of information can be few and far between. High school guidance counselors usually cannot help; oboe performance is too specialized. Private oboe teachers can help, but the quality of their advice depends on their level of experience. College oboe teachers cannot always be relied upon, since some of them will want you to attend their school and can paint a somewhat biased picture. So start by gathering information. Most of it is carried by word of mouth, so find lots of mouths. Go to every oboe event you can. Attend summer festivals. Meet teachers and players and other students. Attend conferences of the International Double Reed Society—many of the teachers you might want to study with will be there. Gradually, you will form an impression of where you can find good teachers teaching at good institutions. As daunting as the field looks at the outset, it is really quite a small world, and you can gain a fair amount of fluency in a reasonable amount of time.

Broadly speaking, there are three kinds of institutions: conservatories, large public universities, and smaller regional universities (the elite private universities—Harvard, Princeton, etc.—by and large do not offer undergraduate music performance degrees). Each of these models has different advantages and disadvantages.

Conservatories offer the most focused music study. Most are in large cities where excellent professional performances take place regularly. Most have fine faculty from the local symphony orchestra. However, that faculty will be largely adjunct, coming to campus only when there are lessons to teach or recitals to hear. There are some institutions calling themselves conservatories that don't fit this model, so do your research. Conservatories also tend to charge the highest tuition (with the exception of the Curtis Institute of Music, which charges no tuition).

Some conservatories are part of a larger university, while others have a relationship with a nearby university to provide nonmusic resources for students. Conservatories come the closest to being a professional trade school for music performers; nonmusic and nonperformance elements are given a lower priority.

Large public universities have full-time faculty for all instruments in addition to all of the traditional university resources. Some of these are located in major metropolitan areas; some are not. Most will have more general studies requirements than conservatories. Some are very large, with correspondingly comprehensive resources. These are often the best choice for the average music student (who is, by definition, already above average). Tuition ranges from very moderate to rather expensive.

Smaller regional universities have full-time faculty for some instruments and not for others. These schools will never have enough oboe students to require hiring a full-time oboe professor, so either they hire a part-time adjunct oboe teacher, or they hire a full-time oboe teacher and assign multiple duties to him or her. So it is not unusual to find the same person teaching oboe, saxophone, music theory, and music appreciation. It is possible that this hypothetical person is really a music theorist or a saxophone player, so you must do your research and make sure that he or she is really an oboist. Earning a music performance degree with a teacher who is not a specialist in your instrument makes no sense.

While it adds considerably to the expense, some students narrow their field of potential schools by visiting them in advance. If this is possible, it is an excellent idea. The institution will always offer some amenities for these travelers: a tour of the school, a tour of the campus, and a lesson with the instructor are all possible. All you have to do is ask.

I would suggest trying to reduce the field to three or four schools: one aspirational school where you fear you might not get in but would go immediately if accepted, one or two good solid schools with slightly less stringent admission requirements but with good programs, and one school where you know you will be accepted. There really is no point in applying to more (if you have done the proper research), since you will most likely just duplicate what you have already done, and the application fees will start to mount up.

Finally the applications are completed, and it is time to make the audition tour. First of all, it is very important to visit the campus in person. Do not audition by audio or video recording. You will spend four years of your life at this place, so visit. If your schedule does not allow attendance at one of the audition days, many schools will be happy to make alternative arrangements. Bring a parent or two. While there, get as much of a feel for the place as possible. If the auditions are scheduled for a weekend, try to spend at least part of Friday or Monday on campus when classes are in session. Attend an orchestra or band rehearsal.

Talk to oboe students. These things can be arranged easily if you plan ahead. Remember that the whole experience is a two-way street—the school is certainly evaluating you, but you are also evaluating the school and the teacher.

For the audition itself, you should prepare about fifteen minutes of material. Some schools have very specific requirements and you should, of course, observe those. When they do not, select a program of contrasting material—something fast, something slow, something traditional, something more modern. It is better to have too much than too little. Single movements are fine, as are etudes and orchestral excerpts. The goal is to give the panel a comprehensive look at your playing. That includes tone, intonation, rhythm, articulation, phrasing, finger technique, and so on. Make sure that your selected material has elements of all of these things. Be prepared to play a few scales and to sight-read. And be prepared to answer a few questions—usually friendly, get-acquainted sorts of icebreakers. Dress well, as though you were going to a job interview, but not formally. Business dress is fine. Make sure your clothes are clean and pressed and your shoes shined. If you are used to expressing yourself through quirky grooming habits, today is probably not the best day to do that. The panel will be trying to gain an impression of your personal qualities as well as your playing, so act professionally.

While on campus, you should get answers to some very important questions. You can ask these of the oboe teacher. If he or she does not know the answer (the teacher should know most of these, though), the teacher can refer you to someone who does. If the audition procedure does not allow for a personal visit with the teacher, you can ask these in writing via e-mail. Often a bit of Internet research or conversations with oboe students will give good information also. Here are the kinds of things you should ask about:

- *What is the size of the oboe studio?* This is important. If it's too small, you will have to play in every ensemble and will never have any time to practice. While this sounds like fun, it is very damaging to your development as a player. If the studio is too large, you may not get much large-ensemble playing for your first couple of years. That is a much better situation than the alternative.
- *What playing opportunities are there?* This is related to the first question. You want to find out how many major ensembles—orchestras and bands—there are. There should be roughly two or three players for each of these. So if you are applying at a school with three orchestras and three bands and there are fifteen students in the oboe studio, that is close to perfect. If there is an orchestra and two bands and only three students, that spells trouble. You do not want to be the best student in the studio the day you arrive there. You are much better off being the worst.

You do not want to be immediately responsible for leading parts in major ensembles. There needs to be a basic training period where you adjust to new demands and expectations and can make a few mistakes without penalty.

- *What opportunities for financial aid are there?* Often music scholarships are available outside the university's financial aid system. The university scholarship office may or may not know much about these. If you get the opportunity, make your financial needs known, but do not be demanding. Even if it is true, do not say that you cannot attend without a full scholarship.
- *What contact will I have with the professor?* Some schools have adjunct oboe faculty—in other words, the teacher comes to campus only to teach the lessons and is otherwise absent. Asking this question also gives you a good idea of the teacher's curricular structure—are there reed-making classes, repertoire classes, studio classes, and the like?
- *What degree program are most of the students following?* If you are interested in a performance degree but you would be the only performance major, perhaps this particular situation is not for you. If you have done good research, you should know the answer to this question already.
- *What is the ratio of graduate students to undergraduates?* Again, this answer can help you decide how comfortable you will feel with the surroundings.
- *What facilities support is there for oboe students?* Is there a reed room? Is there gouging and shaping equipment for the students to use? Everyone will eventually make reeds at home with their own tools, but that can be difficult or impossible for a freshman living in a dormitory.

In order of importance, here are the things you should take into account when making your choice:

- *The quality of the teacher and your rapport with him or her.* This one choice can literally change your life. You will have done your preliminary research, so you have narrowed your choices to a few. Confirm that research—make sure you get a lesson, even if it's brief, while visiting the campus. Teachers are used to this request, and most will accommodate it. Always offer to pay for the lesson, although some teachers will not charge if the student is applying to their school.
- *The quality of the institution.* This will affect you directly and indirectly. If you have a fine teacher at a school with poor major ensembles, a starving library, or a lazy academic faculty, your experience will not be as rich. Do not be too concerned with the

prestige of the institution. Even the most famous schools can have an uneven faculty. Find the best teacher and support for you, and you will do well.

- *Money.* This should come into play only after all other things are equal. This is easy for me to say since it is not my money. But I feel that money is really unimportant in this discussion. A bachelor's degree is not returnable. It's worth paying for the best one. It will repay you many times over. Parents have known for years that their child will one day go to college, and while it sometimes happens that a student gets a huge scholarship to a great school, don't let that be the only feasible alternative. It is a common myth that oboe students receive more generous scholarship offers. I sometimes speak with parents of young (eleven or twelve years old) students who are preparing their children for oboe study "so they can get a scholarship in college." That is just wrong. It is true that there are fewer good oboists in high school than there are, say, flutists. And, every university needs at least a few oboe players to play in its ensembles, so sometimes the school will offer a bit of money for that. But the better schools do not give scholarships on the basis of the instrument you play; they consider only how well you play that instrument. So parents, please encourage your children to play oboe if they love the sound, but don't expect it to save you money.
- *Geographic location.* It doesn't matter whether you spend one hour on the airplane or four hours. In some parts of the country it is possible to find a good program within driving distance, but not everywhere. Expand your search nationwide. Travel is easy.
- *Family considerations.* Again, this is easy for me to say, since it is not my family. But I firmly believe that college should be different from high school and that one of those differences needs to be a change of residence for the student. So even if the college is in the same town as the parents, the student should live on campus and not at home.

Afterward

Now you have applied and auditioned, and you are receiving offers. Professors appreciate it more than you can imagine if you respond quickly. If I make you a financial offer and it is neither accepted nor refused for a month, I cannot offer that money to anyone else. It's your money until the deadline. But when the deadline comes, the next person on my list has probably already decided to go somewhere else. So if you can respond quickly, it helps everyone. Don't be afraid to tell University A that you have decided to attend University B. You will not cause any hurt feelings. We all know that any sensible student will apply to multiple schools and will only attend one. So don't be embarrassed; just send a polite communication saying you have decided to attend University B, and thank the professor very much for all of the help and consideration.

Advice for the Advanced Student
Wishing to Be a Professional

You need experience to get a job, but you need a job to get experience. This is the conundrum that every young musician struggles with. Most undergraduate college students preparing a résumé for the first time are embarrassed to see just how little is there—a couple of gigs, a few private students, the appropriate university ensembles, and that's about it. So the remedy is to build a professional résumé as soon as possible. This is not as difficult as it sounds. There will probably be community orchestras and bands in your region; some will probably even pay a few dollars. It is not important for this to be the Philadelphia Orchestra; it is important that you be able to audition and compete and win *something*. Then you can say that you are the second oboist of the XYZ Symphony Orchestra. If you are interested in a teaching career, you can establish a similar track record with community colleges or independent community music schools. Again, prestige is unimportant; what is important is that somebody hired you to do something.

Note that this is different from performing lots of casual "gigs" or teaching lots of private students. The crucial difference is that someone must officially hire you to do something that pays a salary, even a very meager one. It documents that someone thought highly enough of you to offer you employment, however humble.

Then observe what professional people do and emulate that. There is a saying in the business world that you should dress for the job you want, not the job you have. So act like the musician you would like to be, not the one you are right now. Join the appropriate professional organizations, whether it's the International Double Reed Society or the American Federation of Musicians or the College Music Society or all of them. That one step will repay you many times over in information gained. The International Double Reed Society has an annual conference, as do all professional organizations; attend as many of these as possible.

Attend summer festivals. You will probably have a great experience playing music, and you may get to study with a fine teacher, but the main point (and the point of attending International Double Reed Society conferences) is to network. It is vastly helpful to your life and your career to have as many friends and acquaintances as possible. Develop this early and work on it often. As I've already mentioned, people help those they like, but they have to know you first.

Focus your activities to support your professional goals. If you want to be an orchestra musician, find some orchestras to play in. If you want to be a university professor, observe what professors do: they teach, of course, but they also perform concerts, make recordings, publish research, organize chamber music series, and other activities. Students can do all of these things—on a lesser scale, but they can do them. You can publish an article or two: there are small music journals or newsletters of musical societies that will publish most material submitted to them. Sometimes you have to join their society, but it is money well spent. You can arrange a recital with your trio at a local church or, better, at an out-of-town venue. You can have composer friends write music for you and record it on a privately published CD. You can perform a service to your community: play free concerts in retirement homes, or hospitals, or in facilities for disadvantaged youth. You can volunteer to help an appropriate professional organization; again, the contacts gained in this sort of activity can be invaluable.

The object of all of these suggestions is to build a strong résumé that demonstrates your professional potential. When preparing the résumé, do not be shy. This document is going out into the world as your representative. You can't accompany it to point out particular achievements, so make sure your résumé does it for you. Annotate each line to explain what it is and why it is noteworthy. Think of the résumé as an advertisement, not just a fact sheet.

Audition Recordings

The other representative of yourself that is frequently requested by potential employers is the audition recording. In various professional capacities, I have listened to hundreds of recordings that people have sent as their representative. It is my impression that sometimes people forget that the recording is their only representative. There can be no bonus points for personality, intelligence, fashion sense, or professional demeanor. It either sounds good or it doesn't.

What follows is a little how-to guide for making a recording that will get your message across with a minimum of strain for the listener and a maximum of benefit to you. Most of my suggestions will seem like nothing more than common sense. But I would not be mentioning anything if people hadn't sent me recordings, intended as their best representation of themselves, that did not include this flaw or that. In some cases, that are not as rare as you would hope to believe, recordings are substandard in ways that can hardly be described: unwise microphone placement (in the dishwasher, by the sound of things), external noises (far-off barnyard sounds of some kind), disturbing and mysterious events (huge thumps about twenty times louder than the music), and other distractions. Anyone who listens to lots of audition recordings will corroborate these stories and add their own. Don't be one of the after-dinner stories; make a great recording.

My first, and most important, recommendation is to use a professional recording engineer. Find someone with good equipment who knows how to use it, and who will sit there and listen to playback while you are playing. Better yet, also have your teacher or a trusted colleague in the room listening to you and offering advice on how you might improve your performance (in commercial recordings, this person is called the producer). These steps will avoid countless disappointments and spare you the distraction of operating the equipment while also playing the music. It will also cost money, so you should apply a cost/benefit analysis to this: you are trying to make an impression on someone, probably a stranger, with only this recording as your representative. Yours must be better than the other recordings.

Some recording guidelines are very specific: they might describe exactly what repertoire to perform and exactly which order to follow with the selections; they sometimes even include recommended microphone makes and models and microphone placements. The goal is only partially to make the recordings sound good; it is also to make them sound as uniform as possible, allowing more precise comparison. So if you are given exact guidelines, follow them exactly, even if your recording engineer thinks he or she can make it sound better with some other technique.

Most of the time, however, you have a free choice of program, so you will need to select what you are going to play. Unless you are very fortunate or have performed very extensively for many years, you will probably not be able to use most of the live performances you have participated in. If you want to use something that was recorded live, listen to it very critically, and have someone else listen to it very critically with you. Chances are there will be something wrong. This may have nothing at all to do with you: there might be too much audience noise, or the microphone was too close to the piano, or your friend playing the violin got lost. Perhaps the quality of the recorded sound is a bit fuzzy; perhaps there is water in your octave key. Throughout all of this, your oboe playing might be absolutely first-rate. But if the performance as a whole is not beautiful, it will be difficult for the listener to notice that you, alone, are sounding good. So unless the live material is really convincing, consider making a custom-made audition recording.

However, just in case, if you are giving a performance that you know will be very well prepared and well rehearsed with good musicians—a degree recital, for example—make sure that a good recording engineer with professional equipment is there to capture it. It would be a shame to play beautifully with no record whatsoever of the occasion.

If the recording guidelines specify that the recording must be made live, reconsider what is meant by the word "live." By asking for live performances, they are really asking for unedited recordings; they are not insisting that you expose yourself to all of the random and strange things that can happen during a real performance. So "live" does not mean that there has to be an audience, nor that you cannot play the movement again if you think you can improve it. It does mean that you can't substitute an excellent phrase for a not-so-good one. You can't play three lines, take a break, play two more lines, and edit it all together later. Of course, if the guidelines do not specify "live," then you may edit to your heart's (and your budget's) content. There is nothing dishonest about this—it is still your playing—but it allows the best possible representation of your playing. Some institutions now require a video recording of your playing to assure that the material has not been edited. In this case, make sure that the audio portion of the recording is of the highest possible quality. The video is less important.

Speaking of honesty (and, again, I wouldn't mention this if it had never happened), don't even think about cheating. Cheating, in this case, means passing someone else's recording off as your own. There cannot be any good outcome to this: you will be exposed either sooner or later. Either scenario reflects very badly on you and may cause lasting damage to your future.

The audio quality of the recording should be the best you can afford. Use a good acoustic, use a good piano (and a good pianist), and use a professional engineer with real equipment. Don't make it in your living room, don't use a friend's hobby equipment, and certainly don't just leave your portable recording device in the piano and switch it on for a while. The quality of personal recording equipment continues to improve, while the cost continues to decrease; do not be tempted by the convenience and economy of this. Professionals still have better stuff and know how to manipulate it more skillfully. The oboe is difficult to record without distortion, so you need the best possible microphones.

Recording studios are not ideal—they seldom have a really good piano, and they deliberately have no acoustic at all, so that some artificial reverberation will need to be added. Use a space in which you would be comfortable performing, and have the engineer bring the equipment to you. The expense will be considerable, but reasonable if you compare it to the cost of traveling somewhere for an audition. The judges, of course, are not primarily listening for brilliant audio quality, but they should be able to hear your playing clearly without straining through a fog of boomy echoes and fuzzy distortion. Remember, you want your recording to be the best one, not merely acceptable.

Listen to the recording before you send it out. Even if you paid a professional good money for it, listen to it carefully for any problems. These include ugly thumps and pops between selections, little bits of conversation inadvertently recorded, pointless seconds of audience applause or audience murmuring, abrupt transitions from applause to silence, pitch deviations between selections, volume discrepancies between selections, and so on. About half of the recordings I hear cannot possibly have been listened to. Listen to your recording more than once on different equipment to make sure that it is compatible with a variety of playback apparatus.

Unless required by the guidelines, do not make spoken announcements on the recording. Do include a neatly printed program.

Leave plenty of time in advance of the deadline to fix any problems. Don't rely too much on overnight shipping services.

If the recording repertoire is a list of required pieces or excerpts, which is the case for most competitions and preliminary orchestra auditions, be sure that you can play all of the music with accuracy, conviction, and a sense of the proper style. It stands to reason that somebody somewhere will be able to play it really well, so if it's beyond you, don't enter.

Use a reed with a really clean sound. Microphones tend to pick up treble—hiss and junk in the reed especially—so the nice warm orchestral reed you used in your last concert might sound spitty and fuzzy when recorded. You're best off with a clear, compact sound that you can control with a minimum of effort.

The worst microphone placement for the oboe is near the bell. The best sound of the oboe doesn't radiate from the bell, it radiates out of the tone holes. A good microphone placement has the microphone a foot or two above the player's head and several feet in front. The more distant the microphone is, the higher it should be.

While playing for the recording, don't be seduced by the fact that you can do it over and over. Play the music like it's a performance. There is no good reason why the fiftieth take should be any better than the third. If you can't play the piece to your satisfaction after four or five attempts, it's likely you aren't ready.

Appendix 1

Thoughts for the Complete Beginner

You have just returned from the music store, or your school's storage room, with your new (or not-so-new, but new to you) oboe. What now? Most new things come with an instruction manual. The rest of this book presumes some prior knowledge of and experience with the oboe, but these few paragraphs should help the student who has never played before.

Open the case with care. The handle is usually on the lower part of the case, and the lid is usually the half without the handle. Still, just in case you are holding the case upside down, open it gingerly the first time to make sure the pieces don't tumble out. There will be three joints—the top joint, the middle joint, and the bell—which you have to assemble before playing. The top joint has the smallest diameter, the middle joint is a bit larger, and the bell is the short flared part.

Gently twist the bell onto the middle joint. If there is a key on the bell, there will be a bridge key that connects the two joints; be very careful that this does not snag while you are putting the joints together. Hold the key on the bell closed (that's the low B-flat key) while twisting the joints together; that will give more clearance. Some student oboes are missing the low B-flat.

Bridge keys (there are two linking the middle joint to the top joint) are often badly bent on beginner oboes. Be careful. If the joint does not twist very smoothly on the cork, apply a thin layer of cork grease to the cork and begin again.

After the lower half is assembled, add the top joint. Take note of the location of the two bridge keys and push the top joint straight down into the middle joint without allowing the bridge keys to meet. Then gently turn the top joint until the two joints engage. Again, if the pieces do not join smoothly, apply a thin layer of cork grease.

Set the oboe somewhere safe while you prepare the reed. I often see student oboes set in alarmingly precarious situations. If the oboe is going to be unattended for more than a few seconds, put it in the case. If you are in an ensemble rehearsal with lots of people moving around, the oboe should be either in your hand or in its case. Never leave it lying on your unoccupied chair. Don't leave it unattended on an instrument peg, either. Even when those are very sturdy—many aren't—they can still be knocked over.

The reed needs to be soaked before it can be used. This is best accomplished by standing it in a small container—a shot glass or an empty 35 mm film canister, if anyone still has those—filled with about half an inch of water. Set the reed in there very gently—the tip of the reed is very thin and easily damaged. Leave it in the water for at least five minutes before trying to play. Some players fill the reed tip with saliva and return the reed to its case for a few minutes; this works equally well. Do not allow the reed to soak for more than fifteen minutes or so; it will become waterlogged and require much more effort to control.

Now put the reed in your mouth and make a sound on it. When that sound is a fairly strong C (two octaves above middle C on the piano), you are ready to insert the reed into the oboe. After you have experimented with the oboe for a few hours, the first few chapters in this book should be very helpful.

When you have finished playing, disassemble the oboe and carefully swab out the inside before putting it back in the case. Be careful swabbing: swabs can get stuck inside the bore if not gently used. Also, make sure that the reed is stored safely and that it is permitted to dry completely.

If, after a few days or weeks, you find that playing the oboe is fun and that you like the sound, then find a teacher. Your enjoyment and your progress will be greatly enhanced.

Appendix 2

Fingering Chart
for Oboe and
English Horn

When more than one fingering is shown for a note, they are shown in order of preference from left to right.

Experienced players often alter fingerings slightly to adjust pitch or tone quality. For example, many players like to add right-hand fingers to notes in the high-A-to-C range in order to "lengthen the tube" and thereby enrich the sound. Since there are many of these alterations, I have included only a few suggestions to show the general idea. Students should first learn to play with the standard fingerings.

With rare exceptions, the back octave key should remain pressed when using the side octave key.

Optional fingering alterations are shown in gray. Entirely standard adjustments, like adding the low B key to the upper F-sharp and G, are shown in gray and outlined.

Fingerings marked as "alternate" should only be used to facilitate otherwise unplayable technical passages. They are either awkward to reach (like the "banana" key) or insecure in pitch and/or tone quality, and they should not be used if these problems can be heard. In the extreme high register, however, they should make any passage feasible. Be sure to consult the companion trill chart in appendix 3 for more possibilities.

When choosing fingerings, use common sense. For example, the tonal benefit of using the left F key in a quick passage is sometimes lost because of the audible increase in sloppiness. Listen, and use what sounds best.

Fngerings for extremely high notes (above high G-sharp, on the fourth ledger line above the treble staff) are not well standardized. Use the ones shown here as a basis for experimentation.

Harmonic fingerings should be used when an especially soft sound is wanted or when the composer specifically asks for them by placing a small circle (°) above the note. They are only occasionally useful in normal playing.

The fingerings marked "English horn" may be used in place of the oboe fingerings. Other English horn "help" fingerings (using the side octave key for the upper A-flat, adding the low C key to the upper B-flat, etc.) should not be necessary if the combination of player, reed, and bocal is working properly. The English horn fingerings also work well on oboe d'amore.

These fingerings presume a professional-quality oboe with the full conservatory plateau system and semiautomatic octave keys. Oboes with different systems and student oboes with fewer keys will not be able to use all of the fingerings.

Many oboes are fitted with a third octave key, which allows extreme high notes (high E and above) to speak more easily, especially at soft dynamics. If you have one, experiment with using it in place of the back octave key. When using it, be sure to press only the third octave key, not both the back and the third octave keys together. Some notes (high F-sharp, for instance) also respond much better if the third octave key is pressed but the half hole is closed. The third octave key is not shown on this chart.

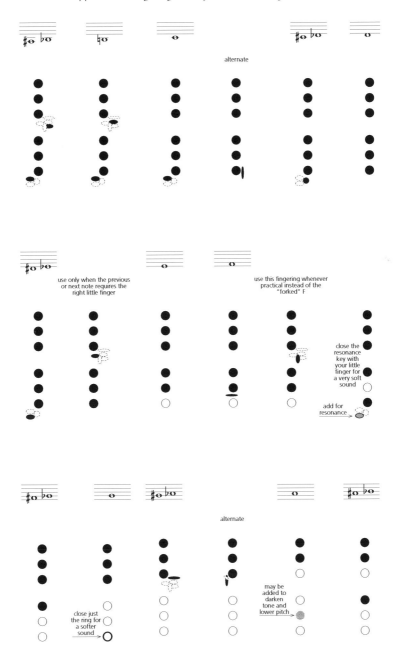

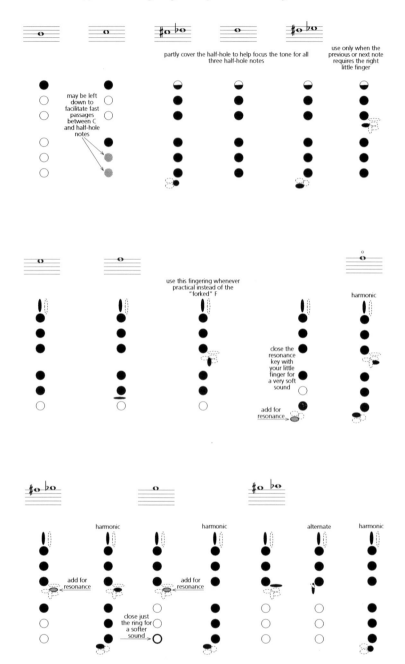

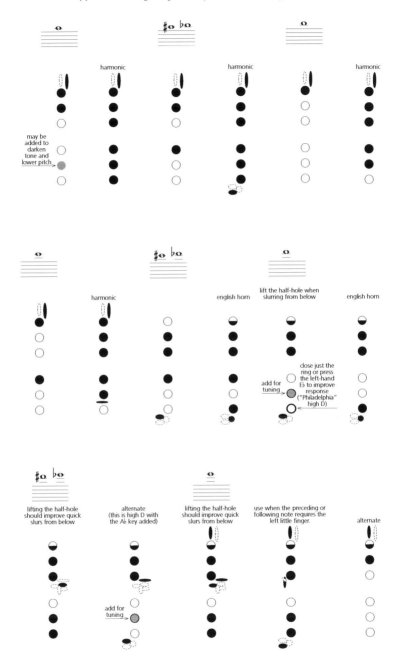

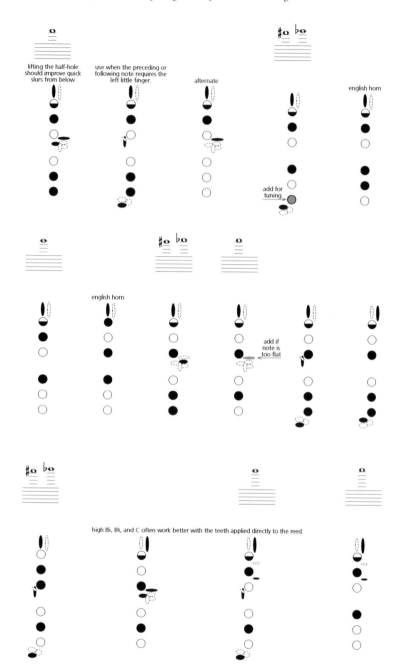

lifting the half-hole should improve quick slurs from below

use when the preceding or following note requires the left little finger.

alternate

english horn

english horn

add for tuning

add if note is too flat

high B♭, B♮, and C often work better with the teeth applied directly to the reed.

Appendix 3

Trill Fingering Chart for Oboe and English Horn

Each fingering shown will produce the lower note of the trill. Alternating the key with the arrow pointing to it will produce the trill. Trills executed by alternating two standard fingerings are omitted from this chart.

Some trills will be impossible or out of tune on oboes without the full conservatory system of keys and articulated mechanisms. Trilling between low B-flat and B-natural is impossible.

These trill fingerings can be used in addition to the alternate fingerings shown on the fingering chart in appendix 2 to facilitate rapid technical passages. Trill fingerings should never be used in slower playing or when their inferior tone quality, pitch, and response can be heard.

Some trills in the extreme high register cannot be played by moving only one finger. In these instances, the two keys indicated by arrows should be beaten together.

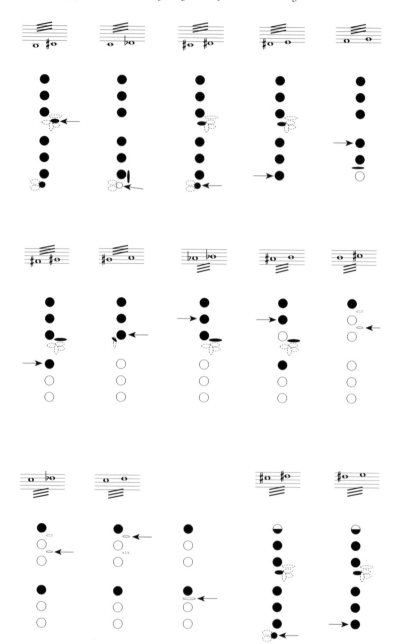

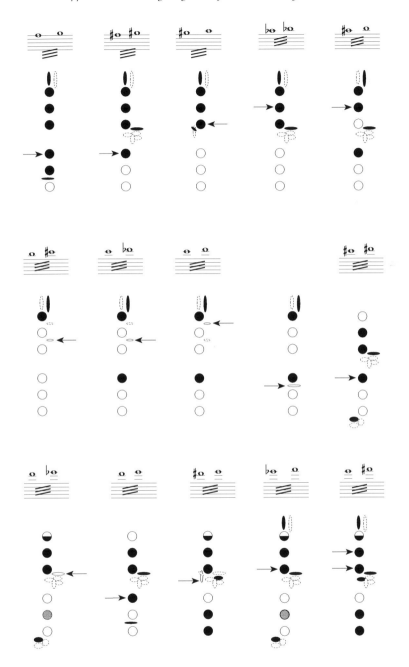

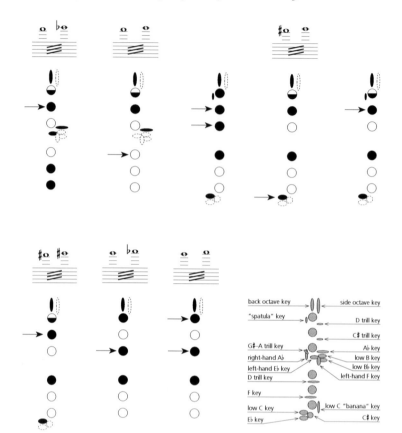

Bibliography

"A Living Legend—Pierre Pierlot: An Interview." *The Double Reed* 23, no. 1 (2000): 83–84.

Andraud, Albert J. *Vade-Mecum of the Oboist.* 9th ed. San Antonio, TX: Southern Music, 1940.

Baines, Anthony. *Woodwind Instruments and Their History.* Corrected 3rd ed. New York: Dover 1991.

Bartolozzi, Bruno. *New Sounds for Woodwind.* Trans. and ed. by Reginald Smith Brindle. London: Oxford University Press, 1967.

Bate, Philip. *The Oboe: An Outline of Its History, Development and Construction.* 3rd ed. New York: W. W. Norton, 1975.

Benade, Arthur. *Horns, Strings and Harmony.* New York: Doubleday, 1960.

Berio, Luciano. *Sequenza VII per Oboe Solo.* London: Universal Edition, 1971.

Berman, Melvin. *The Art of Oboe Reed Making.* Toronto: Canadian Scholars' Press, 1988.

Bleuzet, Louis. *La Technique du Hautbois.* 3 vols. Paris: Alphonse Leduc, n.d.

Burgess, Geoffrey, and Bruce Haynes. *The Oboe.* New Haven, CT: Yale University Press, 2004.

————. *"The Premier Oboist of Europe": A Portrait of Gustave Vogt.* Lanham, MD: Scarecrow Press, 2003.

Debondue, Albert. *Cent exercices pour Hautbois.* Paris: Alphonse Leduc, n.d.

Delaplain, Theresa. My Kingdom for a Reed: Manual for Beginning and Intermediate Reedmakers. Fayetteville, AR: privately printed, 1996.

Ferling, W. F. *48 Famous Studies, Op. 31.* Rev. Albert J. Andraud. San Antonio, TX: Southern Music, 1958.

Florida State University Department of Psychology. "Expert Performance and Deliberate Practice: An Updated Excerpt from Ericsson (2000)." www.psy.fsu.edu/faculty/ericsson/ericsson.exp.perf.html (accessed May 9, 2008).

Gillet, Fernand. *Vingt minutes d'étude: Exercices journaliers pour la technique du hautbois*. Paris: Alphonse Leduc, n.d.

Goossens, Léon, and Edwin Roxburgh. *Oboe*. Yehudi Menuhin Music Guides. New York: Schirmer Books, 1977.

Gorner, Peter. "Virtuoso Ray Still." *Journal of the International Double Reed Society* 8 (1980). www.idrs.org/publications/Journal/JNL8/still2.html.

Haynes, Bruce. *The Eloquent Oboe: A History of the Hautboy 1640–1760*. New York: Oxford University Press, 2001.

———. *Music for Oboe: 1650–1800*. 2nd ed. Fallen Leaf Reference Books in Music 16. Berkeley, CA: Fallen Leaf Press, 1992.

Hewitt, Stevens. *Daily Exercises after Maquarre*. Philadelphia: privately printed, n.d.

———. *Method for Oboe*. Philadelphia: privately printed, 1973.

Joppig, Gunther. *Oboe und Faggot: Ihre Geschichte, ihre Nebeninstrumente und ihre Musik*. Bern: Hallwag Verlag, 1981. In English: *The Oboe and the Bassoon*. Trans. Alfred Clayton. Portland, OR: Amadeus Press, 1988.

Ledet. David A. *Oboe Reed Styles: Theory and Practice*. Bloomington: Indiana University Press, 1981.

Light, Jay. *Essays for Oboists*. Des Moines, IA: Alborada Publications, 1994.

———. *The Oboe Reed Book*. Des Moines, IA: privately printed, 1983.

Marcello, Alessandro. *Concerto in D Minor*. Monteux: Musica Rara, 1977.

Marcello, Benedetto. *Concerto in C Minor*. Bonn: R. Forberg, 1923.

———. *Concerto in C Minor*. New York: International Music, n.d.

———. *Concerto in C Minor*. San Antonio, TX: Southern Music, n.d.

McCall, Bruce D. *The Essential Guide to Adjusting Your Oboe*. Knoxville, TN: McCall Woodwinds, 2005.

McGill, David. *Sound in Motion: A Performer's Guide to Greater Musical Expression*. Bloomington and Indianapolis: Indiana University Press, 2007.

Mozart, Wolfgang Amadeus. *Quartet in F Major, KV 370 (368b)*. Kassel: Bärenreiter, 1987.

Neufeld, Victoria, ed.. *Webster's New World Dictionary of American English*. 3rd college ed. New York: Macmillan, 1994.

Pear, John, Glyn Brown-Evans, and Sandro Caldini. *The Cor Anglais Companion*. 2nd ed. Manchester, UK: Ephemerae, 1998.

Rothwell, Evelyn. *Oboe Technique*. 3rd ed. New York: Oxford University Press, 1983.

Ruiz, Gonzalo X. Post to IDRS-L mailing list. April 20, 2001.

Singer, Lawrence. *Metodo per oboe*. Trans. Reginald Smith Brindle. Milan: Edizioni Suvini Zerboni, 1969.

Sprenkle, Robert, and David A. Ledet. *The Art of Oboe Playing*. Princeton, NJ: Summy-Birchard, 1961.

Stolper, Daniel. "The Robert Bloom Collection: Solo Works and Chamber Music for Oboe." *Notes* 58, no. 1 (2001): 186–91.

Storch, Laila. *Marcel Tabuteau: How Do You Expect to Play the Oboe If You Can't Peel a Mushroom?* Bloomington and Indianapolis: Indiana University Press, 2008.

Van Cleve, Libby. *Oboe Unbound: Contemporary Techniques*. Lanham, MD: Scarecrow Press, 2004.

Veale, Peter. *The Techniques of Oboe Playing: A Compendium with Additional Remarks on the Whole Oboe Family*. Kassel: Bärenreiter, 1998.

Index

9077797R00131

Printed in Great Britain
by Amazon.co.uk, Ltd.,
Marston Gate.